U0930916

中共上海市徐汇区湖南街道工作委员会
上海市徐汇区人民政府湖南路街道办事处 编

陈世东 主编

200031

一個歷史街區的文化記憶（1）

汪觀清

《200031——一个历史街区的文化记忆》

编委会

主　　任：陈澄泉　董　伟

委　　员：郭艳楣　祝　恽　吴　思　张正海　卢　芸
王　华　陈世东

主　　编：陈世东

副 主 编：刘　烨

编　　委：（按姓氏笔画排序）
刘宁路　孙玲弟　邬海佳　严　岷　陈　苏
钱定华　隋淑光

编写人员

撰　　稿：（按姓氏笔画排序）
马信芳　王为松　王伟杰　石纯如　刘光清
刘　烨　朱毅琳　李　卫　陆其国　陈世东
周　楚　徐　达　袁龙海　淳　子　章慧敏

翻　　译：范祥涛　李　健

绘　　画： 汪观清　杨宏富　齐亚明　何祖明　叶　雄
刘为民　忻秉勇　桑麟康　吴耀明　陆小弟
戴晓明　钱定华　王　莳　邬海佳

摄　　影：（按姓氏笔画排序）
马信芳　陆　杨　郭　良　谢云健（部分照片由家属提供）

顾　问

编写顾问： 包南麟

艺术顾问： 汪观清

建筑顾问： 钱宗灏

翻译顾问： 朱亚军

统　筹

中共上海市徐汇区湖南街道工作委员会
上海市徐汇区人民政府湖南路街道办事处
上海梧桐画社

200031—Cultural Memories of A Historical District

Editorial Board

Directors: CHEN Chengquan and DONG Wei

Members: GUO Yanmei, ZHU Yun, WU Si, ZHANG Zhenghai,
LU Yun, WANG Hua and CHEN Shidong

Chief Editor: CHEN Shidong

Deputy Editor: LIU Ye

Editorial Board Members: (Sorted by surname strokes)
LIU Ninglu, SUN Lingdi, WU Haijia, YAN Min, CHEN Su,
QIAN Dinghua and SUI Shuguang

Compilers

Writers: (Sorted by surname strokes)
MA Xinfang, WANG Weisong, WANG Weijie, SHI Chunru,
LIU Guangqing, LIU Ye, ZHU Yilin, LI Wei,
LU Qiguo, CHEN Shidong, ZHOU Chu, XU Da,
YUAN Longhai, CHUN Zi and ZHANG Huimin

Translators: FAN Xiangtao and LI Jian

Painters: WANG Guanqing, YANG Hongfu, QI Yaming,
HE Zuming, YE Xiong, LIU Weimin,
XIN Bingyong, SANG Linkang, WU Yaoming,
LU Xiaodi, DAI Xiaoming, QIAN Dinghua,
WANG Di and WU Haijia

Photographers: (Sorted by surname strokes)
MA Xinfang, LU Yang, GUO Liang and XIE Yunjian
(Some photos provided by family members)

Consultants

Writing Consultant: BAO Nanlin

Art Consultant: WANG Guanqing

Building Consultant: QIAN Zonghao

Translation Consultant: ZHU Yajun

Co-ordination

Hunan Road Street CPC Working Committee of Shanghai Xuhui District
Hunan Road Subdistrict Office of Shanghai Xuhui District People's Government
Shanghai Wutong Painting Society

前　言

上海市徐汇区湖南路街道地处上海市衡山路—复兴路历史风貌保护区，属于邮编为 200031 的区域。这片仅有 1.73 平方公里的社区集中了上海近 15% 的老洋房，是上海花园洋房住宅最集中、优秀历史建筑数量最多、建筑类型最丰富、风貌特色最鲜明的地域。在高大的梧桐树掩映下，一幢幢满布岁月沧桑的西班牙式、英国乡村别墅式、法国文艺复兴式，以及少数地中海式的花园洋房住宅，营造出浓郁的异国风情，东西方文化在此无声地交汇，显现独特的人文特色和深厚的文化底蕴。

这片“花园街道”始于清末，历经民国，迎来中华人民共和国成立。众多政治人物、金融巨头、实业大王、文化名流先后居住于此。晚清重臣李鸿章、辛亥革命先驱黄兴、民国第一任总理唐绍仪、中国社会主义改革开放和现代化建设的总设计师邓小平、中华人民共和国名誉主席宋庆龄、中华人民共和国元帅陈毅、金融奇才周作民、钢铁大王朱垣清、纺织巨头郭棣活、面粉大王孙多森、丝绸翘楚莫觞清、商界女杰董竹君、文学大师巴金、漫画家张乐平、金牌导演汤晓丹、影坛“雄狮”张翼、“电影皇帝”金焰、昆剧泰斗俞振飞……曾在此居住的这些人物，给这片社区的一条条弄堂、一幢幢洋房留下了一个个让人回味的故事，充满戏剧的张力，为湖南路社区赢得了“典雅湖南”和“文化湖南”的美誉。

然而一百多年来，这片宁静的社区也有过无奈和苦涩，穿越历史的尘埃而繁盛起来的街区，见证了人世的沧桑流变，演绎出近现代中国曾经的风云际会，向世人展示具有悠久历史的中华民族如何从沉沦中奋起。

上海自 1843 年开埠，各色外国人纷至沓来，践踏中国主权，形成“国中之国”。殖民者的野心无休无止，到 1914 年法租界第四次扩界（东至沙恩桥，西至徐家汇，南至徐家汇浜，北至大西路一带），覆盖了现在整个湖南路街道区域，使这块土地蒙受了最大的耻辱。一条条马路以洋人名字命名，虽然早已成为历史陈迹，觉醒的中国人却不能忘记这段沉痛的历史。

这里曾响起救亡的号角。1935 年 4 月聂耳在霞飞路（今淮海中路）1258 号为电影《风云儿女》谱写了主题歌《义勇军进行曲》，这首后来成为中华人民共和国国歌的歌曲，轰动了整个中国，唱遍了大江南北，吹奏出中国人民抗日战争的激昂号角。一大批爱国知识分子为了国家存亡，“以笔代戈”不惜牺牲生命。革命烈士郁华、郁达夫兄弟就是千千万万知识分子的代表。

这里还传递过增强国人抗战决心的时代最强音。1938 年，毛泽东《论持久战》英文版从霞飞路 1754 弄 9 号经过中共地下党员杨刚、美国记者项美丽、翻译家邵洵美翻译成英文而走向世界，不仅让外国友人尽快了解中国共产党的抗战方针，更鼓舞国人投入持久抗战的勇气，激励国人争取民族解放的最后胜利。

这里还留下抗日战争胜利结束时的一段秘闻。1945 年，蒋介石通过军统设在福开森路（今武康路）117 号周作民住宅内的秘密电台，电令冈村宁次赴芷江何应钦处接洽投降事宜，有关条款内容以及冈村宁次回复蒋介石的电报等均从此处发收。这是自 1840 年鸦片战争以来，中国人民在反抗侵略斗争中第一次取得完全彻底的胜利。

为了这个时刻的到来，中国人民经历了艰苦的历程。曾居住在这片花园街道的工商业者目睹国家贫弱、民族工业落后的局面，立志实业救国。他们创办各类企业，苦心经营，奋斗多年，为国家发展、民族振兴作出了积极的贡献。

企业家包达三秉持民族气节，拒绝汪伪政府的官职，不顾全家生命安危为新四军捐钱、筹粮、采购药品，支援抗战。出身贫寒的女商人董竹君把以毕生精力创办的锦江饭店，无私地奉献给国家。人称“钢铁大王”的朱恒清，宁愿关厂甚至坐牢也不跟日本人做生意，实现“肉烂了，也要烂在汤里”的诺言。纺织巨头郭棣活为了刚解放的上海的经济发展，不顾个人安危和长辈劝说，毅然决然留在上海，支持国家工商业的发展。中国民族工业的杰出代表、爱国人士、社会活动家刘靖基，在上海解放后积极响应社会主义改造的号召，带头申请纺织行业公私合营，为全国工商业作出表率。1979 年，78 岁高龄的他以“老牛明知夕阳短，不用扬鞭自奋蹄”的精神，带动民建中央和全国工商联骨干，以民间集资方式创办爱国建设公司，为中国工商界的继续发展奉献自己的全部力量。

从沉沦到奋起的历程中，众多文学艺术名流不甘人后。入住于此的他们，抢救历史文献、弘扬传统文化、倡导社会文明、吸取文化精华，为海派文化从孕育、成长走向进步，为中国文化事业的发展作出了不朽贡献。

1942 年，郑振铎先生为抢救沦陷区中国古代文化珍籍，蛰居高邮路 5 弄，虽生活清苦，却不遗余力搜寻整理有珍藏价值的历史文献，在战火纷飞中延续中华文脉。

1949 年，张元济先生为保住合众图书馆，不顾生命危险，以衰迈之躯，坐镇图书馆大门。

一代文化巨匠巴金，用自己的智慧和勇气，回顾个人和民族经历的风风雨雨，挥动如椽巨笔，在武康路 113 号创作《随想录》《再思录》，成为中国文坛上的不朽之作，成为中国人民精神宝库中一份珍贵的财富。

漫画大师张乐平先生，用半个多世纪塑造经典艺术形象——翘鼻、噘嘴、额上飘着三根头发的可爱“三毛”，述说着人世间喜怒哀乐，传递对人生的感慨和美好未来的向往，引得无数人一起品味世态炎凉，共同寻找和创造新的生活，半个多世纪以来始终散发着璀璨光芒，教育影响了几代中国人。有人说看三毛的整个故事，就好像是在看一部中国现代史。

翻译家草婴倾 20 年光阴，译完托尔斯泰的全部小说，成为以一己之力将托翁作品带给中国读者的第一人，完成了我国俄罗斯文学翻译史上的一大壮举。

中国电影一代骄子——电影艺术家郑君里，以独树一帜的艺术实践为我国电影事业的发展作出了重要贡献：他对戏剧、电影理论的执着探索，为后人留下了一份宝贵的遗产。他和蔡楚生联合执导的《一江春水向东流》成为中国电影史上不朽的经典。

电影表演艺术家赵丹，在近半个世纪的艺术生涯中，孜孜以求现实主义的创作风格，不断探索中华民族的表演艺术体系，他那鲜明的艺术形象成为闪烁在中国银幕上的璀璨明珠。

德艺双馨的艺术家张瑞芳，始终把个人命运与民族、国家的命运联系在一起，她主演的影片《李双双》家喻户晓，轰动全国。

昆剧泰斗、京剧大师俞振飞，数十年如一日，为昆剧的延续和发展殚精竭虑。在任上海市戏曲学校校长期间，不仅培养了数以百计的昆、京、沪、越、淮等剧种的演员和评弹演员，还培养了戏剧舞台、化妆、音乐、服装、武功等专门人才。

越剧改革先行者袁雪芬，率先在中国戏曲中建立了编、导、演、音、美齐备的艺术机制，为越剧走向全国乃至世界作出了不朽的贡献。

作曲家、音乐教育家贺绿汀，他创作的歌曲《游击队歌》《垦春泥》《嘉陵江上》，在抗日战争期间流传海内外，对抗日救亡歌咏的大规模发展、对社会音乐生活都产生了至为重要的影响，是中国电影音乐文化中的宝贵财富，至今仍是音乐会和歌咏活动中经常演唱的曲目。

铭记历史，面向未来。我们挖掘整理这一批人文历史资料，目的是更好地传承历史文脉，弘扬核心价值，培养城市精神，增强社区归属。我们认为，优美的环境需要文明的人相协调，温馨的区域需要良好的社会风气相融合，典雅的地段需要高素质的居民相匹配。我们希望，通过品味跨越世纪浮沉的人物及建筑，体验上海梧桐树下的老房子蕴含的文化积淀，更系统地关注和重视我们的城市历史文脉，唤起更多的人参与到整理和保护历史文化资料的工作中，进一步凸现湖南路街道人文环境浓郁，社会秩序和谐稳定，整个社区充满生机活力的新风貌，努力建设彰显海派文化特色的国际化街道，为上海城市文化建设作出有益的贡献。

我们的工作微不足道，我们的心意是真诚的。

陈世东

Preface

The Hunan Road Residential Subdistrict of Shanghai Xuhui District is located in the Historic Conservation Area along Hengshan Road and Fuxing Road in Shanghai, belonging to the district with the zip code of 200031. This community area has only 1.73 square kilometers, but pools nearly 15% of the old foreign-style houses in Shanghai. In this sense it is an area where the foreign-style garden houses in Shanghai are mostly concentrated and there are the largest number of outstanding historical buildings, the most extensive architectural types and the most distinctive features. Against the tall plane trees, various residential buildings of foreign-style garden house are weather-beaten with years of vicissitudes of life—some are of the Spanish style, some are of the British country villa style, some are of the French Renaissance style and a few are of the Mediterranean style—all these constitute characteristic architectures with features of rich exotic flavor, where the Eastern and Western cultures gather together in a silent communication, showing a unique cultural characteristics and profound cultural heritage.

This "Garden-like Residential Subdistrict" traced back to the late Qing Dynasty, went through the period of the Republic of China and ushered in the establishment of the People's Republic of China. Many political figures, financial giants, industrial kings, cultural celebrities have lived here successively. They embrace such big names as LI Hongzhang, minister of the late Qing Dynasty, HUANG Xing, pioneer of the 1911 Revolution, TANG Shaoyi, first premier of the Republic of China, Deng Xiaoping, the general designer of China's socialist reform and opening up and modernization, Song Qingling, the honorary president of PRC, and Chen Yi, the marshal of PRC. In addition there are still the financial wizard ZHOU Zuomin, the steel king ZHU Yuanqing, the textile giant GUO Dihuo, the flour king SUN Duosen, the silk leader MO Shangqing, the outstanding female merchant DONG Zhujun, the literary master BA Jin, the cartoonist ZHANG Leping, the prestigious director TANG Xiaodan, the "Lion" in the movie circle ZHANG Yi, the "Movie King" JIN Yan, the leading authority in Kun Opera YU Zhenfei ... they once lived in this community area, leaving behind them memorable stories in those alleys and foreign-style buildings. All these stories abound with dramatic tension and win the Hunan Road community the good reputation of "Elegant Community" and "Cultural Community".

However, for over a hundred years in the past, this quiet community has also experienced helplessness and bitterness. Passing through the dust of history and flourishing gradually, this community has witnessed the vicissitudes of life, perceived the gathering of the talented in modern China and demonstrated to the world how the Chinese nation with its long history went through the ups and downs and finally rose to the occasion.

Shanghai started opening port since 1843 and mixed varieties of foreigners came over one after another to trample on China's sovereignty with the result of the formation of "states within state". The ambitions of colonialists were endless. By 1914 the French Settlement expanded its boundary for the fourth time (Schaan Bridge in the east, Xujiahui in the west, Xujiahui River in the south and the Great West Road in the north), covering the entire Hunan Road area with the result that this piece of land suffered the greatest humiliations. Roads were named after the names of foreigners. Although they have already become historical traces, the awakened Chinese people can never forget this painful period of time in the history.

Here the horn of salvation once rang. In April 1935 NIE Er wrote the theme song *March of the Volunteers* for the film *Children of Trouble Time* at No. 1258 on Xiafei Road (now Huaihai Road). Later this song became the national anthem of the People's Republic of China and turned into a sensation throughout China. It was once popular across the whole country and blew the heated horn of the war of resistance of the Chinese people against Japanese invasion. A large number of patriotic intellectuals "used pens as weapon" and did not hesitate to sacrifice their lives for the survival of the country. The brothers YU Hua and YU Dafu, two revolutionary martyrs, are the representatives of tens of thousands of these intellectuals.

Here the strongest voice of the era was also passed around to strengthen the people's determination in the War of Resistance against Japanese Aggression. In 1938, the English version of the booklet *On the Protracted War* by MAO Zedong made for the world from No. 9 in Alley 1754 on Xiafei Road by means of YANG Gang, the underground member of the CPC, XIANG Meili, the American journalist and the translator SHAO Xunmei. This not only enabled foreign friends to understand as soon as possible the guidelines of the war of resistance of the CPC, but also excited the courage of the Chinese people for the lasting war and inspired them to fight for the final victory of national liberation.

Here also a secret has remained uncovered after the victory of the War of Resistance against Japanese Invasion. In 1945, JIANG Jieshi ordered Okamura Yasuji by telegraph to go to HE Yingqin at Zhijiang County for the affairs of surrender. The telegraph was sent by means of a secret radio transmitter stationed by the Military Statistics Bureau in the residence of ZHOU Zuomin at No. 117 on Ferguson Road (now Wukang Road). The contents of the relevant provisions and the replies from Okamura Yasuji to JIANG Jieshi were all sent and received from this transmitter. This is the first time since the Opium War in 1840 that the Chinese people achieved a complete victory in the struggle against aggression.

For the arrival of this moment, the Chinese people have gone through a tough and bitter course. Those businessmen who once lived in this garden community witnessed the situation of a poor and weak country and the backwardness of national industry so that they aspired to save the country with industry. They set up various types of enterprises, made painstaking efforts and struggled for many years, dedicating positive contributions to the national development and national revitalization.

The entrepreneur BAO Dasan upheld the national integrity and refused to take official positions of WANG Jingwei's puppet government. Regardless of the life safety of the whole family, he donated money, prepared grains and purchased medicines for the New Fourth Army to support the war against Japanese invasion. DONG Zhujun, a woman merchant born in a poor family, selflessly dedicated to the country the Jinjiang Hotel which she constructed with her lifelong energy. Known as the "Iron and Steel King", ZHU Hengqing would rather shut down the factory and even wear the stripes than do business with the Japanese invaders, realizing the promise that "rotten meat must stay in the soup". The textile giant GUO Dihuo resolutely decided to stay in Shanghai regardless of his personal safety and the persuasion from the seniors in order to support the development of national industry and commerce, and the economic development in Shanghai after its liberation. As one of China's outstanding representatives of national industry, a patriot and social activist, LIU Jingji positively responded to the call of socialist transformation after the liberation of Shanghai and took the lead in applying for public-private partnership of textile industry, setting a good example for the national industry and commerce. In 1979 when he was at the age of 78, he still encouraged himself and brought along backbones of the central committee of China Democratic National Construction Association and All-China Federation of Industry and Commerce to found Patriotic Construction Company in the field of industry and commerce on the basis of civil fund-raising, devoting all his strength to the continuous development of Chinese industry and commerce.

In the course from decline to rise, many literary and artistic celebrities also cherished the desire to overrun others. Those who lived here rescued historical literature, upheld traditional culture, promoted social civilization and absorbed the essence of the world, making invariable contributions to the breeding, growth and progress of Shanghai culture and also to the development of Chinese culture as a whole.

In 1942, Mr. ZHENG Zhenduo lived in seclusion at No. 5 on Gaoyou Road for the rescue of the invaluable books of ancient Chinese culture from the occupied areas. Although his life was full of hardships, he still spared no effort to search for and tidy up historical documents which deserved precious conservation. In this way he was protecting and preserving the Chinese culture in the flames of war.

In 1949, Mr. ZHANG Yuanji braved against the life-threatening danger at the gate of the library with his declining body in order to protect the Public Library.

BA Jin, a great cultural master for a generation, made use of his own wisdom and courage to review the ups and downs of personal and national experiences and waved his giant pen to create *Random Thoughts and Afterthoughts* at No. 113 on Wukang Road, which have become monumental works in Chinese literary world and precious wealth in the treasury of spirit of the Chinese people.

Mr. ZHANG Leping, a master of cartoon, spent over half a century to shape a classic art image—the lovely "Three Hairs" with a tip-tilted nose, sucking mouth and three floating hairs on her forehead, telling about all the sufferings and happiness of the world and passing on the understandings of life and longing for a better future. This image has attracted countless people to taste the fickleness of the world together and find and create new life accordingly. It has always been radiating bright light and educated and influenced generations of Chinese people. Some say that reading the whole story of the "Three Hairs" is just like reading the history of modern China.

The translator CAO Ying poured 20 years of time in translating all the novels of Tolstoy. In this case he became the first person to have translated all of Tolstoy's novels only on the basis of his own efforts, accomplishing a great feat in the history of Russian literature translation in our country.

ZHENG Junli, a film artist and a pride in Chinese film, has made important contributions to the development of China's film industry with his unique artistic practice—his persistent exploration of drama and film theory has left behind a valuable legacy for future generations. The film *A Spring River Flows East* co-directed by him and CAI Chusheng has become a permanent classic in the history of Chinese film.

ZHAO Dan, a film performing artist, industriously pursued the realistic style of creation and constantly explored the performing art system of Chinese nation in nearly half a century of artistic career. His distinctive art images have become bright pearls glittering on the screen in China.

ZHANG Ruifang, excellent both in virtue and art, has always associated her personal fate with that of the nation and the country. The film *LI Shuangshuang* which she starred has become widely known among the audiences and become sensational across the country.

YU Zhenfei, a leading authority of Kunqu Opera and master of Beijing Opera, exerted all his strength and wisdom for the continuation and development of Kunqu Opera for decades like one day. During his tenure as president of Shanghai Opera School, he not only trained hundreds of actors in such opera fields as Kunqu Opera, Beijing Opera, Shanghai Opera, Shaoxing Opera and Huaiju Opera as well as actors of Suzhou Pingtan, but also trained specialists in such spheres as drama stage, make-up, music, costumes and martial arts.

YUAN Xuefen, a pioneer in the reform of Shaoxing Opera, took the lead in establishing the artistic mechanism of the Chinese opera with everything ready including screenwriting, direction, performance, music and artistic decoration, and made monumental contributions to help Shaoxing Opera spread across China and the world as a whole.

HE Luting, a composer and music educator, created such songs as "Guerrilla Song", "Spring Plough" and "On Jialing River", which spread at home and abroad during the War of Resistance against Japanese Invasion and exerted significant impact on the large-scale development of salvation singing against Japanese invasion and on the social life of music. Therefore they are valuable treasures of the Chinese film music culture and are still incorporated in the repertoire of songs often performed at concerts and singing activities up to now.

Bearing in mind the history and opening up the future, we have sorted out and compiled these cultural and historical materials with the purpose to better inherit the historical context, promote the core values, cultivate the city spirit and enhance the sense of belonging of the community. We believe that the beautiful environment requires civilized people for their coordination, that the warm district needs a good social atmosphere for their blending, and that elegant sectors need high quality residents for their matching. We hope that the taste of the ups and downs of the characters and architectures across centuries, the experience of the cultural accumulation implicated in the old houses under the plane trees in Shanghai and more systematic attention to and recognition of the historical context of the city—all these will serve to arouse more people to participate in the compilation and protection of the historical and cultural documents and to further highlight the facts that the Hunan Road is characterized with rich cultural environment, that the social order boasts harmony and stability, and that the whole community is full of vigor and vitality. By doing this, we mean to make great efforts to build an internationalized community area which intensifies the characteristics of Shanghai culture and further make instructive contributions to the construction of urban culture in Shanghai.

CHEN Shidong

目　录

湖南街道

2 0 0 0 3 1

丁是娥
（1923—1988）

浙江湖州人，原名潘咏华，沪剧表演艺术家。9岁开始学沪剧，12岁参加演出，18岁满师，先后应聘到鸣英剧团等艺术团体当演员。1947年秋组织上艺沪剧团，成为台柱。1949年，上海解放不久，就带头演《赤叶河》《小二黑结婚》等新戏，后在《罗汉钱》《金黛莱》《鸡毛飞上天》《芦荡火种》等沪剧中任主要角色。其演唱艺术精湛，并形成绮丽多变、独树一帜的丁派唱腔。曾在上海市戏曲竞赛、华东戏曲会演及全国戏曲观摩演出中获一等奖。曾任上海沪剧团团长兼艺委会主任、上海沪剧院名誉院长。曾当选为上海市人大代表、全国人大代表、全国政协委员、全国文联委员，任中国剧协上海分会副主席，并荣获全国"三八红旗手"和"上海市模范共产党员"称号。1988年6月28日在上海病逝。

吹蜡烛

1954年的华东戏曲会演上，丁是娥因成功主演沪剧《金黛莱》而荣获一等奖。她没有因此而沾沾自喜，相反却寻找起差距。她发现自己在发声换气上不太科学，就想到了歌唱家们的用气方法。电影导演张骏祥曾帮助执导过沪剧《罗汉钱》，其爱人周小燕是著名女高音歌唱家。于是，丁是娥虚心上门请教。周小燕毫无保留，在传授运气技巧的同时，说到"气长"是关键，建议她练习吹蜡烛。

丁是娥真当一回事，回到华亭路的家中就开始练习。她在桌上放几支点燃的蜡烛，隔一段距离吸足气使劲吹，吹灭了再点上，虽枯燥无味，却每天坚持训练。经过一段时间的苦练，她离开放蜡烛的桌子越来越远，吹气的力度越来越大。与此同时，她慢慢练习科学运气。

这，真的管用。科学运气为她后来发展和丰富"丁派唱腔"起了大作用。

沪剧《朵朵红云》中那段"长江滚滚向东流"的"快流水"脍炙人口，至今在观众中传唱不绝。那是丁是娥从京剧传统曲牌"流水"中受到启发而创造的一种崭新的沪剧板式，在演唱这段时正确用气是关键。在《鸡毛飞上天》"教育虎荣"的演唱中，丁是娥冲破"赋子板"从慢到快的传统唱法，当唱到"早思想、夜成梦，盼望有一天，能够堂堂皇皇进课堂"时，有意识地把节奏放慢，唱得委婉而又深情，细致入微地抒发了林佩芬在旧社会因贫苦而失学的不平静心绪。这是她对沪剧"反阴阳"曲调的巧妙运用。这种方法后来又用在演唱《罗汉钱》的"回忆"、《雷雨》中的"盘凤"中。特别是唱《甲午海战》中"祭海"时，"盼你们"这三个字的唱，她能一口气拖十板，以表现金堂妈怀念亲人悲痛欲绝的心境，真是声情并茂、淋漓尽致。

作为沪剧的一代宗师，丁是娥创造的丁派艺术敢于标新立异，无论对润腔处理、节奏力度，还是感情色彩都有发展变化，真正做到声随情走，因人定腔，绮丽婉转，曲折多变。她能在艺术上取得杰出的成就，这与她对其他门类艺术的借鉴和忘我的执着追求是分不开的。

建筑简介：华亭路71弄5号

丁是娥旧居位于华亭路71弄5号，该幢房屋为花园住宅。房屋为二层砖木结构，一层设有架空层，建筑平面近似凸形，其中北立面突出。房屋外立面形式简洁，为淡黄色水泥拉毛墙面，南立面设有木结构雨棚，层间有腰檐，矩形钢门窗，红砖砌筑窗台，红筒瓦坡屋盖，木结构挑檐。一层入口位于房屋北侧，入户为厨房，地面铺设马赛克瓷砖。沿走道向里，东侧为客厅、内阳台，西侧为木结构单跑楼梯、木踏步、木扶手。二层西侧为卫生间和走道，东侧为居住房间。室内走道及房间楼面基本为硬木长条地板、白色涂料内墙面。房屋南侧有小花园，与相邻房屋花园以矮墙相隔。

DING Shi'e

DING Shi'e (1923–1988) has her ancestral family from Huzhou in Zhejiang province. She had a former name of PAN Yonghua and was known as a performing artist of Shanghai opera. At the age of 9, she began to learn it and at the age of 12 she participated in the performance. After she graduated at the age of 18, she served as an actress in such art troupes as Mingying Troupe at their invitation. In the autumn of 1947 she organized the Shanghai Troupe and played leading roles. Soon after the liberation of Shanghai in 1949, she took the lead to perform new operas like in the *Red Leaf River, The Marriage of Young Blacky* and others, and later played leading roles in such Shanghai operas as *Arhat Coin, JIN Dailai, A Chicken Feather Flies up to Heaven, Preserving the Fire in Reed Marshes* and others. Her singing art reached a consummate status, forming her own unique singing style which is beautiful and changeable. Once she won the first prize in Shanghai Opera Competition, East China Opera Joint Performance and National Opera Performance for Communication. She once served as the head and art director of Shanghai Opera Troupe, and honorary president of Shanghai Opera Theater. Also she was elected as representative of the Shanghai Municipal People's Congress and the National People's Congress, member of the CPPCC National Committee, member of the National Federation of Literary and Art Circles. In addition she served as the vice chairman of the Chinese Drama Association Shanghai Branch. Moreover, she was awarded the titles of "March Eighth Red-Banner Pacesetter" and Shanghai Model CPC Member. On June 28, 1988, she passed away of illness in Shanghai.

Blowing Candles

At the East China Opera Joint Performance in 1954, DING Shi'e won the first prize for starring in the Shanghai opera *JIN Dailai*. Instead of feeling complacent for it, she looked for gaps. She found that she was not scientific in sound production and breath exchange and thought about methods of breathing of singers. The film director ZHANG Junxiang once helped direct the Shanghai opera *Arhat Coin* and his wife ZHOU Xiaoyan was a famous soprano. So she went to visit her for advice with an open mind. ZHOU instructed her without reservation, teaching her skills of using breath and at the same time focusing on the importance of "breath length" with a suggestion that she should practice blowing candles.

She took it seriously and started the practice as soon as she was back at home on Huating Road. Putting a few lightened candles

1952 年，上海沪剧团丁是娥（左）、筱爱琴演出沪剧《罗汉钱》
In 1952, *Arhat Coin* performed by DING Shi'e (left) and XIAO Aiqin.

on the table, she breathed fully and blew with force in a certain distance. After blowing out candles, she lightened them again. Though dull, she insisted on training every day. After a period of training with efforts, she stood farther and farther from the table with candles and she blew with growing strength. At the same time, she gradually practiced scientific use of breath.

This practice really worked. The scientific use of breath played a big role for her later development and enrichment of the "DING Style Singing".

The Shanghai opera *Red Clouds* had one section of "the Yangtze River rolling eastward" which was universally praised and so far sung continuously by the audience. It was a new tune of Shanghai opera she created on the basis of inspiration from a kind of tune "running water" from the traditional Beijing opera. In the singing of this section the correct use of breath was the key. Moreover, in singing the section of "Educating Hurong" in *A Chicken Feather Flies up to Heaven*, she broke through the traditional singing method from slow to fast. When singing the part "thinking in the morning and dreaming at night, I hope that one day I could attend school with good reasons", she consciously slowed down the pace and sang with twists and turns as well as affections, which meticulously expressed the restless mood of the heroine LIN Peifen who dropped out in the old society because of poverty. This singing represented her smart application of the tune "anti-yin-yang" in Shanghai opera. This method was later used in singing the part of "memories" in *Arhat Coin*, and the section of "questioning Sifeng" in *Thunderstorm*. In particular, in singing the part of "offering sacrifice to the sea" in *Resisting-Japanese War at Sea*, she could last for ten meters in one breath in singing the three words "I hope you", to show the state of mind of mother of JIN Tang who missed her beloved ones. The singing was really wonderful with a silver voice and deep feeling and was also most vivid and incisive.

As a master of the Shanghai opera for a generation, she created the art of DING Style and had the bravery to be unconventional. In the treatment of singing style, rhythm and force, as well as in emotional coloring, she made development and changes, really realizing the effect of combining voice and emotion, and dependence of singing style on characters. Her singing was truly characterized by beauty and melody, and twists and turns. If she could actualize outstanding achievements in art, it was inseparable from her persistent pursuit of other categories of art for reference.

The former residence of DING Shi'e is located at No. 5 in Alley 71 on Huating Road which is a garden house. With a two-story structure of brick and wood, the first floor has a layer built on stilts. The plane of the building is close to the shape of convex, in which the north facade projects. The exterior facade of the house enjoys simplicity and conciseness and walls have a cement napped surface of light yellow. The south facade is equipped with wooden structure canopy and there are belt eaves between floors. Steel doors and windows are rectangular. Red bricks are used for the masonry of windowsill. The roof has red tiles on slope with wooden structure eaves. The entrance of the first floor is at the north side. Inside the doorway is the kitchen with mosaic ceramic tiles for the floor along the aisle. At the east side there are the living room and the inner balcony; at the west side there are the wooden structure stairs with wooden steps and wooden handrails. On the second floor there are the bathroom and the aisles at the west side; at the east side are the bedrooms. Indoor aisles and the floors are basically featured with hardwood floor boards and white paint interior walls. There is a small garden on the south side of the building, separated by a low wall from the neighboring gardens.

丁是娥 （钱定华画） DING Shi'e （By QIAN Dinghuan）

丁贵堂
（1891—1962）

辽宁海城人。北京税务专门学校毕业。长期在海关工作，曾任总税务司署副总税务司、上海浚浦局局长等职。1949 年参加中国人民政治协商会议第一届全体会议。中华人民共和国成立后，任中央人民政府海关总署副署长、对外贸易部海关管理局局长。1951 年加入民革，任中央委员。为第一、二届全国人大代表。1962 年病逝于北京。

"丁海关"的爱国情怀

1916 年，丁贵堂从培养海关专门人才的北京税务专科学校毕业后，奉派至安东关实习，一年后擢升为帮办。此时，由洋人管理海关的外籍税务司制度所导致的重洋轻华、以洋制华之风仍盛行，华员所遭受的不公正待遇使富有爱国情怀的丁贵堂义愤填膺。为维护华员的权益，他常挺身而出，联合中国职员与洋人交涉。中英文水平高、业务熟练且敢作敢为的丁贵堂在华员中享有很高声望。有口皆碑的丁贵堂于 1919 年调任北京海关总税务司署总务科帮办，并于 1927 年调任上海江海关汉文秘书课秘书，次年升任代理副税务司，是"自有海关以来，华洋关员升任代理副税务司最早最速者"。

1937 年，在抗日战争激烈进行之际，丁贵堂钦佩忠勇爱国的抗战将士，同情流离失所的战区难民，将省吃俭用、辛苦积攒的 5 万元储蓄倾囊捐献以资军需，并号召海关工作人员积极捐款捐物，踊跃救国。

抗日战争胜利后，丁贵堂被财政部委派为"京沪区财政金融特派员办事处"专员，负责接收京沪区海关，并兼任江海关税务司和浙海关税务司及上海浚浦局局长。1949 年 3 月，丁贵堂为祖国的统一及中华的振兴，顺应历史潮流，决定留在上海起义。他敦促总税务司美国人李度电令各关"不得撤退，不得运走档案，不得汇走税款"。丁贵堂承受着巨大的压力与风险，一边对国民党催促海关工作人员速速赴台的紧急通知敷衍应对，一边安抚下属各司其职、严守岗位，以期在解放军到来时将海关财物完整地交给人民。

在中共地下组织的领导和海关工作人员的大力支持与默契配合下，丁贵堂对国民党多次急电下达的将远东最大最好的挖泥船"建设"号火速开往台湾的命令虚与委蛇，以该船亟待修理等理由予以拖延，殚精竭虑保护海关资产。此举惹怒了国民党淞沪警备司令汤恩伯，汤恩伯以拖延执行征调海关船只命令为由，下令逮捕丁贵堂。此时恰逢解放军兵临上海城下，丁贵堂因汤恩伯仓促撤离幸免于难。

1949 年 5 月 25 日清晨，巨幅标语"欢迎人民解放军解放大上海"在江海关大楼迎风飘扬。丁贵堂领导总税务司署和江海关（包括浚浦局、港务科、检疫所等）工作人员起义。承载着悠久历史的珍贵海关档案、数额可观的库存得以完整保留，富有经验的海关员工在丁贵堂的带领下，积极投身中华人民共和国的海关建设。时任上海市市长陈毅称赞丁贵堂"立了大功"。

1949 年 9 月，毛主席热忱地接见他并亲切地称呼他为"丁海关"。

建筑简介：汾阳路45号

丁贵堂旧居位于汾阳路45号，建于1932年。由协澄洋行设计，辛丰记营造厂承建，为典型的西班牙式建筑风格的花园住宅，占地面积8000平方米，建筑面积1236平方米。建筑为假三层砖混结构，正立面竖三段划分，中间底层为三个连续拱券敞廊，以四根圆柱支撑。一层和三层山墙上均有三扇圆拱帕拉第奥式长窗，窗间饰螺旋形柱。二层阳台上为绞绳式铸铁栏杆。白色粉墙，红瓦缓坡顶开单坡老虎窗，屋檐有连续小圈作装饰。主屋东侧有二重拱行门。左右两侧有附屋。

DING Guitang

DING Guitang (1891–1962) has his ancestral family from Haicheng in Liaoning province. Graduating from Beijing Taxation Academy, he worked in the customs for a long time. Once he served as the vice Inspector-General of Chinese Maritime Customs Service, and the director general of Shanghai Junpu Bureau. In 1949 he participated in the first plenary session of the CPPCC. After the founding of the New China, he served as deputy administrator of the General Administration of Customs of the People's Republic of China and director of Customs Administration of Ministry of Foreign Trade. In 1951 he joined Revolutionary Committee of the Chinese KMT and served as member of Central Committee. Also he served as representative of the first and second sessions of the National People's Congress. In 1962 he passed away of illness in Beijing.

The Patriotic Feelings of "Customs DING"

In 1916, DING Guitang graduated from the Beijing Taxation Academy which trained special talents of customs. After his graduation he was sent to Andongguan for internship and was promoted to the deputy leader one year later. At this point, the foreign tax system where foreigners managed the customs resulted in prevalence of valuing the foreign and belittling the Chinese as well as suppressing the Chinese with the foreign. The Chinese staff members suffered unfair treatment and patriotic DING Guitang was filled with indignation. To safeguard the rights and interests of Chinese members, he often stepped forward bravely, uniting the Chinese staff to negotiate with the foreigners. With his high proficiency both in Chinese and English, his proficient skills in his work and his courage and responsibility, he enjoyed a high reputation among the Chinese staff. In 1919, he was transferred to serve as deputy leader of the General Affairs Section of the Beijing Customs General Administration. In 1927, he was transferred to serve as secretary of the Chinese secretarial staff of Shanghai River Customs. In the following year he was promoted to serve as acting deputy commissioner of taxation, who was "the earliest and fastest among the Chinese and the foreigners promoted to the position of acting deputy commissioner of taxation since the founding of the customs."

During the fierce war against Japan in 1937, he admired loyal, brave and patriotic officers and soldiers participating in the war and had sympathy for the destitute and homeless refugees in the war areas so that he lived frugally to manage a hard saving of 50,000

丁贵堂
DING Guitang.

yuan and donate it all to help with military needs. Also he called on customs staff members to donate money and materials for the purpose of taking active actions to save the country.

After the victory of the War against Japanese Invasion, he was appointed by the Ministry of Finance as commissioner of "Beijing-Shanghai Financial Accredited Commissioner Office", who was in charge of receiving the Beijing-Shanghai Customs. Also he served as deputy director general of Shanghai River Customs, director general of Zhejiang Customs Taxation and director general of Shanghai Junpu Administration. In March 1949, he chose to conform to the historical trend and decided to stay in Shanghai for the uprising with a view of the reunification of the motherland and the revitalization of China. For that he urged Lester Knox Little, an American and chief officer of the customs, to order all customs "not to retreat, not to transport files away and not to remit the taxes". Bearing tremendous pressure and risk, he tried to muddle through the emergency notification of the KMT government to urge the customs staff to go to Taiwan quickly, while appeasing the subordinate to take charge of their duties and strictly guard their posts in order that the PLA would arrive to take over the property to the people from the customs.

Under the leadership of the CPC underground organization and the strong support of the customs staff and their tacit cooperation, he dealt courteously with the command by emergency telegraph from the KMT for many times that the largest dredger "Construction" should be rushed to Taiwan. He did so with the excuse that it was in great need of repairs or other reasons in order to play for time, racking his brains for the protection of the customs assets. This move angered TANG Enbo, commander of the KMT Shanghai Garrison, who ordered the arrest of him with the pretext that he delayed the implementation of the command of recruiting customs ships. This coincided with the time when the PLA soldiers besieged the city of Shanghai. In this case he escaped from the military disposal because of the hasty evacuation of the KMT troops

On the early morning of May 25, 1949, a huge slogan fluttered in the wind on the building of the Shanghai River Customs which read "Welcome PLA Liberation of Shanghai". DING Guitang led the uprising of staff members of the Inspector-General of Chinese Maritime Customs Service and the Shanghai River Customs (including Junpu Bureau, Port Department, Quarantine Office and others). Therefore, the precious customs files carrying a history of a long time as well as a considerable amount of inventory could be fully preserved. In the same time, the experienced customs officers actively involved themselves in the construction of the customs in the New China under the leadership of DING Guitang. CHEN Yi, then mayor of Shanghai, praised him for his "making great contributions".

In September 1949, Chairman MAO warmly received him and affectionately called him "Customs DING".

The former residence of DING Guitang is located at No. 45 on Fenyang Road. Built in 1932, it was designed by Xiecheng Architecture and constructed by Xinfeng Factory. As a typical Spanish-style garden house, it covers an area of 8,000 square meters with a construction area of 1,236 square meters. It is a nominally three-storied structure of brick and wood. Its facade is vertically divided into three sections. The bottom floor in the middle has three consecutive arched galleries supported with four round columns. On the gables of the first and third floors there are respectively three long arched windows of Palladian style with spiral-shaped columns for decoration between windows. On the balconies of the second floor there are cast iron railings of the shape of twisted ropes. The building has white walls, gentle slopes of red tiles with dormant windows on one side as well as eaves with consecutive small circles for decoration. At the east side of the main building there are two-fold arched gates. At the left and right sides are attached houses.

丁贵堂　（刘为民画）　　DING Guitang　（By LIU Weimin）

上官云珠
（1920—1968）

江苏江阴人，原名韦均荦，又名韦亚君，电影表演艺术家。1938 年到上海，最初在何氏照相馆当开票员。1940 年考取华光戏剧学校，首次在洪深的独幕剧《米》中登台亮相。不久，进入新华影业公司演员训练班。1941 年，以处女作《玫瑰飘零》登上银幕。在主演新片《王老虎抢亲》时，导演卜万苍专门为其取了“上官云珠”的艺名。中华人民共和国成立后，任上海电影制片厂演员。主演电影《天堂春梦》《一江春水向东流》《万家灯火》《丽人行》《希望在人间》《乌鸦与麻雀》《香飘万里》《南岛风云》《枯木逢春》《早春二月》《舞台姐妹》等。因其在《乌鸦与麻雀》中的出色表演，1957 年在文化部 1949—1955 年优秀影片评奖中获个人一等奖。1962 年，入选新中国二十二大电影明星。1995 年获中国电影世纪奖。

脱胎换骨的“转型”

一没背景、二没靠山的上官云珠，靠着自身的努力，走上了电影演艺之路。抗战胜利后，上官云珠在《天堂春梦》中塑造了一个奢侈、凶狠的腐化女人，在《太太万岁》中又塑造了一个放荡的女子。1947 年进入昆仑影业公司，这是她在人生和艺术道路上的一个转折点。她在影片《一江春水向东流》中饰演了满身珠光宝气的“汉奸夫人”何文艳；在《万家灯火》中饰演了传统型的贤淑主妇又兰；在《希望在人间》中饰演了坚定沉着的教授夫人、妇科医生陶静寰；在《乌鸦与麻雀》中饰演了忍辱负重的华太太。其出色的表演，受到舆论界的高度赞扬和广大观众的热烈欢迎。

中华人民共和国成立时，上官云珠才 30 岁，正是大有作为的年纪。可能是过去饰演的角色关系，有人认为她的相貌、戏路、气质，很不适合演“工农兵”形象。上官云珠不服气，她努力改变戏路，进行脱胎换骨的“转型”。一时没戏演，她就另辟蹊径，为灾区筹款义演，为劳军义演，一连演出了 131 场，直到因过度劳累患急性肺炎昏倒在舞台上。

1955 年，上海电影制片厂准备开拍《南岛风云》。在即将开机之时，女主角护士长符若华的人选迟迟没有敲定。与上官云珠感情深厚的黄宗英想起了三年来一直坐“冷板凳”的上官云珠，便极力向导演白沉推荐。可让上官云珠这样的演员去扮演英姿飒爽、老练果敢的护士长，在一些人的眼里简直是不可思议。好在白沉导演力排众议，坚决起用了上官云珠。

上官云珠不负众望，一改在银幕上似乎早已定型了的“交际花”“阔太太”形象，把一个历经千难万险保护后方伤员的女主人公演绎得令人难忘。她的精湛演技让那些一向带有偏见的人也不得不折服。

此后，她参加了一系列影片的拍摄，其中以《枯木逢春》中的冬哥妈、《早春二月》中的寡妇文嫂、《舞台姐妹》中的商水花最负盛名，给观众留下了深刻的印象。而《今天我休息》中的儿科大夫，戏虽不多，却依然光彩照人。

建筑简介：复兴西路147号

上官云珠旧居位于复兴西路147号，为三层公寓住宅，建于1933年，占地面积1260平方米。建筑为西班牙风格，立面富有变化，室外楼梯到达二层。红瓦多坡顶，烟囱突出于屋面，檐下有齿形饰带。门和窗户的形式多样，窗间有绞绳状柱，黄色水泥拉毛外墙。此处还居住过柯灵、陈国容夫妇，董竹君，陈同生，刘连波，廖沫沙，白薇，陈子展，钟南夫等革命老干部和知名人士。2016年2月6日，此处挂牌“柯灵旧居”，正式对外开放，展示了大量柯灵书信、手稿和日常生活用品，并恢复了楼内原有的一座仅容一人通过的小型旋转楼梯，楼上复原了柯灵的大书房、卧室、厨卫等。

SHANGGUAN Yunzhu

SHANGGUAN Yunzhu (1920–1968) has her ancestral family from Jiangyin in Jiangsu province. She had former names of WEI Junluo and WEI Yajun and was known as an artist in film performance. In 1938, she came to Shanghai and became a billing clerk in HE Photo Studio. In 1940 she was admitted to Huaguang Drama School and made her debut in a one-act play *Rice* by HONG Shen. She soon attended the actor training courses organized by Xinhua Film Company. In 1941, she began her career on the screen with her film debut entitled *Falling Roses*. When she was starring in the new film *A Bride for a Ride*, the director BU Wancang entitled “SHANGGUAN Yunzhu” as her stage name. After the founding of the PRC, she was engaged in the Shanghai Film Studio as actress. The films she starred in include *Spring Dream of Heaven, A Spring River Flows East, Myriad of Lights, Three Women, Hope in the World, Crow and Sparrow, Fragrance Float Miles Away, The Story of Southern Island, Withered Trees Revive, The Threshold of Spring, Sisters on the Stage* and so on. Because of her outstanding performance in *Crow and Sparrow*, she was awarded the first prize in the 1949-1955 Excellent Film Award organized by the Ministry of Culture in 1957. In 1962, she was listed as one of the twenty-two major movie stars in New China. In 1995, she harvested the China's Film Century Award.

Her Reborn “Transformation”

Without any background or patrons, SHANGGUAN Yunzhu embarked on the road of film acting due to her own efforts. After the victory of the War against Japanese Invasion, she shaped a corrupt woman who was lavish and vicious in the *Spring Dream of Heaven*, and a debauchery woman in the *Long Live My Wife*. In 1947, she entered the Kunlun Film Company, which was a turning point in the road of her life and art. She played the role of “Mrs. Traitor” HE Wenyan, glittering with jewels in the film *A Spring River Flows East*, the traditional virtuous housewife Youlan in the *Myriad of Lights*, the firm and calm professor wife and gynecologist TAO Jinghuan in the film *Hope in the World* and the longanimous Mrs Hua in the film *Crow and Sparrow*. Her outstanding performance was highly praised by the media and warmly welcomed by mass audiences.

上官云珠出演电影《一江春水向东流》
SHANGGUAN Yunzhu performed in the film *A Spring River Flows East.*

When the PRC was founded, she was only 30 years old, an age when she was able to accomplish much. Maybe because of the role whom she acted in the past, some people thought that she was not suitable for acting "workers" with her appearance, performance style and temperament. If there was no performance for a while, she tried to change the way that she did charity performance up to 131 times for disaster areas or for troops until she passed out on the stage due to acute pneumonia triggered by working overtime.

In 1955, Shanghai Film Studio was ready to start the production of *The Story of Southern Island*. When the film was about to be shot, the role of a nurse FU Ruohua had not been fixed. Then her friend HUANG Zongying thought of her since she had been waiting in the wilderness for three years. He strongly recommended her to the director BAI Chen. However, allowing her to play valiant, heroic, experienced and courageous nurse would be unimaginable in the eyes of some people. Fortunately, the director BAI Chen prevailed over all dissenting views and firmly invited her.

She lived up to the expectations, changing her stereotypes on the screen which seemed to have been the "social butterfly" and "rich lady". She made the heroine unforgettable who protected the rear area wounded soldiers to go through numerous difficulties and dangers. Her superb acting found admiration in those who had always been prejudiced.

Since then, she participated in a series of films. In these films, the most famous were such of her roles as mother of Brother Winter in the film *Withered Trees Revive*, the widow Sister WEN in the film *The Threshold of Spring* and SHANG Shuihua in the film of *Sisters on the Stage*, leaving a deep impression on audience. The role of a pediatrician in the film *Today, I Rest* did not have much part of performance, but it was still radiant.

The former residence of SHANGGUAN Yunzhu is situated at No. 147 on West Fuxing Road. Built in 1933, it covers an area of 1,260 square meters. It is a three-storied apartment with the stylistic characteristics of Spanish architecture, whose facade is full of changes. Its outdoor stairs reach the second floor. It has a roof of multiple slopes covered with red tiles with chimney protruding from the roof and tooth-shaped ribbons under the eaves. Doors and windows are in various forms with rope-like columns between the windows. It has exterior walls napped with stucco veneer. During that period of time she had neighbors of quite a few elderly revolutionary leaders and well-known public figures, including DONG Zhujun, KE Ling, CHEN Tongsheng, LIU Lianbo, LIAO Mosha, BAI Wei, CHEN Zizhan and ZHONG Nanfu. On February 6, 2016, a brand was put on here with "Former Residence of KE Ling" and it was officially opened to the public. In it are shown a large number of his letters, manuscripts and daily necessities. In addition, the original small rotating staircase accommodating only one person in the building was restored. Moreover, his big study, bedroom and kitchen were also restored upstairs.

上官云珠 （钱定华画）

SHANGGUAN Yunzhu （By QIAN Dinghua）

巴金
（1904—2005）

四川成都人，祖籍浙江嘉兴，原名李尧棠，字芾甘，作家、翻译家、编辑家、出版家、社会活动家、无党派爱国民主人士。1927年赴法国留学，1929年回国后从事文学创作。1953年9月后先后任中国作家协会副主席，《文艺月报》《收获》《上海文学》主编。曾任中国作家协会主席、中国文学艺术界联合会副主席、上海市政协副主席、中国政协副主席。代表性作品有《家》《春》《秋》《寒夜》《再思录》《随想录》等。2003年11月，中国国务院授予巴金“人民作家”称号。

仅有这些不够

1997年5月8日上午，细雨蒙蒙，长年住院的巴金惦记着向上海图书馆捐书一事的进展，在女儿小林等人的陪伴下回到了阔别三年的家。八十多个满满当当的书橱一如三年前，占据了书房、客厅、卧室、阁楼、储藏间、阳台，甚至车库、卫生间、走廊，寓所内无处不在的书香与满院的花香交织在一起。

听说请人整理出的准备捐给上海图书馆的那批书安放在内阳台里的长沙发前，坐在轮椅上的巴金一进门就忙不迭地请护理员小吴帮忙推着轮椅径直前往内阳台。这批堆放整齐的书籍大都是装帧精美的外文画册，有些是他出国访问时购买的，有些是他会见外宾时交换的礼物。

对书由衷的热爱是巴金藏书的最大动力。巴黎的塞纳河畔，东京的神田旧书店，北京的东安市场，上海常熟路的西文旧书店……为寻觅好书，巴金的足迹遍布世界。岁月无情，然而这些为他的写作、翻译和出版提供重要参考的书却如通人性般，大多奇迹般地完好无损。

巴金轻轻摩挲着这些亲笔签名、盖着他的藏书章的书，思绪万千。过了一会儿，他让小吴推着轮椅来到客厅的书橱前，请陪同人员帮忙打开书橱的一扇扇门。他的目光掠过书脊上的每一列文字，若有所思。小林见此情景关切地上前询问：“爸爸，你在找什么？”巴金答道：“捐赠上海图书馆的书仅有这些不够，再增加些。”小林提议增添一些三楼书房里的外文图书，巴金微笑着频频颔首赞同。望着工作人员帮忙从三楼搬下来的《普希金全集》《莎士比亚全集》《托尔斯泰全集》等书纷纷加入捐赠目录，巴金欣慰地笑了。

谁也没有想到，因病情加重，这次因心系捐书事宜而返家竟成了巴金最后一次回家。巴金致力于捐书，默默地为社会、为文化界作贡献，他捐献给上海图书馆的书就多达六千余册。他把“更多的思想，更多的同情，更多的爱慕，更多的欢乐，更多的眼泪”“分散给别人，并不贪图一点儿报酬”，让生命开花。

建筑简介：武康路113号

巴金旧居位于武康路113号，建于1923年，1948年改建，占地面积1080平方米。该建筑为近代独立式花园住宅，门窗、门廊简洁宽大，带有早期现代派特点。三层开圆弧券窗，双坡屋顶出檐较深，坡面有折脊，檐下有木梁外露；外墙以褐色细卵石饰面，墙面开暗绿色长方形木窗，外设木百叶窗。底层南侧原为宽阔的敞廊，上部为贯通二层房间的内阳台，阳台围栏外墙面中央设置菱形组合纹饰。三层为圆弧形立面的内阳台。主入口门廊外侧为水刷石大圆拱造型，拱顶砌筑券心石。1955年，经陈毅市长特批，巴金携家人从霞飞坊（今淮海坊）59号迁入该处。巴金在此完成《创作追思录》《往事与随想》《永夜》《一双标致的眼睛》等译作及小说。1999年9月23日上海市人民政府公布其为市优秀历史建筑。

BA Jin

BA Jin (1904–2005) was born in Chengdu in Sichuan province with his ancestral family from Jiaxing in Zhejiang province. He had a former name of LI Yaotang and a courtesy name of Feigan. He is known as a writer, translator, editor, publisher, social activist and a patriotic and democratic public figure without party affiliation. In 1927 he went to study in France, and engaged himself with literary creation in 1929 when he came back to China. After September in 1953, he successively worked as vice chairman of the Chinese Writers Association, and chief editor of *The Literature and Art Monthly, Harvest, and Shanghai Literature*. Once he was appointed as chairman of China Writers Association, vice chairman of China Federation of Literary and Art Circles, vice chairman of the CPPCC Shanghai Committee, and vice chairman of the CPPCC. His representative works include *Family*, *Spring*, *Autumn*, *Cold Nights*, *More Thoughts*, *Random Thoughts* and others. In November 2003, China's State Council conferred on him the honorary title of "People's Writer".

Only These are Not Enough

On May 8, 1997, it was drizzling outside. BA Jin, who had been in hospital for years, was thinking over the donation of books to Shanghai Library. With the company of LI Xiaolin, his daughter, and others, he returned home after a long separation of three years. Over 80 bookcases full of books, as they were three years ago, occupied the study, parlor, bedroom, attic, storeroom, balcony, and even the garage, toilet and corridor. The scent of books present everywhere in the apartment interwove with the fragrance of flowers in the courtyard.

When getting to know the books, which were packed up to be donated to Shanghai Library, were placed beside the lounge in the inside balcony, BA Jin, still sitting in the wheelchair, asked in a hurry Ms. WU, the nursing assistant, to push the wheelchair straight ahead to the balcony as soon as they entered the room. Most of these neatly piled-up books were beautifully designed and bound ones of painting in foreign languages. Some were bought when he went abroad for visits and others were exchanged presents when he met foreign guests.

巴金正在准备捐赠藏书
BA Jin preparing books for donation.

The love for books from the bottom of his heart was the greatest impetus for BA Jin to collect them. At the banks of Seine River, in the old bookstores at Kanda in Tokyo, in the Dong'an Market in Beijing, in the old bookstores of foreign books along Changshu Road in Shanghai...to seek good books, BA Jin had left his footprints all over the world. Time is merciless to erode everything. Nevertheless, most of these books miraculously remained in good condition as if they understood human feelings. All of these books had provided significant reference for his writing, translation and publication.

A myriad of thoughts crowded into the mind of BA Jin when he gently caressed these books which were affixed with his ownership stamps and his personal signatures. After a while he asked Ms. WU to push the wheelchair to the bookcases in the parlor and asked persons beside him to help open the doors of them. His eyes skated over the lines of words on the spines, as if deep in thought. Seeing this, his daughter came over, asking with concern, "Dad, what are you looking for?" BA Jin replied, "Only these books to be donated to Shanghai Library are not enough. Some more are to be added." When she proposed to add some foreign books in the study on the third floor, BA Jin nodded several times, smiling with assent. Looking at such books as *The Complete Works of Pushkin, The Complete Works of Shakespeare and The Complete Works of Tolstoy*, which were successively taken down from the third floor and were joined into the donation list, he smiled with gratification.

Nobody had expected that his health condition could be so aggravating that his return to home this time for his concern about the book donation turned out in the end to be the last time for BA Jin to be back home. He bent himself to book donation, making silent contribution to the society and the cultural circles. The books he donated to Shanghai Library amounted to as many as over 6000 volumes. He had "more thoughts, more sympathy, more love, more happiness, and more tears" "distributed to others with no expectation of reward" and had his life blossom out.

The former residence of BA Jin lies at No. 113 on Wukang Road, which was built in 1923 and rebuilt in 1948. It covers an area of 1,080 square meters. This building boasts itself an independent garden house in modern times, with compact and broad doors and windows and with some early modern characteristics. On the gable walls of the third floor, arc windows are placed; the double-sloped roof has high eaves and the slope surfaces embrace folding ridges; under the eaves are exposed wooden beams; the exterior walls are decorated with small brown pebbles and in the walls are built dark green rectangular wooden windows, on which wooden shutters are installed. On the south side of the ground floor was formerly a broad open corridor, over which is the inside balcony which connects all rooms on the second floor. On the exterior surface of the balcony enclosure are assorted diamond ornamental patterns. On the third floor the inside balcony has an arc façade. The exterior side of the main entrance porch is a large cement vault, on the top of which a keystone is built. In 1955, with the special approval by CHEN Yi, the mayor of the city, BA Jin and his family moved here from No. 59 in the Xiafei Residential Area (now Huaihai Residential Area). Here BA Jin finished some of his translations and novels such as *Thinking Back on Writing, My Past and Thoughts, Everlasting Nights,* and *A Pair of Beautiful Eyes*. On September 23, 1999, it became a Heritage Architecture issued by the Shanghai Municipal People's Government.

巴金 （汪观清画） BA Jin （ By WANG Guanqing ）

王维
（1919— ）

浙江临海人，原名王茂柏。1940年加入中国共产党。1941年参加新四军，后调任《民族日报》助理编辑。1944年起先后任《前进报》编辑、新华社苏北分社记者、新华社盐阜分社社长、《新华日报》（华中版）副总编辑、《江淮日报》《皖北日报》社长兼总编辑。中华人民共和国成立后历任华东局宣传部报刊处副处长、《解放日报》副总编辑、上海市委宣传部副部长、上海市出版局党委副书记兼副局长、《解放日报》党委书记兼总编辑、上海市记者协会主席、中国记者协会副主席、上海市新四军历史研究会名誉会长等。

为挖掘美好心灵而“拍板”

王维称自己为“老报人”，正规的说法是“老新闻工作者”。掐指算来，自1941年调任《民族日报》当助理编辑算起，他的新闻工作生涯长达60年。这60年中，有近30年的时间是在《解放日报》工作。所以王维说：“我这一辈子，为《解放日报》出力的时间最长，当然得到它的教益也最大。”

1982年4月30日晚9时许，上海某汽车修理厂女工陈燕飞从亲戚家出来，经过苏州河四川路桥，看见桥上和岸边围着许多人，只见水中有个女人时浮时沉在挣扎，不禁叫喊起来：“快救人啊！”但四周无人响应，于是她不顾自己已怀孕五个月，毅然跳入河中，游到落水者身边，揪住她的衣领，拉着她奋力游回岸边。在其他人帮助下，落水者被送进了附近的医院，经抢救脱离了危险。

这一消息很快传到报社，记者及时赶到现场，了解情况后写成了稿子。但当征求陈燕飞所在工厂的意见时，厂方却说，这个同志平时表现一般。所谓一般，就是普普通通，没有什么突出的表现，按照当时的惯例，不值得登报表扬。总编辑王维知道了事情的原委，却认为，平时表现一般，在突发事件中能站出来，更值得赞扬，这有利于把蕴藏在群众之中体现了美好心灵的东西挖掘出来，发扬光大。于是，他果断作出决定：同意值班副总编的意见，发！

这时已过了深夜一时，夜班编辑立即拆版，换稿重新排版。第二天清晨，陈燕飞的名字和救人事迹传遍了上海的大街小巷。这篇报道的及时登报，破除了过去报纸对报道先进人物向来不太讲究时效的“传统”，同时，提示人们对先进人物和思想的认定标准有必要作重新认识。

第二天，王维表扬了报道记者，明确表示，对于这样的报道将给予更大的支持。记者深刻领会，在以后的日子里，与陈燕飞一直保持联系。他图文并用，对她作连续报道，把一个普通女工改变了的人生轨迹宣传得有声有色，在群众中引起较大的反响，被誉为“越开越盛的社会主义精神文明之花”。

建筑简介：五原路253号

王维寓所位于五原路253号协发公寓。建筑为现代风格的成套公寓住宅，建于1933年，混合结构四层（现五层），平面长方形，建筑面积2128平方米，占地面积441平方米，由著名建筑师范文照设计。建筑南立面挑出阳台，北立面中间圆形凸出，底层有方形门洞和水泥雨厦。方形门窗，水泥拉毛墙面，平顶。公寓沿五原路北边布置，平面为一字型，由两个单元组合而成。每个单元标准层平面为一梯一户，每户为四室户型，居室大多为套间，并巧妙地在房间分隔处设置壁橱。起居室通向阳台，有六扇落地长窗，阳光充足，通风良好。厨房特别大，一间用于洗切，另一间用于烹烧。佣人房设在洗切间旁，而且朝南，虽然面宽狭长，但面积不小，在上海公寓中仅此一例。楼梯间半平台悬挑，底层设汽车库、锅炉间，两边尽头各设两室户型。俞振飞、草婴、邵滨孙等文艺界名人都曾在此居住。

WANG Wei

WANG Wei (1919-) is native of Linhai County in Zhejiang province and had a former name of WANG Maobo. In 1940 he became a member of the Communist Party of China. In 1941 he joined the New Fourth Army and was afterwards transferred to serve as assistant editor of *National Daily*. Since 1944, he has served in succession as editor of the newspaper *Advance*, correspondent of the North China branch of the Xinhua News Agency, president of the Yanfu branch of the Xinhua News Agency, deputy editor-in-chief of *Xinhua Daily* (Central China Edition), and president and editor-in-chief of *Jianghuai Daily* and *North Anhui Daily*. After the founding of the People's Republic of China, he served as deputy director of Newspapers and Periodicals of the Publicity Department of the East China Bureau, deputy editor-in-chief of the *Liberation Daily*, vice minister of the Publicity Department of the Shanghai Municipal Committee, deputy secretary and deputy director of the Party Committee of the Shanghai Municipal Publication Bureau, secretary of the Party Committee and editor-in-chief of the *Liberation Daily*, chairperson of the Shanghai Journalists Association, vice chairman of the China Journalists Association, as well as honorary president of the Shanghai Historical Research Society of the New Fourth Army.

"Making a Final Decision" for Finding Out a Better Heart

WANG Wei called himself "an old hand on newspaper", while the formal name should be "a senior journalist". A careful calculation helps to tell that his career as a journalist has lasted for as long as sixty years since he was transferred to the assistant editor of the *National Daily* since 1941. During the years, he worked with the *Liberation Daily* for nearly 30 years of time. For this he said, "I have contributed the longest of my lifetime to the *Liberation Daily* and I have of course benefited the most from it."

At about 9 o'clock on the evening of April 30, 1982, the female worker CHEN Yanfei of an auto repair workshop in Shanghai came out from the house of a relative and crossed the Sichuan Road Bridge over the Suzhou River when she saw many people on the bridge and at the shore. It turned out that a woman was struggling in the water now sinking now floating. CHEN could not help but shout, "Help! Be Quick!" But no one around responded. Regardless of her pregnancy for five months, she determinedly jumped into the river and swam to the side of the woman in the water. Grabbed her collar, she pulled her along and struggled back to the

王维
WANG Wei.

shore. With the help of others, the drowned woman was sent to a hospital nearby and was out of danger after rescue.

The news quickly spread to the newspaper office and reporters rushed to the spot in time to get to know details before a report came out. But when advice was asked for from the factory where CHEN Yanfei worked, the factory authority said that she usually behaved in a mediocre way, which meant being common without outstanding performance. According to the practice at the time, it was not worthy of praise in a newspaper. However, WANG Wei, editor-in-chief, got to know the whole story and believed that a person who could stand out at emergencies was more worthy of compliment even though she manifested common behaviour in general. This was conducive to finding out what was hidden among the masses and embodied the beauty of heart in order to have it fostered and enhanced. So he made a decision with determination to have the news report published, which was in line with the advice of the deputy editor-in-chief on duty.

At this time it was past one o'clock at night. The editor at night shift immediately took apart the type setting and made a re-layout to include the news report. The next morning, the name of CHEN Yanfei and her story spread throughout the streets of Shanghai. The timely report broke the "tradition" that reports on progressive figures in newspapers in the past had never been very particular about time effect. At the same time, the report also served to remind people that there was a necessity to re-examine the standards of confirming progressive figures and their ideas.

The next day, WANG Wei praised the reporter and made it clear that reports of this category would receive greater support. The correspondent obtained a profound understanding of his idea and had been in contact with CHEN Yanfei in the days to come. He combined pictures and words to make continuous reports of her, vividly and impressively publicizing the changed life track of an ordinary female worker, which stirred up a greater response among the masses. This was reputed as the "spiritual civilization in full blossom".

The apartment of WANG Wei is located in Yafa Apartment at No. 253 on Wuyuan Road. The building is a residential apartment of the modern style. Built in 1933, it enjoys a mixed structure of four (now five) floors with a rectangular plane. Designed by the famous architect FAN Wenzhao, it has a construction area of 2,128 square meters and covers an area of 441 square meters. Its south facade has projected balconies and the middle of the north side has circular convexes. The bottom floor has a square door and a cement canopy. The building is equipped with square doors and windows, cement napped walls and flat roof. The apartment is arranged along the north side of Wuyuan Road with its plane being a horizontal line. It has two units, each of which embraces one household with one staircase at one standard plane. Each household enjoys four rooms, most of which are suites, and wardrobes are cleverly installed at the compartment of rooms. The living room leads to the balcony and has six French windows, allowing sufficient sunshine and nice ventilation. The kitchen is particularly large with one room for cleansing and cutting and the other for cooking. The maid room is located at the side of the room for cleansing and cutting and faces the south. Though long and narrow, the area of the room is not small. In addition, it is the only case of its kind among all apartments in Shanghai. At the stairways there are semi-platform cantilevers. At the bottom floor are garages and boilers. At both ends on the bottom floor are house types with two rooms. Celebrities of the literary and art circles, including YU Zhenfei, CAO Ying, SHAO Binsun and others, once lived here.

王维 （邬海佳画） WANG Wei （By WU Haijia）

王一平
（1914—2007）

山东荣成东山镇八河孔家村人。1932 年 10 月加入中国共产党并参加革命工作。1945 年至 1949 年，历任山东军区第四师政委，鲁中军区前方政治部主任，华东野战军第 8 纵队政治部主任、副政委、政委。中华人民共和国成立后，历任第 22 军政委、第三野战军第 8 兵团政治部主任。1952 年起，历任上海市委常委、组织部长，中国科学院上海办事处主任、上海社会科学界联合会副主席、上海博物馆馆长，市委常委、秘书长、书记处候补书记、书记处书记。1977 年起先后担任上海市委书记（当时设有第一书记）、副市长、市第五届政协主席。

三不要

王一平对艺术品收藏有浓厚兴趣，多年来除了家庭生活开支以外，工资几乎都用于购买藏品。他立志将来把收藏都捐给国家。

20 世纪 60 年代，他被明代画家林良的纸本花鸟画佳作深深吸引，由于其价格不菲，他为了筹钱变卖了几年前购买的吴昌硕《秋菊图》，并坚持以原价售出，即使对方告知收购价已远超当年。这反映出王一平“重艺术本原、轻商业价值”的收藏理念。

除了字画，王一平也收藏文房用品，其中有一件宋坑小方壶石，上刻历代名人收藏的题跋，流传有序。一位美籍华人得知后，特意前往王一平住处，提出以 5 万美元购买的意向。见王一平默然不语，对方以为嫌报价太低，说道：“没有人会比我出得更高。”王一平应声说：“你出再多的钱我都不卖！”翌日，他致电上海博物馆，希望博物馆尽快派人来领走这件藏品。博物馆工作人员说：“王老您自己留着吧。”王一平不同意：“我让司机现在就给你们送去。”

晚年，王一平在一次生病出院后，立刻找到上海博物馆的相关负责人，商议将他所藏古代书画捐献给国家。他的妻子去世后，他召开家庭会议，告诉子女，古代艺术品一定要捐给国家，至于朋友送他的现当代画，可留给子女作为纪念。不久，博物馆的几位工作人员前来看望他，恰好看到墙上的现代画，不禁赞美一番，又问：“准备以后怎么处理？”王一平不好意思提要给子女留念，便泛泛地说送朋友，对方的一句“送朋友不如给我们博物馆”使他惊讶原来博物馆也征集现代作品，只是无奈资金有限。王一平立即把家藏的所有现当代绘画都捐给博物馆，甚至连女儿心爱的黄胄《南海养鸡场图》也列入其中。

王一平还与博物馆约定“三不要”：不要宣传、不要捐赠仪式、不要证书。博物馆展出的曾为王一平旧藏的文物，在简介标签上均写着“无名氏捐”。

建筑简介：武康路40弄

王一平旧居位于武康路40弄，属西班牙风格独立花园住宅，建于1923年，由董大酉建筑事务所设计。建筑装饰细腻的主入口，螺旋柱与复合柱式的结合以及两柱之间的券门上贝壳、卷涡和卷草图案，既有西班牙传统的热烈，又有巴洛克艺术的华丽。人字坡顶屋面较陡，南北各设有一座老虎窗，烟囱保存完好。南立面局部结构前出抱厦，构筑为上下两层的内阳台，其外墙皆采用露木结构，抱厦顶部亦为红瓦双坡面，与主体屋檐相互照应。南侧中部建有三联拱式外廊，其上部为宽大的阳台。淡黄色外墙面采用拉毛处理，红砖勾缝装饰门框和窗台。

WANG Yiping

WANG Yiping (1914–2007) has his ancestral family from the KONG village of East Mount Town of Rongcheng County in Shandong province. In October 1932, he joined the CPC and participated in revolutionary work. From 1945 to 1949, he served in succession as political commissar of the Fourth Division of Shandong Military Region, director of the front political department of Central Shandong Military Region, as well as director, deputy political commissar and political commissar of the political department of the Eighth Column of the East China Field Army. After the founding of the New China, he served successively as political commissar of the 22nd Army, and political department director of the Eighth Corps of the Third Field Army. Since 1952, he had served in succession as member of the Standing Committee of Shanghai Municipal Committee and head of the Organization Department as well as director of the Shanghai Office of Chinese Academy of Sciences, vice chairman of Shanghai Federation of Social Science Associations, director of Shanghai Museum, and member of the Standing Committee of Shanghai Municipal Party Committee and its secretary-general, alternate secretary and secretary of its unified secretariat. Since 1977, he served as secretary of Shanghai Municipal Committee (then first secretary), vice mayor and chairman of the fifth session of the municipal CPPCC.

Three Don' ts

WANG Yiping had a strong interest in art collection. In addition to family living expenses, he used almost all his wages to buy art items over the years. Also he was determined to donate the collection to the country in the future.

In the 1960s, he was attracted by the masterpieces of paper flower and bird painting by LIN Liang, a painter in Ming Dynasty, which was not inexpensive. In order to raise money, he sold the painting of *Autumn Chrysanthemum* by WU Changshuo, which he bought several years ago and insisted on selling it at the original price even if buyer told him that its purchase price had far exceeded the price at which he bought it years ago. This reflected his collection philosophy of "valuing art essence and belittling commercial value".

In addition to calligraphy and painting, he also collected study supplies, including a small square inkstone made in Northern

王一平（左）在观赏字画
WANG Yiping (left) was appreciating works of calligraphy and painting.

Song Dynasty. On it were engraved collection inscriptions of ancient celebrities of various dynasties, which indicated the order of circulation. After getting to know this, a Chinese-American deliberately visited his residence and offered $50,000 as the intention purchase price. Seeing that he was silent, the American thought that the offer was too low and said that "nobody could offer a higher price". At this he replied that "I'll not sell it even though your offer is incredibly high". The next day, he called the Shanghai Museum, expecting the museum could send people to take this collection as soon as possible. A staff member of the museum said that "you keep it, Mr. WANG." He did not agree, saying, "I'll ask my driver now to send it to you."

In his later years, he immediately found relevant leaders of Shanghai Museum after he left hospital, talking with them about his determination to donate his collection of ancient paintings and calligraphy works to the country. After his wife's death, he held a family meeting and told his children that ancient art items must be donated to the country. But the contemporary paintings that his friends gave him could be left to children for memory. Soon several museum staff members came to visit him only to see the modern paintings on the wall. They could not help but express their appreciation and admiration, asking, "How will you deal with them?" He felt embarrassed to mention his promise to his children, so he replied in a ambiguous way that he would give them to friends. A quick response was that "you could rather donate them to the museum", which surprised him that the museum also collected modern art works. But its funds were limited. He immediately donated his possession of all contemporary paintings to the museum and even included *South China Chicken Farm*, the painting which was created by HUANG Zhou and was beloved by his daughter.

He also made an agreement with the museum of "three don'ts"—Do not publicize; do not hold any donation ceremony; do not give him certificates. For all the cultural relics on display collected and stored by him, the label of brief introduction only reads "anonymous donation."

The former residence of WANG Yiping is located in Alley 40 on Wukang Road. As a Spanish-style independent garden house, it was built in 1923 with a design by DONG Daqiu Architecture Firm. The main entrance of the building with detailed decoration, the combination of the spiral and the composite columns, and the shell on the arched doors, scroll vortex and curly grass designs between the two columns—all these demonstrate both the warmth of Spanish tradition and the gorgeousness of baroque art. The roof of herringbone pattern is relatively steep. At each of the north and south sides there is a dormant window and the chimney has been well preserved. The south facade has a protruding porch in the local structure, so inner balconies on the upper and lower floors are built. The exterior walls are of a structure of exposed wood. The top of the porch also enjoys double slope with red tiles, which correspond with the main eaves. The middle of the south side has triple-arched exterior corridor, the upper part of which is a large and spacious balcony. Light yellow outer walls are treated with napping and red bricks with glued jointing are used for the decoration of door frames and windowsills.

王一平 （邬海佳画）

WANG Yiping （By WU Haijia）

王元化
（1920—2008）

祖籍湖北江陵，生于湖北武昌，笔名有洛蚀文、方典、函雨等，文学理论家、评论家、作家。1935 年在北平参加“一二·九”学生运动，1937 年后，辗转天津、青岛到上海。1938 年加入中国共产党。1940 年参加编辑《奔流》和《奔流新辑》。抗战胜利后，任国立北平铁道管理学院讲师。中华人民共和国成立后，历任中国作家协会上海分会党组成员、上海文艺工作委员会文学处处长、上海新文艺出版社副社长等。1979 年后任国务院学位委员会学科评议组成员、中共上海市委宣传部部长、华东师范大学教授、中国作家协会顾问、中国《文心雕龙》学会名誉会长、中国文艺理论学会名誉会长等。著有《王元化全集》（10 卷本）。1998 年获上海市文学艺术杰出贡献奖。2006 年获上海市哲学社会科学学术贡献奖。

潜心著述《文心雕龙创作论》

作为中国《文心雕龙》学会的首任副会长（后为名誉会长），王元化的《文心雕龙创作论》是其众多著译中最重要的著作，被誉为新时期我国文艺理论学界和古典文学研究界的最大成果之一。

1946 年至 1948 年，王元化在国立北平铁道管理学院任讲师。有一天，他读到鲁迅的《摩罗诗力说》，文中五次提到《文心雕龙》。《文心雕龙》中有篇《辨骚篇》，刘勰认为后世模仿《离骚》的作家可分为四类：才高者菀其鸿裁，中巧者猎其艳辞，吟讽者衔其山川，童蒙者拾其香草。鲁迅分析说屈原的后世模仿者：“皆着意外形，不涉内质，孤伟自死，社会依然，四语之中，函深哀焉。”读到这里，他不由得佩服鲁迅先生怎么能看出这么深刻的道理。

“不懂这些东西，没法懂中国文化。”王元化由此决定重新审视并转而潜心研究中国传统名著，其中之一就是《文心雕龙》。然而，研究之路艰难曲折。1955 年，他受到胡风案的牵连，被打成胡风分子。1959 年年底，他在经历几乎精神崩溃的数年审查后，被开除党籍，行政降六级。1960 年，被安置于上海作协文学研究所。在这样的情况下，他忍辱负重，重新致力于《文心雕龙》的研究。

王元化一改过去的老方法，对《文心雕龙》重新研究。一是用古今结合的研究视角，二是采用中外比较的研究方法。对《文心雕龙》中重点的名论，皆以西学理论为参照系，在本土资源与外来观念之间，创造出一种沟通对话的可能性，第一次将这部古典名著所包含的思想和观念，上升到与西方文艺理论交流对话的层面。他提出刘勰前后期思想有较大变化，汉晋学术思想系统中刘勰的原道观以儒家思想为骨干，以及刘勰“出身于家道中落的贫寒庶族”等观点，尤其是关于刘勰身世的重新考辨，推翻成说，具突破意义，后为学界大多数研究者认同。

1979 年，《文心雕龙创作论》由上海古籍出版社出版。1992 年，新一版易名为《文心雕龙讲疏》，作者又增添四篇新论。此书获全国首届（1979—1989）比较文学图书评奖荣誉奖。

建筑简介：武康路100弄1号

王元化旧居位于武康路100弄1号，为联列式花园住宅，共4个单元，1号位于房屋东端。房屋为假三层砖木结构，整幢建筑平面近似矩形，建筑面积2114平方米。房屋外立面原为卵石墙面，后涂刷黄色涂料，假三层南间南立面外露木构架。屋面主要为双坡机制平瓦屋面，局部设有老虎窗。1号一层入口位于房屋北侧，入口小门厅地面为红缸砖饰面；1号东端和西北侧各设有一个木楼梯，楼梯与门厅通过北侧东西向走道相连；走道南侧主要分布有三间房屋，走道北侧设有亭子间。二至三层室内走道及房间楼面基本为硬木长条地板。东侧楼梯为木结构单跑楼梯，木踏步、木扶手。楼梯间东墙设有3个长窗。

WANG Yuanhua

WANG Yuanhua (1920–2008) has his ancestral family from Jiangling in Hubei province and was born in Wuchang, Hubei province. He was a literary theorist, critic and writer with pen names of Luoshiwen, Fangdian, Hanyu and so on. In 1935, he participated in the "December 9th" students movement in Beijing. After 1937, he moved from Tianjin to Qingdao and then arrived in Shanghai. In 1938, he joined the Communist Party of China. In 1940, he was engaged in editorial work of *Torrent* and *New Series of Torrent*. After the victory of the War, he served as lecturer at the National Beiping Railway Management Institute. After the founding of the People's Republic of China, he successively held the posts of a Party member of Shanghai Branch of the China Writers Association, director of Literature Section in Shanghai Literature and Art Committee and vice president of Shanghai New Literature and Art Publishing House. After 1979, he was appointed as member of the Disciplinary Review Team of the Academic Degrees Committee of the State Council, director of the Publicity Department of the CPC Shanghai Municipal Committee, professor of East China Normal University, consultant of China Writers Association, honorary president of Chinese Society of *The Literary Mind and the Carving of Dragons as well* as honorary president of Chinese Society of Literary and Artistic Theory. He published the 10-volume book entitled *Complete Works of WANG Yuanhua*. He won the Outstanding Contribution Award in Literature and Art of Shanghai in 1998 and the Academic Contribution Award in Philosophy and Social Sciences of Shanghai in 2006.

Devotion to the Book Writing

WANG Yuanhua was the first vice president and then the honorary president of Chinese Society of *The Literary Mind and the Carving of Dragons*, and his book *On the Creation of the Literary Mind and the Carving of Dragons* is one of his most important works, which is considered as one of the greatest achievements of both the Literary Theory Research Community and Classical Literature Research Community in modern times.

From 1946 to 1948, he served as lecturer of the National Beiping Railway Management Institute. One day when he was reading an article entitled *On the Power of the Satanical School of Poetry* written by LU Xun, he found that the book *The Literary Mind and the Carving of Dragons* was mentioned five times in it. In one chapter *Remarks on Encountering Sorrow* in *The Literary Mind and the Carving of Dragons*, LIU Xie divided writers who imitated it into four categories, i.e. those of unusual literary talent who can learn from its magnificent composition; those of sensibility and intelligence who can learn from its flowery language; those good at

王元化（右）与赵朴初
WANG Yuanhua (right) and ZHAO Puchu.

chanting who can learn from its description of the splendid scenery; and those with their writing in its childhood who can only learn from its words describing *vanilla*. LU Xun made an analysis of the following imitators of QU Yuan, saying, "They only copied the exterior forms of QU Yuan's works rather than its essentials. The spirits of romantic heroes have died and the society remains as it was. The meaning and sorrow lying behind the words are deep and bitter." When he read this part, he could not help admiring LU Xun for his deep insight into the profound truth.

"You won't understand Chinese culture unless you know its background." He thus decided to re-examine and devote himself to studying traditional Chinese masterpieces, one of which is the book *The Literary Mind and the Carving of Dragons*. However, the process of his study was difficult and tortuous. In 1955, he was implicated in HU Feng Event and listed as one of HU Feng's adherents. By the end of 1959, he was deprived of the membership of the Communist Party of China and his administrative ranking was degraded by six ranks after having gone through a devastating and daunting investigation for several years. In 1960, he was arranged to work in the Institute of Literature of Shanghai Writers Association. Although he suffered from unfair treatment under such circumstances, he resumed his research on *The Literary Mind and the Carving of Dragons*.

But he changed the former approaches used in studying *The Literary Mind and the Carving of Dragons* in the past and tried a new approach in his re-study. The approaches he adopted were the research perspective of combining ancient theories with modern ones and the research method of comparing theories in China with foreign ones. He applied the Western literary theories as a reference system in his study of the key statements in *The Literary Mind and the Carving of Dragons*. He created a dialogue between native discourses and alien ones. He was the first to use the theories and concepts contained in this classical masterpiece to dialogue with Western literary theories. A number of arguments he put forward, especially his re-verification of LIU Xie's life experience which had overthrown the former accepted theories, had a groundbreaking significance and were accepted by a majority of researchers in this academic community. For instance, LIU Xie experienced great changes in his early and late years; his views in the essay "Examining Dao" were basically originated from Confucianism in the academic system of the Han and Jin Dynasties; LIU Xie was born in a declining average family, to name just a few.

In 1979, the book *On the Creation of the Literary Mind and the Carving of Dragons* was published by Shanghai Classics Publishing House. In 1992, the name of a new edition was changed into *The Explications of the Literary Mind and the Carving of Dragons*, in which the author added four new essays. This book won the Honor Award in Comparative Literature of the First National Book Awards (1979–1989).

The former residence of WANG Yuanhua lies at No. 1 in Alley 100 on Wukang Road, with 4 units and No.1 unit is located at the east end of the building. The house is of a nominally three-storey structure of brick and wood and the whole building plane is approximate to rectangle with a construction area of 2,114 square meters. The former pebble exterior walls were later painted with yellow coating. Wooden structure is exposed from the south rooms at the south facade. On the double-slope roof covered with flat tiles made by machines, dormant windows are placed. The entrance of the first floor of Unit No.1 is located at the north side of the building with red cylinder brick for decoration in a small hall at the entrance; at the east end and northwest side of Unit No.1 is a wooden stair connecting to the entrance hall through the aisle at the north side; at the south side of aisle are three rooms while at the north side is a garret. The interior aisles and room floors at the second and the third floors are basically made of hardwood stripes. The east stairs are single-flight ones in wooden structure with wooden steps and handrails. On the east wall of the staircase are three long windows.

王元化 （叶雄画）　　WANG Yuanhua （By YE Xiong）

王西彦
（1914—1999）

浙江义乌人，作家。1937年毕业于北平中国大学国学系。从18岁发表第一篇小说《残梦》开始，直到生命的最后一息，他在文学道路上整整跋涉了68个年头，创作了100多部短篇小说和十几部中长篇小说、100多万字的散文以及大量的理论研究文章，作品被选编成《王西彦选集》一套5卷。1948年加入中国民主同盟。1986年加入中国共产党。历任福建永安《现代文学》月刊主编，桂林师范学院、湖南大学、武汉大学、浙江大学教授，上海作家协会副主席。中国作家协会第二、四届理事。

《春回地暖》的创作背景

1956年初，椎间盘突出折磨着王西彦，使他不得不在华东医院卧床整月，但他依旧凭着坚强毅力在2月23日完成了他写作以来篇幅最长、最尽心力的长篇小说《春回地暖》的初稿。他的灵感来源可追溯到1951年任浙江大学中文系教授期间，他亲历了湘东、皖北的土地改革运动，对农民失去土地所受的痛苦有了深入了解。对农民的深切同情呼唤着他全力以赴创作这部描绘土改运动下农民境遇、塑造农村各阶层人物形象的作品。他倾注全力，从动笔到完稿几近两年，期间完成了与武汉话剧演员周雯女士结婚以及儿子降生两件人生大事。

1956年6月，尚在病中的他从淮海中路上海作协宿舍迁到卫乐公寓四楼的新家，自此不再辗转漂泊。他的书房里摆着宽大而适于笔耕的书桌，书柜里排满了心爱的各类文学书籍，文学氛围浓郁。在他的熏陶下，他的夫人发表了第一篇小说《肯帮忙的城隍爷》，刊登于上海《文艺月报》。

他身处上海，而童年、少年时故乡浙东农村的人事、景物却一直萦绕在心头，浮现于脑海，汇聚成浓得化不开的乡愁，幻化为与作品有着千丝万缕渊源的情结。他受过家乡空气和米粮的滋养，他熟悉那里的叔伯、兄弟、姑嫂、姊妹，热爱那里的山丘、溪涧、石桥、泥路、朝晖、晚霞……这便是他对“一个作家的根是什么”问题的回答——“除了自己的家乡、祖国和人民，一个作家没有别的根。”他满怀热情地对《春回地暖》不断修改甚至重写，他诉说道：“因为自己在执笔写作时是的确动了感情的，是脚下带着家乡的尘土和脸上留有为家乡父老们的命运而悲伤的泪痕时的产物。好在我给那部反映农村巨变的作品取了个《春回地暖》的书名，庆幸乡亲们赖以生存的土地不再寒冷如冰，他们的命运也开始了真正的转变。”（《家乡的乡土和童年的泪痕》）

建筑简介：复兴西路34号

王西彦旧居位于复兴西路34号的卫乐公寓，原名卫乐精舍，建于1934年，赉安洋行设计，占地面积1720平方米，建筑面积3797平方米，汽车间附屋802平方米，属现代点式建筑风格的公寓住宅。建筑为十三层钢筋混凝土结构，两翼跌落一层，立面对称，竖三段布置，中间凸出，设一串挑出的半圆阳台为构图中心，两边为卧入式阳台形成竖向线条；水泥砂浆外墙，立面中部竖线条及突出的半圆阳台为暗红色粉刷，其余部分为浅黄色粉刷，山墙顶部及南侧有重复线条装饰，楼前有小花园。1949年后，吕蒙与黄准夫妇、陈鲤庭、吴强、赖少其、峻青、王西彦等一批文化人在此居住。1994年2月15日上海市人民政府公布其为市优秀历史建筑。

WANG Xiyan

WANG Xiyan (1914–1999) has his ancestral family from Yiwu in Zhejiang province and is known as a writer. In 1937 he graduated from the Chinese Department of Beijing University. At the age of 18 he published his first novel *Decrepit Dream*. From then on until the last breath of his life, he traveled for 68 years on the road of literature, creating over 100 short stories, a dozen novels, more than a million words of essays and a large number of theoretical research articles, which were selected and incorporated in the five-volume *Anthology of Works by WANG Xiyan*. In 1948 he joined the China Democratic League. In 1986 he joined the CPC. Successively he served as editor-in-chief of *Modern Literature* in Yongan in Fujian province, professor of Guilin Teachers College, Hunan University, Wuhan University and Zhejiang University, as well as vice president of Shanghai Writers Association. In addition he served as director of the second and fourth sessions of China Writers Association.

The Background of *The Warm Earth in Spring*

At the beginning of 1956, disc herniation tortured WANG Xiyan, so he had to stay in the East China Hospital for a whole month. However, with strong perseverance he still completed the first draft on February 23 of his longest and most dedicated novel *The Warm Earth in Spring*. His inspiration could be traced back to 1951 when he was professor of the Chinese Department of Zhejiang University. At that time he witnessed the land reform movement in eastern Hunan and northern Anhui. He had a deep understanding of the sufferings by the farmers who lost their land. His deep sympathy for them called on him to go all out to create this works which depicted the situation of farmers under the land reform movement and shaped the images of characters from the rural class at different levels. He devoted all his efforts and spent nearly two years from the beginning to the completion of writing, during which he experienced two major events in his life that he got married to ZHOU Wen, actress of Wuhan Drama Troupe, and

王西彦（右二）和巴金（左三）等朋友在一起
WANG Xiyan (second from right), BA Jin (third from left) and others.

witnessed the birth of their son.

In June 1956 when still in illness, he moved from the dorms of Shanghai Writers Association on Middle Huaihai Road to the new home on the fourth floor at Willow Apartment. Since then he no longer drifted from place to place. In his study was a generous working desk suitable for writing as well as bookcases filled with all kinds of his beloved literary books. A rich literary atmosphere filled the room. Under his influence, his wife got her first novel *City God Willing to Help* published in *Literature Monthly* in Shanghai.

Though he lived in Shanghai, people and scenes he experienced in his childhood in the rural areas in eastern Zhejiang province were still lingering in his heart and crossing his mind, gathering as thick and unsolvable homesickness and melting into complex feeling closely connected with his works. Once nourished by the air and food in his hometown, he was familiar with his uncles, brothers, aunts and sisters and had heart-felt love for the hills, streams, stone bridges, mud roads, morning sunshine, sunset there. This was his answer to the question "what is the root of an author"—"He has no other root than his hometown, his motherland and his people." Full of great enthusiasm in his heart, he constantly revised and even rewrote the novel *The Warm Earth in Spring*, pouring out that "I'm indeed writing with true feelings and the works was the result of creation when my feet were on the earth from my hometown and stains of sad tears were on my cheeks left for the fate of the people in my hometown. Fortunately I've selected the title *The Warm Earth in Spring* for the work which reflects the great changes in the countryside. I am glad that the land where the local villagers live their lives is no longer as cold as ice and their fate has witnessed a real change." (*Native Soil from Hometown and Tear Stains from Childhood*)

The former residence of WANG Xiyan is located at Willow Apartment at No. 34 on West Fuxing Road, formerly known as Willow Court. Designed by Leonard-Veysseyre-Kruze Architects and built in 1934, it covers an area of 1,720 square meters with a construction area of 3,797 square meters and attached rooms of 802 square meters for garage. It is an apartment house of point construction and modern architectural style. The building has thirteen floors with a reinforced concrete structure. Its facade is symmetrical with three sections with the middle standing out and the two wings being one floor lower than the middle. A series of projected semi-circular balconies form the center of the composition. At both sides the receding balconies form vertical lines; exterior walls are coated with cement mortar; the vertical lines and prominent semi-circular balconies in the middle section have color of dark red, and the remaining parts are of light yellow. At the top and south side of the gable repeated lines are used for decoration. In addition, a small garden is in front of the building. After 1949, a number of intellectuals once lived here. On February 15, 1994, it became a Heritage Architecture issued by the Shanghai Municipal People's Government.

王西彦 （杨宏富画）　　WANG Xiyan （By YANG Hongfu）

贝祖诒
（1893—1982）

江苏吴县人，字淞荪。1913年任汉冶萍公司上海办事处会计。次年入北京任中国银行总管理处会计。后历任中国银行广州、香港、上海分行代理会计主任、总会计师、营业部主任、副经理、经理等职。1928年当选为中国银行董事兼总行营业部主任。1930年任中国银行外汇部主任。1939年任中英外汇平衡局五人委员会中国代表。1941年参加中英美平衡局工作。是年，出任中国银行代总经理。1944年陪同孔祥熙出席国际金融货币会议，并出席纽约国际通商会议和在旧金山召开的联合国会议。1946年任中央银行行长，次年因“黄金风潮”去职。1948年任出访华盛顿的中国技术代表团团长。1952年至1959年任纽约斯泰公司顾问。1960年任香港上海商业储蓄银行行长。1973年退休，移居美国纽约。1982年病逝。

白银风潮 力挽狂澜

1928年，中国银行总部从北京迁入上海，实行重大改组，并被中央政府和中央银行指定为“政府特许之国际汇兑银行”。贝祖诒因忠于职守的品格及在货币经营和管理上的天才，被委任为改组后的中国银行董事，并出任中国银行总行营业部主任，同时兼任上海分行经理。

1933年，中国曾因白银大量外流而引发一场金融风潮，史称“白银风潮”。许多商人在中国套购白银运往海外，将白银换成美金或英镑后，再回到中国继续套购白银。当时中国的货币主要分银两和银元，银两即白银。通常大额贸易以银两结算，小额贸易以银元结算。白银和银元在短时期内大量外流，导致中国市场出现了货币严重不足的现象，上海的银根奇紧，利息高昂，物价狂跌。钱庄和银行为保全自己，紧缩放款，造成工商业资金周转失灵，许多工厂企业则因流转资金不足而被迫停工歇业。于是，精通套汇业务的贝祖诒被紧急调至中央财政部和中央银行组织的货币改革委员会。贝祖诒提出了应急措施：第一步宣布海关保护，即提高白银出口的关税，以抑制白银外流；第二步废除白银流通，规定以银元作为正式流通货币。贝祖诒力主实行废两改元，并代表中国银行声明：中国银行准备对发行纸币进行公开检查，决不滥发纸币；而且银元库存充足，随时可供应市面。1933年4月5日，财政部正式颁布《废两改元公告》。“废两改元”在一定程度上抑制了白银外流，同时有利于中央银行对全国金融市场的控制。但是，随着世界银价的继续上涨，仍有商人大量套购银元出口；而且，外国银元和地方政府自铸银元同时流通，使得国内跨地区贸易十分困难。贝祖诒等人组成的货币改革委员会于1935年11月2日再次公布实施币制改革，规定由中央银行发行的“法币”为唯一合法货币，其他货币一律退出流通，并规定法币的一元合“废两改元”后的银元一元。

这次币制改革从根本上控制了白银外流，中国货币从此全面改用纸币。贝祖诒对于法币之发行及其信用之维持，作出了巨大贡献。他不仅仅是一位银行家，还无愧于经济学家的称号。

建筑简介：武康路378号

贝祖诒旧居位于原武康路378号。初时，此处有二层五开间洋楼一幢。20世纪20年代末，为国立中央研究院社会科学研究所所在地。20世纪30至40年代，为贝祖诒寓所。解放初，为中国人民银行上海分行租用；1968年，上海中医学院革命委员会请求调换该屋；1977年，为上海市房地产职工医院第一门诊部；1994年，上海市房产管理局将该房屋自公房经营管理处划归办公室管理。20世纪90年代中期，原建筑拆除后在原址建造现在的八层混凝土结构房屋。

BEI Zuyi

BEI Zuyi (1893–1982) has his ancestral family from Wu County in Jiangsu province with a courtesy name of Songsun. In 1913 he served as accountant of Shanghai office of the Hanyeping Company and as accountant of the general office of the Bank of China in Beijing in the following year. Later he served in succession as acting accounting director, chief accountant, business department director, deputy manager and manager of branches of the Bank of China in Guangzhou, Hong Kong and Shanghai. In 1928 he was elected board director of the Bank of China and director of the business department of the head office. In 1930 he served as foreign exchange department director of the Bank of China. In 1939 he served as the Chinese representative of the Five-person Commission of the Sino-British Foreign Exchange Balance Administration. In 1941 he participated in the work of the Balance Administration of China, UK and USA. In the same year, he served as acting general manager of the Bank of China. In 1944 he accompanied KONG Xiangxi to attend the international financial and monetary conference as well as the New York International Trade Conference and the United Nations conference in San Francisco. In 1946, he served as governor of the Central Bank and resigned the next year due to the Gold Storm. In 1948 he was head of the Chinese technology delegation to Washington. From 1952 to 1959, he was appointed advisor to the Steyr Company in New York. In 1960 he served as governor of the Shanghai Commercial Savings Bank in Hong Kong. In 1973 he retired and moved to live in New York of the United States and passed away of illness in 1982.

Turning the Tide in Silver Trend

In 1928, the headquarters of the Bank of China moved from Beijing to Shanghai and implemented a major reorganization. Also the bank was designated by the Central Government and the Central Bank as "the international exchange bank authorized by the government". BEI Zuyi was appointed director of the Bank of China after reorganization and head of the office of the headquarters of the Bank of China as well as manager of the Shanghai branch, because of his dedicated character and genius in currency operation and management.

In 1933, a financial storm was triggered in China due to a large amount of silver outflow, known as the Silver Storm in history. Many merchants in China fraudulently purchased silver and shipped it to foreign countries. After the silver was exchanged into

贝祖诒全家合影
BEI Zuyi and his whole family.

US dollars or British pounds, it was then taken back to China to continue to illegally buy silver. At that time, China's currency was divided into two main categories—tael and silver dollar, and the former was silver in reality. Usually large amount of trade was settled with tael and small amount of trade was settled in silver dollar. Consequently large amounts of silver and silver dollar flew outside in a short period of time, resulting in a serious shortage of currency in the Chinese market as well as particular tightness of money in Shanghai, and high interest rates. In consequence, prices plummeted. To protect themselves, money houses and banks tightened approving loans with a result of a failure of industrial and commercial capital flow. In addition, factories and enterprises were forced to suspend business due to lack of working capital funds. As a result, owing to his proficiency in arbitrage business, BEI Zuyi was transferred to the monetary reform committee organized by the Ministry of Finance of the Central Government and the Central Bank. He proposed emergency measures. The first step was to declare customs protection, that is, to raise the export tariffs on silver in order to curb the silver outflow; the second step was to abolish silver circulation and it was provided that silver dollars should be the official currency of circulation. He forcefully proposed the implementation of abolishing silver and replacing it by silver dollar, and made a statement on behalf of the Bank of China—Bank of China was ready to make public inspection of issuing bank notes to absolutely avoid junk currency; moreover, silver dollar stock was sufficient to supply the market at any time. On April 5, 1933, the Ministry of Finance promulgated the *Announcement on the Replacement of Silver by Silver Dollar*, which at once inhibited the silver outflow to a certain extent and was conducive to the control of the national financial markets by the Central Bank. However, with the world silver prices continuing to rise, there were still a large number of businessmen who fraudulently purchased silver dollar for export. Moreover, foreign silver dollars and those cast by local governments circulated at the same time, making it very difficult for domestic cross-regional trade. The Monetary Reform Commission composed of BEI Zuyi and others announced the implementation of another currency reform on November 2, 1935, providing that the "legal coins" issued by the Central Bank should be the only legal currency and all other currencies exit from circulation and also providing one dollar of "legal coins" was equal to one silver dollar on the basis of "replacement of silver by silver dollars".

The currency reform fundamentally controlled the silver outflow and since then the Chinese currency switched to paper money in the round. BEI Zuyi made a great contribution to the issuance of the legal coin and the maintenance of its credit. He is not just a banker, but also worthy of the title of economist.

The former residence of BEI Zuyi is located at No. 378 on the former Wukang Road. At the beginning, there was a two-story Western-style building with five open rooms. In the late 1920s, it was the site of the Social Sciences Institute of the National Academia Sinica. In the 1930s and 1940s, it was the apartment of BEI Zuyi. In the beginning after the liberation, it was rented by the Shanghai branch of the People's Bank of China. In 1968, the revolutionary committee of Shanghai Traditional Chinese Medicine College requested the exchange of the house. In 1977, it was used by the first out-patient department of the Worker's Hospital of Shanghai Real Estate. In 1994, the Shanghai Real Estate Administration shifted it from public housing management office to the office management. In the middle of the 1990s, the present eight-story building with a concrete structure was constructed at the former site after the removal of the original construction.

贝祖诒 （邬海佳画） BEI Zuyi （By WU Haijia）

包玉刚
（1918—1991）

浙江宁波人，世界船王。13 岁到上海求学，不久后进入吴淞船舶学校学习。后辗转到重庆银行当职员。1938 年回上海，供职于中央信托局保险部。7 年里，从普通职员升至衡阳银行经理、重庆分行经理、上海市银行副总经理。1949 年春，携眷迁香港，开始从事进出口贸易，后矢志发展海洋运输业。1955 年成立环球航运集团有限公司。1967 年扩为环球航运集团，任主席、名誉主席。1978 年，其事业达到顶峰，包玉刚也成为华人世界船王第一人，第一个进入英资汇丰银行的华人董事。他热情支持祖国建设，捐献巨资为家乡兴建兆龙学校、中兴中学、宁波大学等，还建有北京兆龙饭店、上海交通大学包兆龙图书馆、包玉刚图书馆，设立包兆龙、包玉刚留学生奖学金等。

世界船王圆梦之路

1955 年，37 岁的包玉刚开始他的“船王”之梦时，连一艘旧船都买不起。包玉刚几经周折，在日本一家银行申请到了贷款。他凑足 77 万美元前往英国，买下了一艘以烧煤为动力的旧货船。包玉刚像得了稀世珍宝一样，请人将它整修并油漆一新，取名为“金安”号。“金”字表示要赚钱，而“安”字表示要稳中求胜。这，正是他对经营航运业的构想。

当“金安”号从英国驶向香港，途经印度洋的时候，包玉刚已经办好了两件事，一是成立了环球航运集团有限公司；二是与日本一家船舶公司谈妥，将“金安”号转租给它，从印度运煤到日本。

当时，世界各国航运主都采用短期出租方式，这样收费高，且可随时提价。闻名于世的船王们都例行这样的做法。包玉刚却采取长期出租的经营方式，租金标准也低很多，被一些同行讥笑为“门外汉”。然而包玉刚却有自己的算盘，长租既可持续、稳定地获得租金收入，又可在这个过程中逐渐熟悉航运业务。

包玉刚买下“金安”号的第二年，由于苏伊士运河因埃及战争而关闭，航运费猛涨。当年年底，“金安”号赚的钱，就足够买 7 艘新船了。到 1957 年下半年，航运业出现萧条，运价跌到最低点，那些搞短期出租的船主每天都在赔钱，而包玉刚却凭着合约稳收租金。

这次低潮过后，不少人都学包玉刚的办法，开始买旧船长期出租。而包玉刚又改变了方针，将新船长期租给人家，旧船留着自己经营。因为，新船出租，租金自然比旧船高；而旧船自己用，效果则与新船一样。

尽管连战皆捷，包玉刚仍不满足，他认为单靠经营利润来买新船，发展速度太慢了。他凭着对银行业务的熟悉和经营的长期信用，争取到汇丰银行大量的低息贷款。

在包玉刚的精心经营下，环球公司的船队迅速壮大，1980 年船数达到 200 多艘，总吨位达 2000 万吨。第二年，包玉刚的船队总吨位达到 2100 万吨，成了名副其实的“世界船王”。

建筑简介：淮海中路1818弄1号

包玉刚旧居位于淮海中路1818弄1号。淮海中路1818弄1至8号建于1934年，由中国建业地产公司设计，中法营造厂承建，建筑面积1356平方米。该建筑群由8幢法式建筑风格的花园住宅组成，住宅行列式排列。建筑为假三层砖木结构，南立面入口前凸，底层为门廊，以爱奥尼克式柱支承。二层为阳台，立花式铸铁栏杆。复折式屋面，上部为跌檐式山墙，双坡瓦顶，门、窗楣饰红色弧形砖券嵌白色券心石。白色水泥外墙凸出红砖砌层间腰线，有砖雕巴洛克式垂花饰。现为民居。1999年9月23日上海市人民政府公布其为市优秀历史建筑。

BAO Yugang

BAO Yugang (1918–1991) has his ancestral family from Ningbo in Zhejiang province and known as ship king in the world. At the age of 13 he arrived in Shanghai for study and soon after that entered the Wusong Ship School. After the outbreak of the War against Japanese Invasion, he travelled a long way and finally entered the Chongqing Bank to serve as a staff. In 1938 he went back to Shanghai and worked in the Insurance Department of the Central Trust Agency. Within 7 years, he was promoted from a common staff member to manager in Hengyang Bank and Chongqing Bank Branch as well as deputy general manager of Bank of Shanghai. In the spring of 1949, he moved to Hong Kong with his family and began to engage himself in import and export trade. Later he was committed to the development of marine transport industry. In 1955, he established the Global Shipping Group Co., Ltd. In 1967 it was expanded to the Global Shipping Group and he served as chairman and honorary chairman. In 1978, his enterprise reached its peak and he became the first of ship kings in the Chinese world and the first Chinese director who entered the British-funded HSBC. Enthusiastic in the support of the construction of the motherland, he donated a large amount of funds to build Zhaolong School, Zhongxing High School and Ningbo University, to list only a few. Also he built Beijing Zhaolong Hotel as well as BAO Zhaolong Library and BAO Yugang Library in Shanghai Jiaotong University, and established BAO Zhaolong and BAO Yugang Scholarships for International Students.

The World Ship King and his Road to Dreams

When BAO Yugang started his dream of "ship king" at the age of 37 in 1955, he even could not afford to buy an old ship. After twists and turns, he succeeded in the application for a loan in a bank in Japan. He collected 770,000 US dollars to go to the United Kingdom and bought a coal-driven old cargo ship. As if he had got a rare treasure, he had it renovated and painted anew and named it "Jin'an". The character *jin* (gold) meant to make money and the character *an* (security) meant to win in stability. This was exactly his idea of operating the shipping industry.

When the "Jin'an" sailed from the UK to Hong Kong via the Indian Ocean, he had made two preparations, i.e. the establishment

包玉刚（右）与李嘉诚
BAO Yugang (right) and LI Jiacheng.

of "the Global Shipping Group Co., Ltd."; the negotiation with a Japanese shipping company to sublease "Jin'an" to it to transport coal from India to Japan.

At that time, the world's shipping companies in various countries adopted the way of short-term rent in order to charge high fees and raise prices at any time. Kings of ship famous worldwide routinely adhered to this practice. BAO chose a long-term rental mode of operation and the rent was also much lower, which was ridiculed by some peers as a "layman". However, he had his own abacus since long-term rent could have sustained and stable access to rental income, but also help gain familiarity with the shipping business in the process of operation.

In the second year after he bought the ship, the closure of the Suez Canal due to the Egyptian War resulted in a rapid increase of shipping costs. At the end of the year, the money earned by the ship was enough to buy seven new ships. In the second half of 1957, the shipping industry experienced a depression and the shipping prices fell to the lowest point. Those engaged in short-term rent lost money every day, but he obtained rent steadily by right of the contract.

After the low tide, many ship owners learned from his approach and began to buy used ships for long-term rent. In the meantime, he changed its policy to lease new ships to others on a long-term basis while he reserved the used ships to do his own business. This was because the rent of new ships was naturally higher than that of the used ones while the used ships could be operated with the same effect as that of the new ships.

Although success came one after another, he was still not satisfied because he believed that the pace of development was too slow only by means of buying new ships to gain operating profit. With his familiarity with the banking business and long-term credit, he obtained a large number of low-interest loans from HSBC.

Under his careful management, the fleet of his global company made rapid growth. In 1980 the number of his ships reached over 200 and the total tonnage amounted to 20 million tons. In the second year, the total tonnage of his fleet added up to 21 million tons. Consequently he became a veritable "ship king of the world".

The former residence of BAO Yugang is located at No. 1 in Alley 1818 on Middle Huaihai Road. Buildings from No. 1 to No. 8 in this alley were built in 1934, which were designed by China Jianye Real Estate Company and constructed by Sino-French Construction Company with a construction area of 1,356 square meters. The building complex consists of eight garden houses of French style with a layout of lines and rows. It is a nominally three-storied structure of brick and wood with the south facade projected at the entrance and the bottom as the porch supported by Ionic columns. The second floor is for balcony with rails of fancy cast iron. The double folding roof has a falling eaves gable at the upper part and has two slopes covered with tiles. The lintels of doors and windows are decorated with red arched bricks in which white arched stones are embedded. Lines of red bricks are projected in the middle of white cement wall with Baroque encarpus carved from bricks. Now it is a residence for common citizens. On September 23, 1999, it became a Heritage Architecture issued by the Shanghai Municipal People's Government.

包玉刚 （邬海佳画）

BAO Yugang （By WU Haijia）

包达三
（1884—1957）

浙江镇海人。16岁到上海当纸店学徒。1914年赴日本留学，在日本加入中国同盟会。辛亥革命时，秘密回国，加入上海民军敢死团，攻打江南制造总局。1918年，与人创办开封大昌制蛋厂，任经理。次年，在上海创办黄海渔业公司。1920年，参加由虞洽卿等筹建的上海证券物品交易所，为常务理事。后又与黄楚九等合办上海夜市物券交易所。20世纪30年代，投资江湾上海新市区建设，营建江湾跑马厅，并集资开办房地产公司，建造大批民居。1937年上海沦陷后，靠变卖古董书画维持生活。抗日战争胜利后，与陈叔通、马叙伦、盛丕华等从事民主活动。1946年，加入民主建国会。是年6月，作为上海人民和平请愿代表团的代表，与马叙伦、阎宝航等赴南京请愿。1949年，出席中国人民政治协商会议第一次全体会议，当选为全国政协委员。1950年，任浙江省副省长、华东军政委员会委员、浙江省工商联主任委员、民建浙江省主委。为全国人大代表、全国政协委员等。1957年4月6日在杭州病逝。

邂逅周恩来

1927年初春的一天，包达三从证券交易所出来，他刚想上车便听见有人叫他："包先生，请留步！"包达三回头看着眼前这个英气勃勃的男人，却想不起他是谁。"我能上车吗？"那人问道。

包达三虽然有些迟疑，但还是点了点头。两人刚坐定，那人就自我介绍说："我叫周恩来，你不认识我，我可认识你！"

"您就是周恩来？久仰！早听说黄埔军校有位周恩来，无缘见面，真是幸会！"包达三欣喜地说道。轿车沿着马路兜着圈儿，他们谈得十分投机。也就是因为这次见面，二人的接触频繁了起来，周恩来也成了包达三在赵主教路（今五原路）家中的常客。

包达三十分看重气节，1939年10月，汪伪成立上海特别市政府，请他出任实业部长等职，被他一口回绝。为了躲避伪市长傅筱庵及其手下的迫害，他改名包光周，依靠变卖家产和古董度日。可是，只要是战斗在抗日一线的新四军有需要，他就义无反顾地帮助采购药品和粮食，同时还帮助在上海的爱国青年去苏北抗日根据地参加抗日救亡运动。

1957年初，周恩来总理特意看望了在杭州休养的包达三。总理对身边工作的同志说："包达三跟随孙中山先生参加过辛亥革命，对我们共产党是有感情的。"

建筑简介：五原路252弄11号

包达三旧居位于五原路252弄大通别墅11号，建于1938年，占地面积约340平方米，其中建筑占地面积145平方米。11号与12号住宅相毗连，又与毗连的13号和14号共同组成外观和结构完全相同的两幢住宅楼，呈东西向并列分布。整幢建筑中轴对称，高3层，每层左右各设一套居住单元，立面设计运用了转角窗、悬挑阳台和弧线墙面等现代元素，但入口处等局部仍带有少量装饰艺术派的纹饰。孙毅、彭新琪夫妇曾住在大通别墅13号。

BAO Dasan

BAO Dasan (1887–1957) has his ancestral family from Zhenhai in Zhejiang province. At the age of 16 he came to Shanghai as a paper shop apprentice. In 1914 he went to study in Japan, where he joined the United League of China. During the Revolution of 1911, he came back secretly and joined the Shanghai Civilian Army Dare-to-die Corps to attack Jiangnan Manufacturing Bureau (King-Nan Arsenal). In 1918, he co-founded with others the Dachang Egg Factory in Kaifeng and he served as manager. In the following year, he established the Yellow Sea Fishery Company in Shanghai. In 1920, he participated in the Shanghai Stock and Goods Exchange prepared and founded by YU Qiaqing and others and he served as executive director. Later he co-founded with HUANG Chujiu and others the Night Market in Shanghai Securities Exchange. In 1930s, he invested in the construction of a new urban district at Jiangwan in Shanghai and the construction of Jiangwan Racecourse and raised funds to start a real estate company to build a large number of citizen residences. After the fall of Shanghai in 1937, he maintained a life by selling antique calligraphy and painting works. After the victory of the War of Resistance against Japanese Invasion, he engaged himself in democratic activities together with CHEN Shutong, MA Xulun, SHENG Pihua and others. In 1946, he joined the China Democratic National Construction Association. In June of the same year, he went to Nanjing as one of the representatives of the Shanghai People's Peace Petition Delegation to make a petition together with MA Xulun, YAN Baohang and others. In 1949, he attended the first plenary session of the CPPCC and was elected as member of its National Committee. In 1950, he served as vice governor of Zhejiang Province, member of East China Military and Political Committee, chairman of Zhejiang Provincial Federation of Industry and Commerce, and chairman of Zhejiang Provincial Committee of China Democratic National Construction Association. Also he was member of the National People's Congress and member of the CPPCC National Committee. On April 6, 1957, he passed away of disease in Hangzhou.

包达三（左一）与陈叔通（左二）等民主人士
BAO Dasan (first from left), CHEN Shutong (second from left) and other democratic figures.

Meeting ZHOU Enlai by Chance

One day in the early spring of 1927, BAO Dasan went out of the stock exchange building. He was about to get on the car when he heard someone calling, "Mr. BAO, one moment please!" He looked back at the man with vigor and courage in front of him, but he did not remember who he was. "Can I get on your car?" asked the man.

He was a little hesitant, but nodded his head. When they just sat down, the man introduced himself, "My name is ZHOU Enlai. You don't know me, but I know you!"

"You are ZHOU Enlai? I'm very pleased to meet you. I've heard long ago that there was a ZHOU Enlai in Whampoa Military Academy, but no chance of meeting. Really nice to meet you!" said BAO with delight. The car ran on by circling the streets and they talked very agreeably. It was because of this meeting that the two persons contacted frequently and ZHOU also became a regular visitor at his home at Bishop ZHAO Road (now Wuyuan Road).

He valued moral courage and integrity. In October 1939, the puppet government of WANG Jingwei established the Shanghai Special Municipal Government and asked him to serve as minister of industry, which he rebuffed. In order to avoid the persecution of the puppet mayor FU Xiaoan and his subordinates, he changed his name as BAO Guangzhou, making a living by selling family possessions and antiques. But as long as the New Fourth Army needed anything in the frontline of the War against Japanese Invasion, he would not hesitate to help with the procurement of medicines and food. In addition, he helped the patriotic youth in Shanghai to go to the resistance base areas in Northern Jiangsu and participate in the national salvation movement against the Japanese aggression.

In the early 1957, Premier ZHOU specially visited BAO in his recreational stay in Hangzhou. ZHOU said to employees around him, "BAO Dasan followed Mr. SUN Yat-sen and participated in the '1911 Revolution' and had a relationship with the Communist Party."

The former residence of BAO Dasan is located in Datong Villa at No. 11 in Alley 252 on Wuyuan Road. Built in 1938, it covers an area of about 340 square meters with a construction area of 145 square meters. No. 11 and No. 12 houses adjoin with each other, which are adjacent to No. 13 and No. 14. The four of them make up of two buildings with exactly the same appearance and structure in a parallel distribution from the east to the west. The whole building is symmetric along the central axis with three floors, and each floor has a residential unit at both sides of the gate. The design of the facade makes use of such modern elements as corner windows, cantilevered balconies and curve line wall surface, but some local parts like the entrance still have some patterns of deco art. SUN Yi and his wife PENG Xinqi once lived at No. 13 in Datong Villa.

包达三 （齐亚明画）　　BAO Dasan （By QI Yaming）

叶浅予
（1907—1995）

浙江桐庐人，原名叶纶绮，笔名初萌、性天等，从事绘画教学和以舞蹈、戏剧人物为主的国画创作。1926 年起在上海当过柜台伙计，画过广告、教科书插图，并从事时装设计、舞台美术布景。1928 年，与张光宇等创办中国美术刊行社，创刊《上海漫画》周报，任编辑。创作长篇漫画《王先生》，在《上海漫画》《晨报》连载长达七年之久，影响很大，成为有名的漫画家。后集成《王先生别传》和《小陈留京外史》。

王人美
（1914—1987）

湖南长沙人，原名庶熙。1927 年底赴上海就读于美美女校（后改为中华歌舞团、明月歌舞团）。1931 年随明月歌舞团加入联华影业公司。曾主演《野玫瑰》《渔光曲》《风云儿女》等故事片，并出演话剧《回春之曲》《保卫卢沟桥》等。中华人民共和国成立后，长期在北京电影制片厂演员剧团工作，相继参演了《两家春》《青春之歌》等影片。1979 年加入中国共产党。为第六届全国政协委员、中国影协名誉理事。

磕磕碰碰三十年

王人美在回忆录《我的成名与不幸》中如此形容与她共度三十余载的丈夫——“倔老头叶浅予”，她写道，“叶浅予是个好画家，却不是个好丈夫。他除了懂画，别的什么都不懂，家中里里外外的事全要我操心……”叶浅予在剖析自己婚姻生活的回忆作品《爱怨四人传》中则提到：“在我一生的四次婚姻中，王人美是和我共同生活最长的，但是由于我们在世界观、人生观和生活习惯等方面差异很大，三十多年来始终磕磕碰碰，貌合神离，两人都不幸福。”两人的婚事，是朋友们有意促成的，1955 年经朋友介绍见了面，步入中年的他们考虑到年事渐高，需要相互照顾的伴侣，仅过几个月便结了婚。结婚当日，王人美这样描述：“我们想老头儿老太太结婚不要声张，可不知怎么，风声还是漏出去了。朋友们纷纷送来贺礼。怎么答谢呢？叶浅予说请老朋友们聚聚餐吧。几十个人拥进四川饭店……叶浅予花了近 200 元钱。回来的路上，他告诉我，他已经破产了，因为他的全部财产也只有 200 元。我又好气又好笑，只好自己掏钱去买必需的日用品……”

婚后一个月，他们发生口角，王人美甚至提出离婚。叶浅予问：“这到底为什么？”她生气地说：“你有大男子主义，我受不了！”他反诘：“若是你头脑里没有大女子主义，怎能感到我有大男子主义呢？”她哑口无言。

这样磕磕绊绊多年，他终于意识到自己在婚姻生活中不够宽容，而她也逐渐体谅包容，目睹丈夫对青年画家的爱之深、责之切，以及情愿过俭朴生活也不肯卖画的品格，无不让她心生崇敬。当她病倒不省人事，他为她的病情忧心而心脏病发入院，只能用文字寄托怀念：“我躺在病床上，想着这位共同生活了三十年的伴侣，不由心中黯然，只能默默地祝愿她的灵魂获得解脱。”

建筑简介：淮海中路1842—1858号武康大楼

叶浅予、王人美旧居位于淮海中路1842—1858号武康大楼，旧称东美特公寓，又称诺曼底公寓。建于1924年，万国储蓄会投资建造，克利洋行邬达克设计，高30米，占地面积1580平方米，建筑面积9755平方米，属法国文艺复兴式建筑风格的公寓住宅，是上海最早的外廊式公寓建筑。建筑为八层钢筋混凝土结构，平面依楔状地形布置，楼身狭长似船。其前部为骑楼，骑楼形式为连续券廊。立面作横三段划分，第一、二层处理成基座，连续半圆券廊，水泥仿石墙面。三层挑出长阳台，四至七层挑出小阳台。一、二层为水泥墙面，三至七层为清水红墙外砖。顶层由连续的挑出阳台和女儿墙构成双重檐部水平线脚。1930年，又在该楼东侧再建五层混合结构新武康大楼1幢，建筑面积1700平方米。底层为商店，二至五层为住宅。1945年抗战结束后多为国民政府官员居住。1953年改名为武康大楼，许多文艺界名人在此安家。1994年2月15日上海市人民政府公布其为市优秀历史建筑。

YE Qianyu and WANG Renmei

YE Qianyu (1907–1995) has his ancestral family from Tonglu in Zhejiang province with a former name of YE Lunqi and some pen names like Chumeng and Xingtian. He engaged himself in teaching of painting and creation of Chinese paintings with the themes of dancer and drama character. Since 1926 he had the experiences of working as a counter man, painting advertisements and illustrating textbooks and also engaged himself in fashion design and stage art setting in Shanghai. In 1928, he co-established China Art Publishing House with ZHANG Guangyu and founded the weekly *Shanghai Sketch* and served as editor. In addition he created long comics *Mr. Wang* serialized in the *Shanghai Sketch* and *Morning Newspaper*, which lasted as long as seven years and exerted a great influence. In this way he became a famous cartoonist. Later twc collections were published, including *Mr. Wang's Supplementary Biography* and *An Unofficial History of Jr. CHEN Liujing*.

WANG Renmei (1914–1987) has her ancestral family from Changsha in Hunan province with a former name of Shuxi. At the end of 1927 she went to Shanghai to study in the Meimei Girls School (later renamed as Chinese Song and Dance Troupe, and Bright Moon Song and Dance Troupe). In 1931 she joined Lianhua Film Company together with Bright Moon Song and Dance Troupe. Once she starred in feature films including *Wild Rose, Song of Fisherman, Children of Trouble Time* and others, and performed in such dramas as *Song of the Return of Spring* and *Defending the Lugou Bridge* and others. After the founding of the PRC, she worked for a long time in the actor and actress troupe in Beijing Film Studio, participating in the performance of films including *Spring Comes to Both Families, Song of Youth* and others. In 1979 she joined the CPC. She was member of the National Committee of the CPPCC for six times and also honorary director of China Film Association.

Stumbling and Bumping for Three Decades

In her memoir *My Fame and Unhappiness*, WANG Renmei described her husband, who had been with her for over thirty years, as "a stubborn old man YE Qianyu". She wrote, "YE Qianyu is a good painter, but not a good husband. Except painting, he knows nothing else. I've got to care about all things inside and outside our home..." In his memoir *Biography of Four in Love and Resentments*, which makes an analysis of their marriage life, the husband wrote, "In the four marriages in my life, WANG Renmei lived the longest together with me, but

叶浅予和王人美
YE Qianyu and WANG Renmei.

because of the differences in our world view, life philosophy and life habits, we have experienced stumbles and bumps and have been apparently of one accord but divided in heart all along for over 30 years. Neither of us has lived a happy life."Their marriage was promoted intentionally by friends. In 1955 they got to see one another with the introduction of friends. Middle-aged, they took into account the increasing age and needed partners to take care of each other. After only a few months they got married. The wife described the wedding day in this way, "We thought that a marriage between an old man and an old woman should not be made public, but I did not know how it was still leaked out. Friends gave gifts one after another. How shall we express our thanks? YE said we should invite old friends to have a gathering. Dozens of people thronged into the Sichuan Restaurant... YE spent nearly 200 yuan. On the way back, he told me that he had gone bankrupt because all his wealth added up to only that number. I was between anger and laughter and had to take out my money to buy necessary commodities."

One month after their marriage, they quarreled and the wife even proposed a divorce. The husband asked, "Why did all this happen at all?" She answered angrily, "You have male chauvinism, which I can not stand!" He quipped, "If you don't have female chauvinism in your mind, how could you feel that within me?" She was speechless.

After many years of stumbles and bumps, he finally realized that he was not tolerant in marriage and she gradually learned to forgive and tolerate. Witnessing with her own eyes her husband's deep love for and severe scolding of young painters as well as his willingness to live a frugal life rather than to sell his paintings, she couldn't help but spontaneously have reverence for him from the bottom of her heart. When she was so ill as to be unconscious, he worried about her condition and a heart disease attacked and took him to hospital. What he could do was to write letters to express his yearning for her, "I'm lying in sickbed. When I think about the companion who has lived a common life with me for thirty years, I can't help but feel sad in my heart. I can only wish silently that her soul will get relieved.

The former residence of YE Qianyu and WANG Renmei is located in Wukang Building at No. 1842-1858 on Middle Huaihai Road, formerly known as East Meite Apartments and also known as Normandy Apartments. Founded in 1924 by the International Savings Society and designed by Ladislaus Edward Hudec from R. A. Curry Company, the building is 30 meters in height and covers an area of 1,580 square meters with a construction area of 9,755 square meters. It is an apartment of French Renaissance style and is the earliest apartment building with outside corridor in Shanghai. With eight stories of reinforced concrete structure, it has a wedge-shaped layout and its body part long and narrow like a boat. Its front is of an arcade, which takes on the form of continuous arched corridors. The facade adopts the horizontal division of three sections with the first and second floors as the foundation, which have continuous semicircular arched corridors and wall surface of cement imitation stone. At the third floor long balconies are projected and from fourth to seventh floors small balconies are protruded. Wall surfaces from the first to the second floor are of cement and those from the third to seventh floors are of exposed red brickwork. At the top floor continuous projected balconies and parapets constitute the horizontal architrave of double eaves. In 1930, a new Wukang Building of a five-story mixed structure was constructed to its east side with a construction area of 1,700 square meters. The bottom floor is for stores and floors from the second to the fifth are for residence. After the end of the War in 1945, it was mostly occupied by national government officials. In 1953 it was renamed as Wukang Building and many literary celebrities once lived here. On February 15, 1994, it became a Heritage Architecture issued by the Shanghai Municipal People's Government.

王人美 （刘为民画） WANG Renmei （By LIU Weimin）

艾明之
（1925—2017）

祖籍广东英德，生于上海，原名黄志堃，作家、剧作家。少年时代当过学徒、报童，后考入救济会办的免费中学，因日军入侵而辍学。1944 年赴重庆任中学教员，发表第一部中篇小说《上海二十四小时》。抗战胜利后返沪，供职于上海、香港和北平生活书店。1949 年 7 月，任上海第三钢铁厂副厂长。1952 年，调任上海电影剧本创作所担任编剧。历任中国电影家协会第一至第三届理事、中国作家协会第四届理事、上海作家协会副主席、中国电影文学学会副会长。著有长篇小说《浮沉》《火种》《燃烧吧，上海》等。创作《伟大的起点》《护士日记》《幸福》《黄浦江的故事》《青山恋》《海上生明月》等近 20 部电影剧本。出版全部创作作品合集《艾明之文集》（6 卷）。

作家当厂长

解放战争以迅雷不及掩耳之势迅速推进，继辽沈战役和淮海战役取得辉煌胜利后，又传来了北平和平解放的喜讯，接着上海也解放了。这时，正在北平生活书店工作的艾明之坐不住了。他强烈地意识到，展现在他面前的将是陌生而新奇的全新生活。他更知道，如果不去体验，要想写出像样的文学作品来，无异于缘木求鱼。于是，他决定辞去生活书店的工作，回到自己熟悉的上海，为写出新上海而努力。

离开北平前夕，艾明之到北京饭店向茅盾先生辞行。茅公肯定了他的意愿，并说把写作暂时放下一段时间没有关系，要紧的是应有长期深入生活的准备，为今后的写作开辟新的起点。说着，写了一封信，托艾明之带给时任华东局统战部副部长的周而复。艾明之不知信中内容，回沪后就将茅盾的信转交了。周而复看了信后对艾明之说，茅公在信上说，你回上海是想深入生活，要我给予帮助。听到这话，一股热流涌上艾明之的心头，感慨于自己和茅公没有太多交往，他对于一个文学青年，竟是如此提携和深切关爱。

果然，艾明之接到了通知，让他去上海市政府重工业处报到。他没想到，自己已被分配到上海第三钢铁厂任军管会助理员。一年后，他当了副厂长。上钢三厂是个万人大厂，它像一座富矿，等待着艾明之的勘探和开采。艾明之除了做好领导工作外，更用心地沉入下去，和工人们打成一片。三年后，艾明之又来到江南造船厂继续体验生活一年多。这一切都为他创作城市题材的作品提供了素材和养料。

期间，他先后创作了他在中华人民共和国成立后的第一部长篇小说《不疲倦的斗争》、独幕剧《炉边风波》、三幕话剧《钢铁的力量》、短篇小说集《竞赛》等。接着又创作了第二部长篇小说《浮沉》，不久被改编成电影《护士日记》。片中插曲《小燕子》经著名演员王丹凤演唱后传遍全国。艾明之的“上海题材”创作越发强劲，他积极酝酿长篇系列“火焰三部曲”——接着，《火种》《燃烧吧，上海》相继问世。

建筑简介：淮海中路1350弄12号

艾明之旧居位于淮海中路1350弄12号。1至15号建于1941年，16号建造时间稍晚，总建筑面积5877平方米。建筑由4排16幢三层砖混结构住宅组成，入口上方书“愉园”两字。单幢正立面左侧入口以爱奥尼克式柱支承二层阳台，右侧三层退为阳台，钢窗，缓坡红瓦屋顶，水泥拉毛外墙，用红砖砌窗框和窗间柱，房前为花园。1949年前，潘汉年曾住愉园5号，那里同时也是中共地下党机关所在地。2005年10月31日上海市人民政府公布其为市优秀历史建筑。

AI Mingzhi

AI Mingzhi (1925–2017), born in Shanghai, has his ancestral family from Yingde County in Guangdong province. As a writer and playwright, he was formerly known as HUANG Zhikun. When young, he worked as an apprentice and newsboy and later was admitted to the high school free of charge and run by the Relief Office. Because of the Japanese invasion, he dropped out of school. In 1944 he went to Chongqing as a secondary school teacher and published his first novella *Twenty-four Hours in Shanghai*. After the victory of the War against Japanese Invasion, he returned to Shanghai, and worked in the Life Bookstore located in Shanghai, Hong Kong and Beiping. In July 1949, he served as deputy director of Shanghai Third Steel Plant. In 1952, he was transferred to Shanghai Film Script Writing Office and worked as a playwright. After that, he successively served as director of China Film Association from the first to the third sessions, director of China Writers Association for the fourth session, vice chairman of Shanghai Writers Association, and vice president of China Movie Literature Association. He is the author of such novels *Ups and Downs, Fire* and *Wake Up, Shanghai*. In addition he created nearly 20 film scripts including *A Great Starting Point, Nurse's Diary, Happiness, The Story of the Huangpu River, Love Castle, Bright Moon at Sea*, etc. Also he got published *Collection of Works by AI Mingzhi* (6 volumes).

Writer Serving as Director

The War of Liberation advanced at a lightning speed. Following the brilliant victories in the Liaoning-Shenyang Campaign and the Huaihai Campaign, came the good news of the peaceful liberation of Beiping. Then Shanghai was also liberated. At this time, AI Mingzhi was working in the Life Bookstore in Beijing, but he could not sit still any more. He was strongly aware that the founding of the New China would exhibit in front of him an unfamiliar and novel life. He also knew that, if he did not experience it, it would be impossible for him to create literary works of high quality. Therefore he decided to resign from the work at the Life Bookstore and

艾明之伏案写作
AI Mingzhi at work.

returned to Shanghai familiar to him to strive to write about a new Shanghai.

On the eve of his departure from Beiping, he went to Beijing Hotel to say good bye to Mr. MAO Dun, a well-known writer in contemporary China. The latter affirmed his will and said that it didn't matter to put aside writing for some time temporarily and what was important was to have a good preparation to get deep into life for a long time to open up a new starting point for future writing. Then Mr. MAO wrote a letter for him to bring to ZHOU Erfu, vice minister of United Front Work Department of the East China Council. AI Mingzhi did not know the content of the letter and transferred it to ZHOU when he was back in Shanghai. After reading the letter, ZHOU told him that MAO Dun asked ZHOU in the letter to give a hand to him since he came back to Shanghai in order to go deep into life. Hearing this, a surge of warmth arose in his heart. He was moved since he didn't have much contact with Mr. MAO, but he actually supported and cared a literary youth so much.

As expected, he received a notice, telling him to get registered with the heavy industry office of Shanghai Municipal Government. He did not expect that he was assigned to Shanghai Third Iron and Steel Plant to serve as assistant to the Military Control Commission. One year later, he became deputy director. The Third Plant was a large factory of over ten thousand people, which was like a rich ore and waited for his exploration and mining. In addition to the work as a leader, he went deep into the factory and identified himself with workers. Three years later, he further went to Jiangnan Shipyard to continue his experience of life for over a year. All this provided materials and nourishment for his works of urban themes.

During this period, he created in succession his first novel *Tireless Struggle* which he finished after the founding of the New China, one-act play *Storm at Fireplace*, three-act drama *Power of Steel* and short story collection *Contest*. And then he created his second novel Ups and Downs which was soon adapted into a film *Nurse's Diary*. The original song "Little Swallow" interpreted by well-known actress WANG Danfeng spread all over the country. After this, his creation of "Shanghai theme" became more powerful. Moreover, he actively brewed the long series of "flame trilogy" and his novels *Fire Seeds* and *Wake Up, Shanghai* were published one after another.

The former residence of AI Mingzhi is at No. 12 in Alley 1350 on Middle Huaihai Road. Buildings here from No. 1 to No. 15 were built in 1941 and Building No. 16 was completed a little later. It has a total construction area of 5,877 square meters with four rows and 16 three-storied residential buildings of brick and concrete structure. On the top of the entrance are written two Chinese characters which mean "Happy Garden". At the entrance to the façade of each single building the Ionic pillars are used to support the balcony of the second floor; the third floor recedes as a balcony. It enjoys steel windows, a roof with gentle slopes and red tiles, and walls napped with cement. Red bricks are used for window frames and columns between windows. In front of it is the garden. Before 1949, PAN Hannian lived at No. 5 in "Happy Garden", where the office of the CPC underground organization was also situated here. On October 31, 2005, it became a Heritage Architecture issued by the Shanghai Municipal People's Government.

艾明之 （叶雄画） AI Mingzhi （By YE Xiong）

任德耀
（1918—1998）

江苏扬州人，笔名王十羽，儿童剧作家、导演。1940 年毕业于国立戏剧专科学校。1947 年在上海参与宋庆龄创办的中国福利基金会儿童剧团筹建工作，任剧团负责人之一。中华人民共和国成立后历任团长、院长、名誉院长兼艺术指导。1988 年被评为国家一级导演。先后创作了 23 部儿童剧（3 部被改编拍摄成电影），导演各类剧目 38 部，其中有 10 部获得省市和国家级奖励。《友情》《马兰花》《小足球队》《宋庆龄和孩子们》《魔鬼面壳》等剧目已成为中华人民共和国成立后中国儿童戏剧各个时期的代表作。先后荣获上海市首届儿童少年工作白玉兰奖、第五届宋庆龄樟树奖、第二届中国话剧荣誉金狮奖、首届宝钢高雅艺术特别荣誉奖。曾任中国儿童戏剧研究会理事长，中国文联第四届委员，中国戏剧家协会第二、三届常务理事，中国戏剧家协会上海分会（第三届）副主席，中国舞台美术学会顾问，中国作家协会会员，上海市作家协会会员，第一至六届上海市政协委员，上海市宋庆龄基金会理事。

余晖同样耀目

1987 年，中国福利会儿童艺术剧院为任德耀老院长从事儿童戏剧 40 年举办隆重的艺术档案展览，回顾他在建设儿童剧院及创作儿童剧等领域的伟大成就。然而，已退居二线、担任儿艺名誉院长兼艺术指导的任德耀并未在探索儿童剧的漫漫征程中止步。对祖国少年儿童深切的爱使年近古稀的任德耀“老骥伏枥，志在千里；烈士暮年，壮心不已”。他仍然骑着那辆陪伴他数十年的“老坦克”，每天到中国福利会儿童艺术剧院上班。他深入基层，关注儿艺的发展状况，尤为重视剧本的品质，因为这是剧院之魂。

一天，任德耀被《人民文学》登载的童话《魔鬼面壳》深深吸引了。全文虽然只有寥寥几千字，却生动细腻地勾勒出一个猴子的世界。作者刘厚明正巧是任德耀相识多年、共同在儿童文艺领域奋战的老友。任德耀按捺不住激动的心情，在第一时间与刘厚明联系，探讨如何将这个蕴含哲理、不落俗套的儿童剧素材改编成儿童剧。刘厚明对老友这个提议非常支持，鼓励有更多创作时间的任德耀着手改编。

艺术创作在任德耀心目中是神圣的。他认为“有了材料，并不是等于有了剧本。这就像馒头和面粉的关系一样，尽管做馒头少不了面粉，而面粉却不是馒头”。艺术创作就像制作馒头，要经历一个发酵的过程，而想象力扮演着酵母的角色。作家只有体验到生活的真谛、认识到生活的本质，才能激发出想象力。1987 年，任德耀在全国儿童戏剧创作研讨会上，把根据《魔鬼面壳》改编的新作《我一点也不快活》的详细提纲在小范围内向同行们征询意见。作品被公认为是一块难得的璞玉，精心雕琢必将成为儿童戏剧界的瑰宝。

深受鼓舞的任德耀全身心地投入改编创作中。此时正值酷暑时节，空调尚未普及，任德耀狭小的居室如同蒸笼般炎热。考虑到电扇打出的风会吹乱稿纸，任德耀伏案创作时仅仅准备了一条凉毛巾。一滴，又一滴，任德耀肘部淌下的汗珠常常打湿稿纸。长时间伏案导致腰酸背痛，任德耀便起身踱步沉思。月光柔柔地照进窗户，孤灯下任德耀仍笔耕不辍，逐字逐句地反复推敲。功夫不负有心人，新奇曲折、发人深省的儿童剧《我一点也不快活》（后改名为《魔鬼面壳》）诞生了。在上海公演大获成功后，儿童剧《魔鬼面壳》被文化部选调参加第二届中国艺术节，向中华人民共和国成立 40 周年献礼。

任德耀以生命和灵魂关爱孩子们的成长，将毕生心血倾注于儿童戏剧事业，践行宋庆龄“提高儿童素质、点燃他们想象力”的嘱托，无愧为“儿童戏剧事业拓荒者”。

建筑简介：五原路205弄5号

任德耀旧居位于五原路205弄（来斯南村）5号，建于1938年，美商普益地产公司建造，占地面积746.67平方米，建筑面积1075平方米。建筑群由5幢假三层砖木结构楼房组成，建筑入口位于背面中间，有雨篷。每幢右面为连续玻璃窗，左面后退为阳台。通高窗套，窗间有几何图案装饰。四坡屋顶，檐下有券齿带修饰，水泥砂浆压花墙面。因安福路上已有来斯别业，故名来斯南村，以示区别。现为民居。1999年9月23日上海市人民政府公布其为市优秀历史建筑。

REN Deyao

REN Deyao (1918–1998) has his ancestral family from Yangzhou in Jiangsu province. WANG Shiyu as his pen name, he is a playwright and director of children's drama. He graduated from the National Academy of Drama in 1940. In 1947, he was involved in the preparation of the Children's Troupe of China Welfare Foundation established in Shanghai by SONG Qingling and served as one of the leaders of the company. After the founding of the New China, he served in succession as head, president and honorary president and art director of the troupe. In 1988 he was rated as a national first-class director. He created 23 children's dramas (3 were adapted and shot into film), and directed a repertoire of 38 dramas, among which 10 won provincial and national awards. Dramas including *Friendship, The Magic Aster, The Small Football Team, SONG Qingling and the Children, Devil's Face Shell* and other plays have become representative works of Chinese children's dramas of various periods after the founding of the New China. He successively won the honors of the First Shanghai Magnolia Award for Children's Work, the Fifth SONG Qingling Camphor Tree Award, the Second Chinese Drama Honorary Golden Lion Award, the First Baogang Elegant Art Special Award. One of the first to enjoy special government subsidies, he once served as director-general of the Chinese Children Drama Research Society, member of the fourth session of China Federation of Literary and Art Circles, routine director of the second and third sessions of China Theatre Association, vice chairman of the Shanghai Branch of China Theatre Association (the third session), consultant of China Stage Art Society, member of China Writers Association, member of Shanghai Writers Association, member from the first to the sixth session of the CPPCC Shanghai Committee, and director of Shanghai SONG Qingling Foundation.

Equally Shining Years in his Later Life

In 1987, the Children's Art Theatre of China Welfare Association held a grand art file exhibition for REN Deyao, the former president, for his work in the field of children's drama for 40 years, looking back at his great achievements in such fields as the construction of the Children's Theatre and the creation of children's dramas. However, he didn't stop on the long journey of exploring children's drama even though he had taken a back seat and served only as honorary president and art director of the Children's Theatre. His deep love for children of the country enabled him to "aim for the far-off future and retain a high aspiration" even though he was nearly 70 years of age. He still rode on the "old tank" that accompanied him for decades and went to work at the Children's Art Theatre of China Welfare Foundation. He went to the grass-roots level and paid close attention to the development of children's arts, especially to the quality of plays because it was the soul of the theater.

任德耀在创作
REN Deyao in creative writing.

One day, he was deeply attracted by the fairy tale *Devil's Face Shell* published in *The People's Literature*. Though the full text of the original only covered a few thousand words, it vividly and delicately outlined a monkey in the world. The author LIU Houming happened to be his friend for many years who also worked in the field of Children's art. He felt very excited and contacted Liu as soon as he could, and they explored how to adapt the philosophical and unconventional tale into a children's drama. He was supported in this proposal of adaptation and encouraged to start the adaptation since he had more time for creation.

Artistic creation was sacred in the eyes of REN Deyao. He believed that "material at hand does not equal the script itself. This is just like the relationship between bread and flour. Even though bread can never be made without flour, flour is not bread". Artistic creation was like making bread, which underwent a fermentation process and in which imagination played the role of yeast. Writers could stimulate their imagination only when they experienced the true meaning of life and understood its essence. On a national seminar of children's drama creation in 1987, he consulted a small circle of peer writers for advice with a detailed outline of a new drama *I'm Not Happy Any Bit* adapted from *Devil's Face Shell*. The work was recognized as a rare jade, which would become the treasure of children drama after fine carving and polishing.

REN was considerably inspired and devoted heart and soul to the creative adaptation. It was at a time of summer and air conditioning was not yet popularized. His narrow room was burning hot. He knew that the electric fan would blow paper away. When he was writing at the desk, he only prepared a cold towel. Drop after drop of sweat from his elbow often wetted paper. Long time of work at desk led to backache in him so that he stood up to walk back and forth in meditation. The moonlight softly shone through windows while he was sitting at a lonely desk, still writing continuously and repeatedly polishing word by word and sentence by sentence. Hard work paid off quickly. *I'm Not Happy Any Bit* (later *Devil's Face Shell*), was a new, labyrinthian and thought-provoking children's drama. Its debut in Shanghai was a great success, so the drama was selected by the Ministry of Culture to participate in the Second China Art Festival as a dedication to the 40th anniversary of the founding of the People's Republic of China.

REN cared for children's growth with his life and soul and devoted all his energy to the cause of children's drama, fulfilling the expectation of SONG Qingling to "improve the quality of children and light up their imagination" and deserving the title of "pioneer of the cause of children's theater".

The former residence of REN Deyao is situated at No. 5 in Alley 205 on Wuyuan Road. Built in 1938 by Asia Realty Company, an American firm, it covers an area of 746.67 square meters and a construction area of 1,075 square meters. The architecture complex is composed of five three-tiered buildings of brick and wood. The building entrances are located in the middle of the back and all have canopies. The right side of each building has continuous glass windows and the left side falls back to form balconies. Full-height window covers are used and between windows are geometric pattern decorations. The roofs have four slopes and under the eaves are arch teethed belts of decoration and walls with embossed patterns of cement mortar. On Anfu Road there has been a Laisi residence. Therefore this building is named Laisi South Village to make a difference. It is now a residential house. On September 23, 1999, it became a Heritage Architecture issued by the Shanghai Municipal People's Government.

任德耀 （邬海佳画） REN Deyao （By WU Haijia）

刘亚楼
（1911—1965）

福建武平人，原名刘振东。1929年加入中国共产党，同年参加中国工农红军。曾任红十二军营长兼营政委，红四军十二师三十五团政委、第十一师政委，红一军团第一师师长，陕甘支队第二纵队副司令员。随中央红军参加长征。抗日战争时期，任抗日军政大学训练部部长、教育长。1939年赴苏联伏龙芝军事学院学习。1946年回国后，任东北民主联军参谋长、东北野战军参谋长、东北军区参谋长、第四野战军十四兵团司令员。中华人民共和国成立后，任人民解放军空军司令员、国防部副部长、国防科委副主任、国防委员会委员。1955年被授予上将军衔。在中国共产党第八次全国代表大会上当选为中央委员。1965年5月7日在北京病逝。

“30个小时就够了”

1949年1月，中国人民解放军东北野战军参谋长刘亚楼，指挥野战军主力5个纵队22个师和特种兵司令部炮兵、坦克、工兵等共34万人攻取天津。战役开始前，中共平津前线总前委委员罗荣桓听了刘亚楼汇报的作战计划后询问：“军委限令三天拿下天津。你需要几天？”“30个小时就够了。”刘亚楼满怀自信。另一位委员聂荣臻不由一怔：“军中无戏言喽！”

总攻前一天夜晚，刘亚楼亲自前往前沿阵地观察敌情。当他途经敌我阵地间的一座坟冢时，一束光忽然照到他身上，那是敌军搜查队的手电筒。“什么人？”盘问的同时伴随着拉枪栓声。刘亚楼急中生智，喊道：“混蛋，大声嚷什么？小心共军听见了！”正当对方犹豫疑惑时，他和警卫员掏出枪向敌方射去，趁他们混乱之际，拔腿就跑。回到指挥部，警卫员直冒冷汗，忙问刘亚楼：“前线指挥员要是真有个闪失，怎么交代？”刘亚楼一边洗脸一边说：“好兆头！好兆头！他们这次没抓住我，咱们就该抓住他们的主帅了！”

敌军主帅是国民党军天津警备区司令陈长捷，他对“大天津堡垒化”亦是自感把握十足。对于夺取天津这场攻坚战，刘亚楼打算把敌军主力引向城北加以牵制，使城中心地带防卫空虚，以利于东西两方夹攻。正巧，陈长捷又派代表前来谈判，刘亚楼计上心来，让人安排四位谈判代表到指挥部隔壁屋中休息，告诉他们说：“刘总指挥正在路上，半个小时才能赶到。”刘亚楼在指挥部坐了片刻，从后门离开，乘吉普车绕天津发电厂转了一圈后再回到指挥部，犹如外出赶回。走进休息室，他拂去衣服上的尘土，对代表们说：“对不起，我紧赶慢赶，还是晚了，让诸位久等了。”代表瞅了眼手表，已过将近一小时，不正是从天津北面的杨村回来的路程所需？代表们将这一“发现”汇报给陈长捷。

刘亚楼则继续实施计策——“咱们再加加温，从城北放它几炮，让陈长捷坚信我们从城北进攻。”这天下午，部署于城北的第四野战军炮火延续了半个小时，给敌军工事不小的打击。夜里，陈长捷便将守城主力115师从城中心调至城北，这样一来，防御体系在中心区域出现薄弱环节。东北野战军给予致命一击，全歼敌军13万人，活捉陈长捷。陈长捷叹道：“我上了刘亚楼的圈套！圈套啊！”

从攻城到大捷，一共用时29小时。

建筑简介：安福路271号

刘亚楼旧居位于安福路271号，为独立式花园住宅。房屋为三层砖混结构（局部二层），建筑平面近似矩形。北立面楼梯间设有上下通长的矩形钢长窗，该区域为白色涂料饰面，其余部分主要为清水红砖外墙面，平拱钢窗；机制平瓦不规则坡屋面，屋顶有出屋面烟囱。一层设有架空层，入口位于房屋北侧中部，三层北立面西侧退为露台，二层南立面中部设有半圆形露台。房屋北侧为入户庭院，东侧、南侧为花园。

LIU Yalou

LIU Yalou (1911–1965) has his ancestral family from Wuping County in Fujian province with a former name of LIU Zhendong. In 1929, he joined the Communist Party of China and participated in the Chinese Red Army of Workers and Farmers in the same year. Once he served as battalion commander and commissar of the Twelfth Army of the Chinese Red Army of Workers and Farmers, commissar of the Thirty-fifth Regiment of the Twelfth Division of the Fourth Army, commissar of the Eleventh Division, commander of the First Division of the First Army and vice commander of the Shaanxi-Gansu Column of the Second Army. He participated in the Long March together with the Central Red Army. During the War against Japanese Invasion, he served as director of the Training Department and provost of Chinese People's Resisting-Japanese Military and Political College. In 1939, he attended the Combined Arms Academy of the Armed Forces of the Russian Federation. When he returned to China in 1946, he was appointed as chief of staff of the Northeast Democratic Allied Army, the Northeast Field Army and the Northeast Military Command as well as commander of the Fourteenth Army Corp of the Fourteenth Field Army. After the founding of the People's Republic of China, he served as commander of Air Force of the People's Liberation Army, vice minister of the Ministry of National Defense of the People's Republic of China, deputy director of the Commission of Science, Technology and Industry for National Defense and member of the National Defense Commission. In 1955, he was granted the rank of General and elected as member of the Central Committee in the Eighth National Congress of the CPC. On May 7, 1965, he passed away of illness in Beijing.

"30 Hours is Enough"

In January of 1949, LIU Yalou was chief of staff of the Northeast Field Army of Chinese People's Liberation Army. He commanded a total of 340,000 soldiers, including artillery, tank soldiers and engineer soldiers from both five different Columns of the Field Army and Special Troops to attack the city of Tianjin. Before the campaign, he reported his campaign plan to LUO Ronghuan, member of the General Frontline Committee of Beiping-Tianjin front-line. After getting to know his plan, LUO asked him, "The Central Military Commission has ordered you to occupy Tianjin within 3 days. How long do you actually need?" "30 hours is enough." He answered full of confidence. NIE Rongzhen, also member of the General Frontline Committee, was shocked by his

刘亚楼上将
General LIU Yalou.

words and said, "No joke is allowed in terms of battle!"

During the night before the attack, he went to the frontline to observe the enemy situation in person. When he went through a graveyard between them and the enemy's positions, a light suddenly shone upon him. The light came from the torch of searching team of their enemy. "Who are you?" the enemy interrogated, pulling the bolt at the same time. With quick wits in this emergency, he shouted, "Idiot! You shouted so loudly! Be alert, or you will be discovered by the Communist soldiers!" While the enemy soldiers felt puzzled and hesitated for a moment, he and his guard took out the gun and shot the enemy soldiers. During the chaos, they ran away as fast as possible. When they got to their headquarters, his guard still felt frightened and nervous. He said to LIU anxiously, "What if anything should go wrong? You are the Commander of the frontline!" He washed his face, saying, "It is a good luck! They didn't catch me this time and it's our turn to catch their general!"

The general of the enemy was CHEN Changjie, commander of Tianjin Garrison of the KMT Army. He was also full of self-confidence of his "Impregnable Tianjin". In order to win this battle of heavily-fortified Tianjin, LIU Yalou intended to attract the main forces of the enemy to the north of the city to pin them down, thus resulting in the absence of defense in the center of the city, which would help them attack the city from both the west and east sides. It happened that CHEN Changjie sent representatives to make negotiations with him and an idea occurred to him suddenly. He ordered one of his men to arrange for the four negotiators to have a rest in the neighboring room of the headquarters and to tell them, "Commander LIU is on the way and he will arrive in half an hour." He sat in the headquarters for a moment and left through the rear door. After driving a jeep around the Tianjin Power Plant for some time, he returned to the headquarters as if he had just gone back from outside. He went into the lounge of the representatives, brushed off the dust from his clothes and said, "I am sorry for being late and keeping you waiting for such a long time." The representatives took a look at their watches and found it was nearly an hour after their arrival. Wasn't it exactly the time required to go back from Yangcun Village at the north side of Tianjin to the headquarters? The representatives of the enemy reported this "discovery" to their commander.

He continued his manoeuvre, saying, "Let's redouble our efforts by blasting in the northern part of the city so as to convince CHEN Changjie of our attack from the north." In that afternoon, the Fourth Field Army, which was deployed in the north of the city, had been firing for half an hour, brought a terrible blow to the fortification of their enemy. At night, CHEN Changjie transferred his 115th Division, the main force of guarding the city, from the city center to the northern part. In this way, the defense in the central area became weak and was attacked by a knockout blow from the Northeast Field Army. All the 130 thousand enemy soldiers were wiped out and Commander CHEN was captured alive. CHEN sighed, "I got trapped by LIU! It's a trap!"

It just took 29 hours for him to achieve the victory.

The former residence of LIU Yalou is situated at No. 271 on Anfu Road. This house is an independent garden-style house. It is a three-storeyed building of mixed structure of brick and concrete (two-story at parts) and the building plane is approximate to rectangle. The north side of the staircase has long rectangular steel windows of equal length, which is coated with whitewash, and the remaining parts are external walls made of water red bricks. The walls have flat arch steel windows and irregularly machine-made flat tile roof with a chimney outside. There is an overhead layer on the first floor and the entrance is located in the middle of the north side of the house. The west of the north side of the third floor becomes the terrace and the middle of the south side of the second floor is a semi-circular terrace. There is a courtyard for entrance on the north side of the house and on the east and south sides is a garden.

刘亚楼 （钱定华画） LIU Yalou （By QIAN Dinghuan）

刘靖基
（1902—1997）

江苏常州人，中国民族工商业者的杰出代表，爱国人士和社会活动家。早年就读于江苏省立第二工业专科学校。1920年后，与他人合办常州大成纱厂，并任经理和常务董事。1938年，在上海公共租界创办安达纱厂，任董事兼总经理。1942年，任上海棉纺同业公会收花处常务理事和总经理。抗战胜利后，任南京江南水泥厂副董事长、董事长，上海大丰纱厂常务董事和全国纺织业联合会常务理事。1948年任上海市商会常务理事、市参议员。1949年8月被推选为上海市工商业联合会筹备会常务委员。1981年协助政府组建上海市投资信托公司，任董事长。1985年，任上海工商学院董事会主席、上海沪港经济发展协会名誉会长。是中国人民政治协商会议第六、七、八届全国委员会副主席，中华全国工商联合会副主席，中国民主建国会中央委员会顾问。

心里始终想着国家

刘靖基早年目睹国家贫弱、民族工业落后的局面，立志实业救国，苦心创办企业，奋斗多年终于成为在上海纺织业与工商业具有相当影响力的民族企业家。

上海解放前夕，刘靖基曾考虑是否应把工厂迁往香港，他在香港遇到了爱国进步人士黄炎培等朋友，深受他们宣传共产党统一战线与保护民族工商业政策的鼓舞和感召，且难以割舍亲属和经营多年的企业，于是在1949年4月搭乘泛美航空最后一次飞沪航班回上海。汤恩伯送来飞往台湾的机票，要他尽快迁离大陆，但他已下定决心留在上海，为防不测，他到机场假装候机，飞机起飞后便悄悄折返，躲到医院里等待解放。

1949年6月，他受到陈毅市长邀请，倾听陈毅市长对于民族资产阶级政策的阐述，这更坚定了他为国出力的决心。他发表文章，宣传介绍“公私兼顾、劳资两利”之举措，在棉纺工业界率先创建劳资协商会，又把解放前留在香港和海外的资产设备调回上海，在浦东北蔡镇扩建上海安达纺织新厂和化纤厂。

20世纪50年代，他积极响应社会主义改造的号召，首批带头申请纺织行业进行公私合营，为全国工商界作出表率。此后，他还承担起很多社会工作，为上海市工商联和政协不辞辛劳奔走效力。

1979年，78岁高龄的他以“老牛明知夕阳短，不用扬鞭自奋蹄”的自我勉励，率先捐款并带动民建中央和全国工商联骨干，以民间集资方式创办工商界爱国建设公司。他还率领上海工商界代表团赴香港访问、赴美国探亲访友，以亲身经历宣传国内政策，吸引侨胞回故乡投资。

1980年，他将精心珍藏的张即之行书《待漏院记卷》、吴琚行书《五段卷》、王蒙的《天香深处图轴》、倪瓒的《六君子图轴》、朱德润行书《田园杂兴诗轴》等40件最珍贵的书画捐赠给了上海博物馆。

建筑简介：武康路99号

刘靖基曾居住的武康路99号，建于1928年，占地面积1105平方米，建筑面积563平方米，属英国乡村建筑风格的花园住宅。建筑为假三层砖木结构，平面略呈L型，中间凸出门廊，二层为阳台，立镂花栏杆。右侧坡檐至二层，陡坡屋面，开双坡老虎窗。外墙为白色水泥拉毛墙面，露红色木构架，上有齿形装饰，砖砌锯齿平面状烟囱，局部墙体转角及北立面窗框处均有红砖砌筑屋角石。建筑原为英商正广和洋行大班住宅。20世纪30年代，这里又成了宋子文亲信、江海关监督唐海安的住宅。中华人民共和国成立后，潘汉年、魏文伯、王震都曾在此居住过。后来又作为市委招待所、华东局机要局的办公室。后刘靖基返沪，市政府安排其全家入住。1994年2月15日上海市人民政府公布其为市优秀历史建筑。

LIU Jingji

LIU Jingji (1902–1997) has his ancestral family from Changzhou in Jiangsu province. He is known as one of China's outstanding representatives of national industry and commerce as well as a patriot and social activist. In his early years he studied in Jiangsu Province-run Second Industrial College. After 1920, he set up with others Changzhou Dacheng Cotton Factory and served as its manager and executive director. In 1938, he founded Anda Cotton Factory in Shanghai International Settlement and served as its director and general manager. In 1942, he served as managing director and general manager of the Cotton Collection Division of Shanghai Cotton Textile Association. After the victory of the War against Japanese Invasion, he served as vice chairman and chairman of Nanjing Jiangnan Cement Factory, executive director of Shanghai Dafeng Mill and managing director of China National Textile and Apparel Council. In 1948 he served as executive director of Shanghai Chamber of Commerce and senator of the city. In August 1949 he was elected as member of the standing committee of the preparatory meeting of Shanghai Federation of Industry and Commerce. In 1981 he assisted the Government to organize Shanghai Investment Trust Company and served as its chairman. In 1985, he served as chairman of the director board of Shanghai Industry and Commerce College, and as honorary president of Shanghai and Hong Kong Economic Development Association. Also he was vice chairman of the sixth, seventh and eighth sessions of the National Committee of the CPPCC, vice chairman of All-China Federation of Industry and Commerce, and consultant of the Central Committee of China National Democratic Construction Association.

Always with the Country in his Heart

LIU Jingji witnessed the situation of national poverty and backwardness of national industry in the early years so that he was determined to save the country by industry, painstakingly setting up enterprises. After struggling efforts for many years he finally became a national entrepreneur with considerable influence in the field of textile industry as well as the field of industry and commerce in Shanghai.

刘靖基（左四）参观考察

LIU Jingji (four from left) on an inspection tour.

On the eve of the liberation of Shanghai, he once considered whether he should move the factory to Hong Kong. At this time, he met in Hong Kong some patriotic and progressive friends, including Huang Yanpei and was deeply moved and inspired by their publicity of the united front of the CPC and its policy of protecting national industry and commerce. Moreover, it was difficult for him to part with the relatives and the business he had run for many years. Therefore, in April 1949 he took the last flight of Pan American Airlines to fly back to Shanghai. TANG Enbo, the KMT general, sent him air tickets to Taiwan and asked him to move out of the mainland as soon as possible, but he had determined to stay in Shanghai. For protection against accident, he pretended to go to the airport, but quietly returned after the aircraft took off. After his return, he hid himself in the hospital to wait for the liberation of the city.

In June 1949, he was invited by CHEN Yi, mayor of the city, to listen to his elaboration of policies to national bourgeoisie, which strengthened his determination to make his own contributions to the country. He published articles, publicizing the measures of "considering both public and private, and benefiting both the labor and the capital". Also he took the lead to create the first labor and capital consultation society in cotton industry. Furthermore he moved assets and equipment from Hong Kong and overseas factories back to Shanghai, which remained there before the liberation. With these he expanded to found a new Shanghai Anda Textile Factory and a chemical fiber plant at Beicai Town in Pudong District.

In the 1950s, he actively responded to the call of socialist transformation and took the lead in the textile industry to apply for public-private partnerships, setting a good example for the national business community. Since then, he also assumed a lot of social work, contributing tirelessly to Shanghai Federation of Industry and Commerce and the municipal CPPCC.

In 1979 when he was at the age of 78, he still encouraged himself and took the lead to donate and bring along backbones of the central committee of China Democratic National Construction Association and All-China Federation of Industry and Commerce to found Patriotic Construction Company in the field of industry and commerce on the basis of civil fund-raising. Also he led a delegation of businessmen from Shanghai to visit Hong Kong and went to visit relatives and friends in the United States, publicizing domestic policies with his own experiences in order to attract overseas Chinese to return home for the purpose of investment.

In 1980, he donated 40 pieces of most precious calligraphy and paintings to Shanghai Museum.

LIU Jingji once lived at No. 99 on Wukang Road. The building was finished in 1928, which covers an area of 1,105 square meters with a construction area of 563 square meters. It is a garden house of rural architecture of British style. It is of a nominally three-storied structure of brick and wood and its plane is L-shaped. In the middle there is a protruding porch and the second floor is for balcony, where railings with ornamental engravings are used. At the right side eaves and slope reach the second floor. The roof has steep slopes with luthern on both slopes. The exterior walls have napped stucco veneer with white cement and the red wood frame is exposed with toothed decorations and chimneys of brick. Local wall corners and window frames at the north facade have red brick as corner stones. Formerly the building was the residence of Calbeck Macgregor & Co. Building. In the 1930s, it became the residence of a confidant of SONG Ziwen. After the founding of the New China, quite a few well-known people once lived here. Later it was used as City Guest House and office of East China Bureau. After LIU returned to Shanghai, the city government arranged this building for the whole family. On February 15, 1994, it became a Heritage Architecture issued by the Shanghai Municipal People's Government.

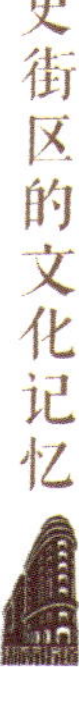

刘靖基　（吴耀明画）　LIU Jingji　（By WU Yaoming）

向梅
（1937— ）

祖籍河南巩县，生于北平，原名武相梅，电影表演艺术家。1957 年，于天津大学建筑系求学时参加影片《女篮 5 号》拍摄而获得观众好评，并由此改变了她的专业，同年进入上海天马电影制片厂任演员。1985 年任上海电影演员剧团团长。其表演质朴自然，戏路很宽，先后在《红色娘子军》《北国江南》《夜航》《保密局的枪声》《蓝色档案》《月随人归》《琴童》《永不凋谢的花朵》《流逝的岁月》《丁香别墅》《西游记》等影视剧中饰演各类角色。因在《流亡大学》中饰演校长夫人，荣膺上海市文联首届文学艺术奖优秀电影表演奖、中国电影表演学会表演奖。

黑丝绒旗袍艳压群芳

在向梅参演的众多电影中，有两部最为著名，那就是《保密局的枪声》和《蓝色档案》。在这两部影片中，她演的两人都是我党地下工作者，应该说是同一类型的角色。

艺术最忌重复。1979 年，向梅饰演了《保密局的枪声》中的史秀英，于 1980 年又接演《蓝色档案》中的沈亚奇。所不同的是，沈亚奇具有三重身份（地下工作者、中统红人、银行经理）。向梅知道，要抓住特点，这才是塑造好人物的关键。可解放时她才 12 岁，以上这三种人都未见过。为此，只有向生活求教了。她开始查阅文史资料，走访地下党老干部，听他们讲述斗争经历。但现实生活和文艺作品毕竟不同。于是，她来到市工商联，找女实业家座谈，请她们介绍上流社会各种女人的生活细节和风采。向梅受益颇多，经过仔细分析、消化吸收，她把学到的融进了角色。银幕上的沈亚奇，与敌特周旋于舞场、宴会厅、宾馆等交际场所，被誉为“东方美人”。

那么，当她在大型舞会上首次露面，又该如何呢？作为演员，身材、体形、容貌是客观存在，所以，只有在举止风度、气质和服饰穿着上别出心裁、高人一着，才能凸显她的个性。但这又不能哗众取宠，因为沈亚奇有特殊政治身份。为解决这个难题，向梅一方面注意从沈亚奇的站坐姿势、说话神情等生活细节上来体现上层社会女人的高雅气质；另一方面思索该穿什么服装，戴什么样的饰品。当工作人员选了件红色的挑花丝绒旗袍时，她突然冒出一个大胆的想法：可否穿黑丝绒旗袍出席舞会？没想到，这个设想立即遭到主创人员的否定。理由有三：一是黑色服装在中国习俗中为丧服，不太吉利；二是彩色胶片最忌黑色，有技术难度；三是中国银幕上，还没出现过美丽女人穿黑色服装出席交际场所的。

向梅据理力争，并举出托尔斯泰名著《安娜·卡列尼娜》中女主人公穿黑色服装出席舞会的实例。为什么不能打破传统观念，树立新的审美观呢？向梅把大家说服了，她的建议得到认可，不少人反过来为之献计献策。

就这样，向梅穿着“安娜式”黑丝绒旗袍来到拍摄现场，她胸前挂着晶晶闪亮的项链，气度不凡地款款步入舞厅，顿时吸引了所有目光，赢得一片惊叹。她塑造的沈亚奇美而不媚、正气端庄，犹如鹤立鸡群，达到了预想的艺术效果。一时，那一袭“安娜式”黑丝绒旗袍成为女性话题。她那艳压群芳的形象至今仍被观众奉为经典。

建筑简介：永福路147弄33号

向梅寓所位于永福路147弄33号。永福路147弄原是永福路(旧名古神父路)上的曹家巷，北临复兴西路。20世纪初这里人烟稀少，多为菜地，法租界越界筑路后，开始建独院式别墅，但直至中华人民共和国成立后还夹杂着简屋和空地。20世纪80年代为解决住宅困难，见缝插针建了33号一幢六层公房，配套有煤卫设施。

XIANG Mei

XIANG Mei (1937–) has her ancestral family from Gongxian County in Henan province and was born in Beijing. She had a former name of WU Xiangmei and was known as a film performance artist. In 1957, she won the praise of audience for her participation in the film *Woman Basketball Player No. 5* when she was studying in the department of architecture in Tianjin University. For this she changed her major. In the same year she entered Shanghai Tianma Film Studio and worked there as actress. In 1985 she served as head of Shanghai Film Actor Troupe. Her performance was natural and unpretending. In addition she was capable of a wide range of performance, playing various roles in films and television plays, including *Red Detachment of Women, The Spring in Northern China, Night Flight, The Gunshots of Secrecy Bureau, The Blue File, Return With The Moon, Child Violinist, The Flower That Never Fades, The Passing Years, Lilac Villa, Journey to the West* and others. Because of her role as the wife of the president in *University in Exile*, she won outstanding film performance award of the first literary and artistic award of Shanghai Federation of Literary and Artistic Circles as well as performance award of Performing Art of China Film Society.

Against All Others with Black Velvet Cheong sam

Among the many films where XIANG Mei played roles, two were best known, which included *The Gunshots of Secrecy Bureau* and *The Blue File*. In these two films, the two persons she played were both underground party members, so it could be said that they were of the same type of role.

Art dislikes repetition most. In 1979, she played the role of SHI Xiuying in *The Gunshots of Secrecy Bureau*, and in 1980 she played the role SHEN Yaqi in *The Blue File*. The difference was that SHEN had a triple identity (underground member, favorite of the CISB and bank manager). As far as she knew, the key to shape good characters was to catch hold of their characteristics. But at liberation, she was only 12 years old and did not see any of the three types of above-mentioned people. In this case she had to learn from life. She began to get access to the historical and cultural documents, visited the veteran leaders of former underground

向梅在《蓝色档案》中饰演沈亚奇
XIANG Mei played the role of SHEN Yaqi in *The Blue File*.

organization and listened to them telling the experience of struggle. But real life and literary works were after all different. Consequently she came to the Association of Industry and Commerce in the city, looking for businesswomen to make discussion with them and ask them to introduce a variety of life details and style of women in high society, from which she benefited a lot. After careful analysis, digestion and absorption, she melted what she learned into the roles. On the screen she circled round the enemy and special agents in the dance hall, banquet hall, hotel and other communication sites, known as the "Oriental Beauty".

So, when she first appeared in a large ball, how should she perform? As an actress, stature, shape and appearance were objective realities. Therefore she could only adopt an original approach and took a higher position in manners, temperament and dress in order to highlight her personality. But this was not grandstanding, because the character she played in the film had a special political identity. To solve this problem, she paid close attention to the sitting position, expression of speaking and other life details in a view of reflecting the elegant temperament of the upper class women. On the other hand she was thinking about what clothes to choose and what kind of jewelry to wear. When the staff members selected a piece of red velvet cheongsam with cross-stitch work, she suddenly had a bold idea in her mind—whether it was possible to wear black velvet cheongsam when she was present at the dance ball? Unexpectedly, this idea was immediately denied by the production team. There were three reasons. First, black clothes were for mourning in the Chinese customs, which was not auspicious; second, color roll films were most sensitive to black, which posed technical difficulty; third, on the Chinese screen, there had not been such a case that a beautiful woman wearing black clothes attended a communication site.

She argued on the basis of reason and cited as an example the heroine in *Anna Karenina*, a well-known novel by Tolstoy, who attended dance balls in black dress. Why not possible to break the traditional concept and establish a new aesthetic outlook? She persuaded and convinced everyone and her proposal was recognized. In addition quite a few persons offered advice and suggestions to her in turn.

In this way, she was in black velvet cheongsam to appear at the shooting scene. With a sparkling necklace on her chest, she walked gracefully into the ballroom, attracting all eyes all of a sudden and winning acclamation on the spot. The role she shaped was beautiful, elegant, and outshining, having achieved the desired artistic effect. For a time, the "Ana style" black velvet cheongsam became a topic among females. Her beautiful image over all others is still regarded as classic by the audience up to today.

The former residence of XIANG Mei is situated at No. 33 on Yongfu Road. The Alley 147 on this road was formerly the CAO Alley on Yongfu Road (Gushenfu Road), with Fuxing Road in the north. In the early 20th century, this place was sparsely populated and most parts were vegetable fields. After the French settlement crossed its border to construct roads, an independent courtyard-style villa was started, but until after the founding of the People's Republic of China this place was still mixed with simple houses and open spaces. During the 1980s, to solve the housing difficulty, every single empty space was used to build a 6-storey public apartment at No. 33 supported with facilities of gas and toilets.

向梅 （钱定华画） XIANG Mei （By QIAN Dinghua）

吕蒙
（1915—1996）

浙江永康人，版画家。17岁入广州市立美术学校学习西画。1936年参加上海文艺界救亡协会。1938年加入中国共产党，后辗转皖南，在新四军里担任政治部宣传科长和文艺科长等职，创作木刻《磨炼》和连环木刻《铁佛寺》。中华人民共和国成立后，曾任上海市美术家协会副主席、中国版画家协会理事、上海中国画院院长等职。版画作品有《共和新路旱桥》《翱翔》《菊》等。出版《吕蒙画集》等。

黄准
（1926— ）

浙江黄岩人，原名黄雨香，作曲家。1938年在贵州参加抗日民族先锋队，同年进延安鲁迅艺术学院学习。1942年加入中国共产党。1945年先后在东北西满军区文工团和鲁艺文工一团任演员。1947年入东北电影制片厂任演员和作曲。1948年任北京电影制片厂作曲。1950年后任上海电影制片厂作曲，先后为《红色娘子军》《牧马人》等三十余部故事片以及《新中国的诞生》等多部纪录片、美术片、电视剧作曲。其中美术片《小猫钓鱼》主题歌《劳动最光荣》、《在老师身边》获全国儿童歌曲奖；《娘子军连歌》获"建国四十周年歌曲奖""20世纪华人音乐经典著作奖"。曾任中国音乐家协会常务理事、中国电影音乐学会副会长、中国影协理事、上海文联委员。出版歌曲集《黄准歌曲选》以及音乐论著《生活与旋律》等。

不离不弃

携手走过的四十多年岁月中，黄准与吕蒙相辅相佐、互相支持，不仅是生活中的伴侣，亦是事业上的忠实伙伴。每当黄准创作一首新歌，吕蒙便是她的第一位听众，直抒己见、展开评论；每逢吕蒙完成新的画作，黄准则成为他的第一位观赏者，端详体会、分享心得。

他如兄长般关心呵护着她，为她分担家庭重任，使她感受到家的温暖，支持着她投入音乐创作。

吕蒙中风偏瘫后，黄准感受到他急于重握画笔的焦虑，想尽一切办法帮助他康复。1981年，黄准赴香港参加作曲家会议时，专程把吕蒙接到广州，安排他泡温泉疗养以及与多年未见的挚友会面诉衷肠。艺术的召唤以及爱人的照料，使他更为强烈地渴望抒发对生活的爱，"右手残了，他开始用左手握画笔，刻刀拿不住，就改用毛笔创作国画"，从此，他决心让左手点燃他生命的火花，来照亮他的余生。1984年，黄准为《滴水观音》作曲时，向摄制组提议与吕蒙一起前往云南拍摄外景，借大好河山激发他们共同的创作灵感。功夫不负有心人，1986年吕蒙第一次小型画展的成功举办，使他信心大增，与此同时又接到了赴美举办画展的邀请，他心情更加激动，整日奋笔于画案边。1987年，黄准陪伴丈夫到安徽疗养，吕蒙以顽强的意志刻苦锻炼，又渐渐恢复了画国画的能力。"他又不停地画着，要把他心中的画，一幅幅地跃于纸上，这时期他的国画技艺更加成熟了。从他那鲜明的风格和那独特而又新颖的着色，很难相信他原来是个功成名就的版画家。"

吕蒙生命的最后两年，虽是在医院度过，但始终有黄准的相伴相守。她天天去医院送去他喜欢吃的饭菜，守护着他。有时出差回来，不进家门先去医院。连着两个春节，她都在医院里与丈夫共守年夜，给了吕蒙莫大的精神慰藉。

建筑简介：复兴西路34号

吕蒙、黄准寓所位于复兴西路34号卫乐公寓，原名卫乐精舍，建于1934年，赉安洋行设计，占地面积1720平方米，建筑面积3797平方米，汽车间附屋802平方米，属现代点式建筑风格的公寓住宅。建筑为十三层钢筋混凝土结构，两翼跌落一层，立面对称，竖三段布置，中间凸出，设一串挑出的半圆阳台为构图中心，两边为卧入式阳台形成竖向线条；水泥砂浆外墙，立面中部竖线条及突出的半圆阳台为暗红色粉刷，其余部分为浅黄色粉刷，山墙顶部及南侧有重复线条装饰，楼前有小花园。解放后，陈鲤庭、吴强、赖少其、峻青、王西彦等一批文化人在此居住。1994年2月15日上海市人民政府公布其为市优秀历史建筑。

LÜ Meng and HUANG Zhun

LÜ Meng (1915–1996), a printmaker, has his ancestral family from Yongkang in Zhejiang province. At the age of seventeen, he was admitted to the Guangzhou Municipal Fine Arts School to learn Western painting. In 1936 he participated in the Shanghai Literature and Art Salvation Association. In 1938 he joined the CPC. Later he tossed about to reach the south of Anhui province to join in the New Fourth Army, served as head of the Political Department of Publicity and the Department of Literature and Art and created woodcut *Annealing* and serial woodcut *Iron Buddhist Temple*. After the founding of the PRC, he once served as vice chairman of Shanghai Artists Association, director of China Printmakers Association, and president of Shanghai Chinese Painting Academy. His block print works include *Republican New Road Crossroads, Hover* and *Chrysanthemum*. He also got published *Collection of Paintings by LÜ Meng*.

HUANG Zhun (1926–) has her ancestral family from Huangyan in Zhejiang province with a former name of HUANG Yuxiang and was known as a music composer. In 1938 she participated in the National Vanguard of the Resisting-Japanese War and in the same year she was admitted to the LU Xun Art Academy at Yan'an. In 1942 she joined the CPC. In 1945 she served as actress successively in the art troupe of Northeast Ximan Military Region and the first art troupe of LU Xun Art Academy. In 1947 she got into Northeast Film Studio to serve as an actress and music composer. In 1948 she served as music composer of Beijing Film Studio. Since 1950, she served as music composer of Shanghai Film Studio, composing for over 30 feature films such as *The Red Detachment of Women* and *Herdsman* as well as many documentaries, art films and teleplays such as *The Birth of New China*. Among them the theme songs "Labor is the Most Glorious" and "Beside the Teacher" of the art film *Cat Fishing* won the National Award for Children's Songs; "Company Song of the Detachment of Women" won "The Music Award of the 40th Anniversary of the PRC" and "The 20th Century Chinese Music Classics Award". She once served as executive director of Chinese Musicians Association, vice president of China Film Music Society, director of China Film Association, and member of Shanghai Federation of Literary and Art Circles. She got published a collection of songs *Selected Songs by HUANG Zhun* and a book on music *Life and Melody*.

吕蒙用左手作画，黄准在旁观看
LÜ Meng was painting with his left hand and HUANG Zhun was watching by his side.

Never Give Up

Hand in hand for over forty years, HUANG Zhun and LÜ Meng complemented and supported each other, being both partners in life and faithful partners in career. When the wife created a new song, the husband would be her first audience and directly express his views and comments; each time when the husband completed a new painting, the wife became his first viewer, making detailed observation and sharing experience.

He was like an elder brother and took care of her and shared family responsibilities with her, enabling her to feel the warmth of home and supporting her in her music creation.

After he got the stroke and hemiplegia, she felt his eagerness to take up the painting brush again and tried every possible means to help him recover from illness. In 1981, she went to Hong Kong to participate in a conference of composers, when she made a special trip to take him to Guangzhou and arranged for him to take a spa treatment and meet with his friends absent from each other for many years. With the call of art and the care of wife, he got stronger desires to express his love for life. "When the right hand was crippled, he began to use his left hand to hold the brush; when he could not hold the knife, he shifted to learn Chinese painting." Since then, he was determined to use his left hand to ignite the spark of his life and illuminate the rest of his life. In 1984, she composed music for *The Statue of Guanyin* and made a suggestion to the film crew to go to the shooting location in Yunnan with her husband to inspire their common creative inspiration with the beautiful scenes of rivers and mountains. Efforts paid off. In 1986, the husband successfully held his first small-scale exhibition so that his confidence greatly increased. At the same time he received an invitation to hold an exhibition in the United States. More excited, he bent over the desk to paint every day. In 1987, the husband and wife went to Anhui for convalescence. With his tenacious will and hard exercise, he gradually restored the ability to paint traditional Chinese painting. "Again he went on with his painting to put all pictures in his heart on paper one by one. During this period his painting skills gained more maturity. From his distinctive style and the unique and innovative coloring, it was hard to believe that he had been an accomplished printmaker".

The last two years of his life was spent in the hospital, but he was always accompanied by his wife. She went to the hospital every day to send to him his favorite food and guard him. Sometimes when she came back from travel, she went to the hospital first before she went home. For two consecutive years during the Spring Festival, she was in the hospital to enjoy the eve with her husband, giving him great spiritual comfort.

The apartment of LÜ Meng and HUANG Zhun is located in Willow Apartment at No. 34 on West Fuxing Road, formerly known as Willow Court. Designed by Leonard-Veysseyre-Kruze Architects and built in 1934, it covers an area of 1,720 square meters with a construction area of 3,797 square meters and attached rooms of 802 square meters for garage. It is an apartment house of point construction and modern architectural style. The building has thirteen floors with a reinforced concrete structure. Its facade is symmetrical with three sections with the middle standing out and the two wings being one floor lower than the middle. A series of projected semi-circular balconies form the center of the composition. At both sides the receding balconies form vertical lines; exterior walls are coated with cement mortar; the vertical lines and prominent semi-circular balconies in the middle section have color of dark red, and the remaining parts are of light yellow. At the top and south side of the gable repeated lines are used for decoration. In addition, a small garden is in front of the building. After the liberation, a number of intellectuals once lived here. On February 15, 1994, it became a Heritage Architecture issued by the Shanghai Municipal People's Government.

吕蒙、黄准 （钱定华画）

LÜ Meng and HUANG Zhun （By QIAN Dinghua）

孙瑜
（1900—1990）

原籍四川自贡，生于重庆，原名成玙。1914—1919 年就读于天津南开中学。“五四”时期参加反对北洋军阀的游行。后进入清华大学文学系，毕业后在威斯康星大学、哥伦比亚大学和纽约摄影学院学习文学、戏剧和电影。1927 年回国加入长城影片公司和民新影业公司，编导《渔叉怪侠》和《风流剑客》。30 年代初，转入联华影业公司，执导《故都春梦》和《野草闲花》。1932 年完成影片《野玫瑰》。与蔡楚生、史东山合作编导的《共赴国难》，是中国电影史上最早的抗日故事片。1933 年中国电影文化协会在上海成立，当选为执行委员，同年编导《天明》和《小玩意》。1934 年编导以筑路工人生活为题材的《大路》，成为其代表作。抗日战争全面爆发后，到重庆担任中国电影制片厂编导委员，编导影片《长空万里》和《火的洗礼》。1948 年加入昆仑影业公司。1950 年编导《武训传》。1956 年编导《乘风破浪》《鲁班的传说》和黔剧戏剧片《秦娘美》。为中国影协执行委员、常务理事。著有回忆录《银海泛舟》等。

第一部“有声片”

1930 年 12 月 3 日，由孙瑜编导的影片《野草闲花》在上海与观众见面。作为 30 年代初联华影业公司倡导的“复兴国片”运动中的代表作品之一，《野草闲花》在大批粗制滥造的神怪武侠片中脱颖而出，尤其受到了知识阶层和青年学生的青睐，使联华影业公司成为“复兴国片之革命军、对抗舶来影片之先锋队”，引领了 30 年代中国电影新潮流。

孙瑜将全部精力与激情都投入到这部自编自导的影片拍摄过程中。在分镜头、镜头处理和摄影技巧上，孙瑜采用了象征、对比、叠印、序幕等在当时十分新颖的手法，大量运用了出色的蒙太奇电影语言，镜头流畅简洁。他将国外所学的电影拍摄技巧灵活运用到创作实践中，创造了独具一格的“浪漫写实”的艺术风格和影像风格，令观众耳目一新。

更难能可贵的是，《野草闲花》虽然是一部默片，却是中国第一部有专门作词配曲的电影插曲的影片。该片的插曲《寻兄词》由孙瑜作词，其三弟孙成璧作曲，委托大中华唱片公司灌制成蜡盘唱片。虽然当时有声电影还没有在中国问世，但许多影院为放映外国有声片已配备了相关的设备。1930 年深秋，寒风萧瑟。作为《野草闲花》的编导，孙瑜亲力亲为、废寝忘食，整整三天驻扎在上海首映该片的影院放映室里，全神贯注、目不转睛地注视着银幕。每当银幕上出现阮玲玉和金焰唱歌的画面，孙瑜就立刻把电唱机的唱针放到事先标好印记的唱片上，从而使观众第一次在观看国产影片时听到了与剧情完全吻合的并且由剧中演员亲口所唱的歌声。这首插曲在影片中共出现两次，且与故事情节紧密相联，增加了影片的感染力，体现了孙瑜作为编导的社会责任感，诗意地表达了强烈的反封建意识和对下层劳动人民的深切同情，再加上两位明星阮玲玉和金焰的倾情演唱，很快便传遍学校和街头。

《野草闲花》由此被冠以“中国第一部配音有声片”的称号。孙瑜以独创的诗性电影美学谱写了中国电影史崭新的篇章，被誉为“诗人导演”。

建筑简介：武康路240号

孙瑜旧居位于武康路240号开普敦公寓，建于1942年，占地面积126.7平方米，建筑面积429平方米。建筑为四层混合结构，立面竖三段划分，中部凸出，东侧一二层之间有白色凸起线条装饰，左侧有通高二到四层的长窗。方形门窗，楼梯间开圆形窗洞，本色水泥外墙，平顶。底层为附屋，楼上是住宅，每层一套，共三层。公寓的三棱体外形带有明显的欧洲现代派建筑风格，也呈现出流线型风格，明快流畅。公寓的锐角转角的弧形处理非常巧妙，以细小白色转角窗点缀，又与沿街立面窗形走势连贯，使整幢楼看似正在行走的船只。中华人民共和国成立初以所在道路序号称呼，又名二四〇公寓。

SUN Yu

SUN Yu (1900–1990), born in Chongqing with a former name of Chengyu, has his ancestral family from the city of Zigong in Sichuan province. From 1914 to 1919 he studied at Nankai High School in Tianjin. During the May Fourth Movement he took part in parades in opposition to the Northern Warlords. Later he entered the Department of Literature in Tsinghua University. After graduation he attended University of Wisconsin, Columbia University and New York Institute of Photography to learn literature, drama and film. He returned to China in 1927 to join the Great Wall Studio and the Minxin Film Company and wrote and directed such films as *Strange Knight* and *Rose and Beauty*. At the beginning of 1930s, he transferred to the Lianhua Film Company and directed *Between Tears and Smiles* and *Wild Flower Among the Weeds*. In 1932 he completed the movie *Wild Rose*. He also co-directed with others the film *Share the Burden of the National Crisis*, which was the first film of story about resistance against Japanese invasion in the history of film in China. In 1933, China Film Culture Association was established in Shanghai and he was elected to the executive committee. In the same year, he directed *Crossroads Daybreak* and *The Little Toys*. In 1934 he directed *The Bid Road: Queen of Sports*, which was based on the life of roadmen and became one of his representatives. After the outbreak of the War of Resistance against Japanese Invasion, he went to Chongqing to serve as a member of director committee of China Film Studio, directing such films as *Wings of China* and *A Baptism of Fire*. In 1948 he joined the Kunlun Film Company. In 1950 he directed the film *The Life of WU Xun*. In 1956 he directed two films of *Braving Wind and Waves* and *The Legend of LU Ban*, and a Guizhou Opera film of *QIN Niangmei*. Once a member of the Executive Committee and a standing director of China Film Association, he authored books like a memoir *Boating on Silver Screen* and others.

The First "Sound Film"

On December 3, 1930, the film *Wild Flower Among the Weeds* directed by SUN was released in Shanghai. This film was one of the representatives produced in the movement of "revitalizing national film" advocated by Lianhua Film Company in the early 1930s and stood out among a large number of crudely-made fantasy and martial arts films. It was especially favored by the intellectuals and

电影《乘风破浪》工作照，中为孙瑜
A work photo of the film *Braving Wind and Waves* (SUN Yu in the middle).

young students. This made the company "the revolutionary army for the renewal of national films and the pioneer against imported videos", which took the lead of the new trend of Chinese film in the 1930s.

He put all his energy and passion into this self-written and self-directed film. In terms of breakdowns of scenes and photographic techniques, he adopted symbolism, contrast, overprint, and preludes which were very novel techniques at that time. Also he made extensive use of outstanding movie language of montage so that scenes in the film were smooth and concise. By flexibly putting into practice the shooting skills of foreign movies, he created a unique art style of "romantic realism" and image style so that the audience found themselves in an entirely new world.

More importantly, though a silent one, it was China's first film with specially written words and music. The song "Seeking Brother" had words by SUN himself and music by his third younger brother, Sun Chengbi. The Greater China Record Company was commissioned to make shellac discs. Although there were no sound films in China at that time, many theaters had been equipped with relevant facilities for the projection of foreign sound films. In the late autumn of 1930, cold wind rustled in the air. As the director of *Wild Flower Among the Weeds*, he took a hands-on approach and neglected sleep and meals for three full days to stay in the projection booth of a theater in Shanghai for the debut of the film. He was all ears in it and stared at the screen. Each time when the two film stars appeared on the screen to sing, he immediately played the record so that the audience, who were watching a domestic film, heard for the first time the song which was quite consistent with the story and sung by the actor and actress in person. The theme song appeared twice in the film and closely connected with the story, which enhanced the appealing effect of the film. This consequently reflected his sense of social responsibility as a director and poetically expressed his strong consciousness of anti-feudalism and his deep sympathy for the working people of the lower class. In addition the emotional singing of the two film stars enabled this film to spread quickly through schools and streets.

From then on, the film *Wild Flower Among the Weeds* got the title of "the first Chinese sound film". In this sense, SUN wrote a new chapter in the history of Chinese film with the original poetic film aesthetics and he was called "the poet director".

The former residence of SUN Yu is situated in the Cape Town Apartment at No. 240 on Wukang Road. It was built in 1942, covering an area of 126.7 square meters with a construction area of 429 square meters. A building of four-storied mixed structure, it has a front of three sections. The central side projects; the eastern side has white bulged lines as decoration between the first and second floors; the left side has high windows from the second to the fourth floors. The building has square windows and doors, round windows at staircases, outside walls of cement and flat roof. The bottom floor has attached rooms and the upstair rooms are for residence. There is one suite on each floor and there are three floors in total. The prismatic appearance of the apartment enjoys a clear style of modern European architecture, which also takes on a streamlined style, both straightforward and smooth. The sharp corners of the apartment are craftily treated as arc turns decorated with slim white corner windows which are coherent with the front windows along the street, so that the whole building seems like a moving ship. In the beginning of the New China, it was called by its street number, so also known as the No. 240 Apartment.

孙瑜 （叶雄画）　SUN Yu （By YE Xiong）

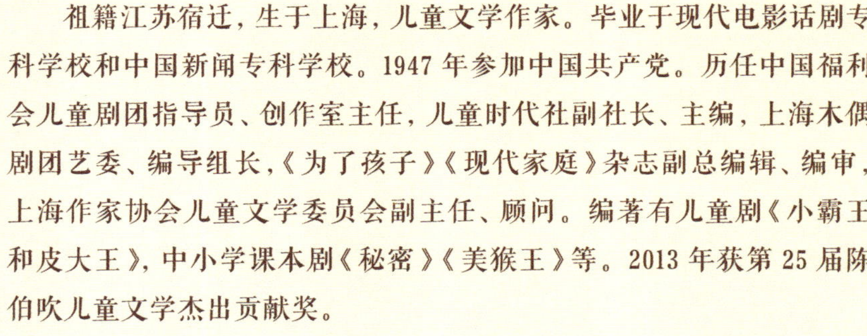

祖籍江苏宿迁，生于上海，儿童文学作家。毕业于现代电影话剧专科学校和中国新闻专科学校。1947 年参加中国共产党。历任中国福利会儿童剧团指导员、创作室主任，儿童时代社副社长、主编，上海木偶剧团艺委、编导组长，《为了孩子》《现代家庭》杂志副总编辑、编审，上海作家协会儿童文学委员会副主任、顾问。编著有儿童剧《小霸王和皮大王》，中小学课本剧《秘密》《美猴王》等。2013 年获第 25 届陈伯吹儿童文学杰出贡献奖。

孙毅
（1923— ）

彭新琪
（1929— ）

祖籍湖南浏阳，生于浙江绍兴，原名彭逸兰，作家、编辑。毕业于复旦大学中文系。历任中国福利会文化馆文艺组组长，《儿童时代》《收获》《上海文学》杂志编辑、编审。1948 年开始发表作品。1988 年加入中国作家协会。著有《动画大师万籁鸣》《包身工的眼泪》《巴金的世界——亲情、友情、爱情》等。1988 年获全国文学期刊优秀编辑奖。作品《偷橘》《巴金的世界》分别获 1994 年、1998 年青少年优秀读物奖。

文学伉俪夕阳红

1953 年 2 月，宋庆龄签发中福会调令，将孙毅调任儿童时代社副社长兼主编。在这里他遇到了当编辑的彭新琪。从相识到相知，1955 年，两人结为秦晋之好。相濡以沫六十余年，文学把他们紧紧连在了一起。孙毅，不论是在儿童时代社，还是 1981 年调任上海市妇联，创办《为了孩子》和《现代家庭》杂志，他从未放弃儿童文学创作。多年来，他利用业余时间写了《一张电影票》《小白兔和小花猫》《翻筋斗》等五本儿童剧、儿童相声集子。

2002 年，《少年文艺》给任溶溶、圣野和孙毅颁发了突出贡献奖，捧着鲜花和奖状，孙毅夜不能寐。彭新琪早就读懂了孙毅，在夫人的帮助下，一个出版《孙毅儿童戏剧快活丛书》的计划酝酿起来。在少年儿童出版社与上海教育出版社支持下，孙毅编著的“儿童戏剧快活丛书”：原创儿童剧《小霸王与皮大王》、小学课本剧《秘密》、中学课本剧《美猴王》、木偶剧《小小五彩鸡》、儿童相声《嘻嘻哈哈》和《娃娃剧场开演了——孙爷爷教你写剧本》等六本书正式出版。

作为编辑，彭新琪甘当人梯，培养作者无数。如“上海 LADY”程乃珊、旅美作家曹冠龙、茅盾文学奖得主周大新等当今享誉文坛的作家都受过她的教诲。当她退休后，又为“老祖母”们当起了主编。在她建议下：一本《七人集》应运而生。这七位上海女作家是：罗洪、欧阳翠、欧阳文彬、黄宗英、姚芳藻、黄屏和她自己。她们在步入八十、九十，甚至临近百岁高龄时仍笔耕不辍，以丰厚的历史积淀和思想感悟，向我们真实展现了中国文化界让人刻骨铭心的一段段历史。

2009年，《七人集》由上海文艺出版社出版，甫一亮相就获得好评。而孙毅对夫人的评价却是："她是个平凡的俗人，平生没有伟大的追求抱负，凡事适可而止，不过，她做到了处事认真诚信，待人热情真诚，这也是我最为欣赏的。"

所谓"妇唱夫随""夫唱妇随"。孙毅近年来诗作不断，创作的童谣《两个钉》在2013年全国童谣大赛中荣获成人组一等奖。而彭新琪的编辑生涯仍没停息，她编选的《巴金萧珊双叶集》《生活如此多彩》已与读者见面。

建筑简介：五原路252弄13号

孙毅、彭新琪寓所位于五原路252弄13号。五原路252号又称大通别墅，建于1938年。13号占地面积约340平方米，其中建筑占地面积145平方米。13号与14号住宅相毗连，又与毗连的11号和12号共同组成外观和结构完全相同的两幢住宅楼，呈东西向并列分布。整幢建筑中轴对称，高3层，每层左右各设一套居住单元，立面设计运用了转角窗、悬挑阳台和弧线墙面等现代元素，但入口处等局部仍带有少量装饰艺术派的纹饰。爱国民主人士、全国政协委员包达三曾住在大通别墅11号。

SUN Yi and PENG Xinqi

SUN Yi (1923–) has his ancestral family from Suqian of Jiangsu province. Born in Shanghai, he is known as a writer of children's literature. He graduated from the Modern Film Drama Academy and the Chinese News Academy. In 1947, he joined the Communist Party of China. Successively he served as instructor and director of Creation Section of Children's Theater Troupe affiliated to China Welfare Institute, vice president and editor-in-chief of *Times for Kids*, member of art committee and leader of director team of Shanghai Puppet Theatrical Company, and deputy editor-in-chief and editor of the two magazines *For the Children* and *Modern Family*. Apart from that, he was also deputy director and consultant of Children's Literature Committee of Shanghai Writers Association. He wrote a children's drama *The Bully and the Naughty Boy*, and textbook plays used in primary and secondary schools such as *Secret* and *Monkey King*. In 2013, he won the Outstanding Contribution Award of the 25th CHEN Bochui Children's Literature.

PENG Xinqi (1929–) has her ancestral family from Liuyang in Hunan province. Born in Shaoxing in Zhejiang province, she has a name of PENG Yilan and is known as a writer and an editor. Graduating from the Chinese Department of Fudan University in Shanghai, she served successively as leader of the Literature and Art Team of Culture Center affiliated to China Welfare Institute, as well as editor of magazines like *Times for Kids, Harvest* and *Shanghai Literature*. She began her writing career in 1948 and joined the China Writers Association in 1988. Her works included *Cartoon Master WAN Laiming, Tears of Indentured Laborers, BA Jin's World—Kinship, Friendship and Love* and so on. In 1988, she won the Outstanding Editor Award of National Literary Magazines. Both of her works *Stealing Oranges* and *BA Jin's World* were granted the Excellent Books Award for Juvenile in 1994 and in 1998 respectively.

A Couple of Writers in their Twilight Years

In February of 1953, SONG Qingling issued an order of China Welfare Institute to transfer SUN Yi to the new post of vice

孙毅、彭新琪在西湖留影

SUN Yi and PENG Xinqi at the West Lake.

president and editor of *Times for Kids*. There he met another editor PENG Xinqi. They gradually got acquainted with each other and got married in 1955. Closely linked by literature, they helped and cherished each other for more than sixty years. The husband never gave up the creation of children's literature, whether when he was working for the magazine *Times for Kids* or in 1981 when he was transferred to the Shanghai Women's Federation where he initiated such magazines as *For the Children* and *Modern Family*. For years, he spent his spare time completing *A Movie Ticket, the Rabbit and the Cat, Somersault* and two other children's dramas as well as a collection of children's crosstalk.

In 2002, the magazine *Juvenile Literature* granted Outstanding Contribution Award to REN Rongrong, SHENG Ye and SUN Yi respectively. Thinking of the flowers and the award given to him, he spent a sleepless night, feeling a great responsibility on his shoulders. He made a plan to publish *A Happy Series of Children's Drama by SUN Yi* with the help of his wife, who understood him all the time. Supported by Children's Publishing House and Shanghai Educational Publishing House, *A Happy Series of Children's Drama* was published, including an original children's drama *The Bully and the Naughty Boy*, a drama for primary school textbook *Secret*, a drama for secondary school textbook *Monkey King*, a puppet play *Little Colorful Chicken*, a children's crosstalk *Laughing and Joking*, and *Children's Theater Begins—Grandpa SUN Teaches You to Write Scripts*.

As an editor, the wife was willing to help cultivate numerous authors. Such famous writers in the literary arena as "Shanghai Lady" CHENG Naishan, the Chinese-American writer CAO Guanlong and ZHOU Daxin, a winner of Maodun Literature Prize—all have received her teachings. After her retirement, she became an editor-in-chief again for the "Elderly Grandmothers". With her suggestion, *The Collection of Seven People* came into being. The seven women writers in Shanghai include LUO Hong, OUYANG Cui, OUYANG Wenbin, HUANG Zongying, YAO Fangzao, HUANG Ping and PENG Xinqi herself. They were still actively producing new works in their eighties and nineties and even when they were centenarians. Full of rich historical deposit and profound thoughts, their works present a precious record of unforgettable moments in the cultural circles of China.

In 2009, *The Collection of Seven People* was published by Shanghai Literature and Art Publishing House, which was well received upon its publication. The husband's evaluation of his wife was like this, "She is an ordinary woman without great ambitions, satisfied with what is proper. However, she has done things in good faith and treats others warmly and sincerely. That is why I've admired her most."

As the old sayings go, a husband is his wife's echo and a wife is also her husband's echo. This couple is an example of this kind. The husband has created a lot of poems consecutively in recent years, among which the nursery rhyme *Two Nails* won the first prize of National Nursery Rhymes Contest (adult group) in 2013. The wife's editorial career did not cease either, and the two books she compiled, *Double Collections of BA Jin and XIAO Shan* and *Life So Colorful*, have already been published.

The apartment of SUN Yi and PENG Xinqi is situated at No.13 in Alley 252 on Wuyuan Road. The Alley 252 on Wuyuan Road is also known as Datong Villa, which was built in 1938. Apartment No. 13 covers an area of about 340 square meters with a construction area of 145 square meters. Apartment No. 13 and No. 14 adjoin with each other, which are adjacent to Apartment No. 11 and No. 12. The four of them make up of two buildings with exactly the same appearance and structure in a parallel distribution from the east to the west. The whole building is symmetric along the central axis with three floors and each floor has a residential unit at both sides of the gate. The design of the facade makes use of such modern elements as corner windows, cantilevered balconies and curve line wall surface, but some local parts like the entrance still have some patterns of deco art. BAO Dasan, a democratic patriot and a member of the National Committee of the CPPCC, once lived at No.11 in Datong Villa.

孙毅、彭新琪（钱定华画）　　SUN Yi and PENG Xinqi （By QIAN Dinghua）

孙多森
（1867—1919）

安徽寿州（今寿县）人，字荫庭。1898年与其兄孙多鑫在上海创办阜丰面粉公司。1911年武昌起义后，经袁世凯举荐任清廷内阁和议代表。1913年任中国银行总裁，同年，袁以“皖人治皖”名义令其接替革命党人柏文蔚安徽都督等职务，遭省议员反对，遂被软禁。1914年任参政院参政，并创办通惠实业特种公司等企业。1916年开办中孚银行，在全国设分行，自任总经理。1919年7月6日在天津病故。

中国第一个银行条例缔造者

孙多森生于书香门第，父辈为官，母亲是李鸿章的侄女，她教育孙多鑫、孙多森兄弟说：“当今欧风东渐，欲求子弟不坠家声、重振家业，必须攻习洋文，以求洞晓世界大势，否则断难与人争名于朝，争利于市……”这一观念深深影响了孙多森。

清朝末年，清政府开始鼓励工商业，对面粉生产给予免税优惠，而国产面粉在质量上仍明显逊于进口面粉，孙多森看到了机制面粉的广阔前景，下决心要生产出质量与价格均有竞争力的国产面粉。孙氏兄弟将厂址定于地价低廉的苏州河边，并认真考察了刚落成的英商增裕面粉厂，详细了解制粉全过程，又花费白银5万两从美国购得16部钢磨，使面粉产量可达增裕面粉厂的三倍，并不分国籍广纳贤才，以提升管理水平。经过精心筹备，阜丰面粉厂于1900年投产，孙氏兄弟决定以自行车图形作为面粉商标，寓意着如新生事物般充满活力、蓬勃向上。刚投产时，面粉厂每日产量为2500包，4年后新建车间落成，使每天产量增至7000余包。通过改进面粉原料，以进口小麦与国产小麦混合，使产品更合乎国人口味且物美价廉，并推出几斤装的小包装，向点心店推销，打开了市场。

孙多森兴办实业的成功，令袁世凯瞩目。1912年袁氏就任大总统后，孙多森当选为国会议员，并被委任为中国银行总裁。1913年由孙多森主持修订的《中国银行条例》是民国财政部公布的第一个中国银行条例。不久，袁世凯野心膨胀，向孙多森提出由中国银行发行准备金以筹措经费。孙多森婉言拒绝道：“发行准备金关系国家大信，一旦基金动摇，失信于民，则国家不幸，亦即于我公不利，不如另筹他法。”

1913年6月，孙多森被免去中国银行总裁职务。之后不久，孙多森赴日本调查实业，回国后又创办了通惠实业公司、中国实业公司等。

孙多森旧居位于华山路 831 号，建于 1918 年，占地面积约 3200 平方米，建筑面积 825 平方米，属西班牙建筑风格的花园住宅。建筑为三层砖混结构，正立面一层底部架空，开券形门洞，有螺旋纹柱。二层退为露台，有连续的拱券门洞，方形窗洞和券形窗洞相间，上有红色筒瓦雨厦。黄色水泥拉毛墙面，红筒瓦四坡顶。屋前有花园。现为上海市拥军优属基金会使用。2005 年 10 月 31 日上海市人民政府公布其为市优秀历史建筑。

SUN Duosen

SUN Duosen (1867–1919), with a courtesy name of Yinting, has his ancestral family in Shouxian County in Anhui province. In 1898, he and his brother founded Fufeng Flour Company in Shanghai. In 1911 after the Wuchang Uprising, he served as the peace-making representative of the cabinet of the Qing Dynasty under the recommendation of YUAN Shikai. In 1913 he served as president of the Bank of China. In the same year, YUAN ordered him to take the place of a revolutionist to serve as the military governor and other posts in the name of “governance of Anhui by people from it”. But this was opposed by some members of provincial government and he was subsequently under house arrest. In 1914, he served as councilor of the State Council of the YUAN Government. In addition, he founded such enterprises as the Tonghui Industrial Special Company. In 1916 he set up Zhongfu Bank with branches opened in the whole country and served as its general manager. He died of illness in Tianjin on July 6, 1919.

The Creator of the First Bank Statute in China

SUN Duosen was born in a family of scholar and his forefathers were officials. His mother was a niece of LI Hongzhang and instructed her two sons by saying that “the western civilization has influenced China and you need to learn foreign languages in

阜丰面粉厂的“自行车”商标
Trademark “Bicycle” of Fufeng Flour Factory.

order to revitalize the prosperity of the family and have a clear understanding of the trend of the world. Otherwise it would be absolutely difficult to strive for a name in the country and contend for benefit in the world...” He was deeply affected by this idea.

At the end of the Qing Dynasty, the government began encouraging industry and commerce. It imposed free tax on the production of flour while the quality of domestically produced flour remained significantly worse than the imported. Seeing the broad prospects for the machine-made flour, SUN made up his mind to produce domestic flour with competitive quality and price. He and his brother selected the site of the factory at the riverside of the Suzhou River where the price of land was low. They also carefully investigated the Zengyu Flour Factory newly completed by British merchants and got a detailed understanding of the milling process. Then they spent fifty thousand taels of silver in purchasing 16 steel mills from the United States in order that their flour yield could be three times more than that of Zengyu Flour Factory. Moreover they recruited talents regardless of their nationality to enhance the management. After careful preparation, the Fufeng Flour Factory went into operation in 1900. The brothers decided to use the figure of bike as the trademark of their flour, meaning that their factory was energetic and vigorous. In the beginning, the daily production of their flour mill added up to 2500 bags. Four years later after the completion of the new workshop, the daily output increased to more than 7000 bags. By improving the flour raw materials with the mixture of imported and domestic wheat, the floor product was more in line with the tastes of the people and was less expensive. Also they adopted small packaging of a few kilograms to satisfy the needs of dim sum shops, thus establishing the market.

His industrial success attracted the attention of YUAN Shikai. After YUAN became the president in 1912, SUN was elected as member of the Congress and was appointed as president of the Bank of China. In 1913, the *China Bank Regulations*, the revision of which was chaired by SUN, was the first of its kind issued by the Ministry of Finance of the Republic of China. Soon YUAN was so ambitious as to propose to SUN that the Bank of China should issue reserves to raise funds. SUN politely declined, saying that “issuing reserves is associated with the national trust and once it is shaken and the government loses the confidence of the people, that would be the disaster of the state and could not be beneficial to us. So I would rather suggest seeking for other ways.”

In June 1913, SUN was removed from the post of president of the bank. Soon after that he went to Japan to do investigation of industry. After he came back he founded such companies as Tonghui Industrial Company and China Industrial Company.

The former residence of SUN Duosen, situated at No. 831 on Huashan Road, was built in 1918, covering an area of about 3,200 square meters with a construction area of 825 square meters. The building is a garden house of the Spanish architectural style. It is a three-storied structure of brick and concrete. The front first floor was built on stilts with open arch-shaped gate and columns of swirl marks. The second floor recesses to form colonies and has continuous arch doorways. Square and arch windows alternate with each other with red pantile as canopies. It has yellow walls with napped stucco veneer and a four-sloped roof with red tiles. In front of house is a garden. It is now occupied by the Shanghai Municipal Army-Supporting Fund. On October 31, 2005, it became a Heritage Architecture issued by the Shanghai Municipal People's Government.

孙多森 （齐亚明画）　SUN Duosen （By QI Yaming）

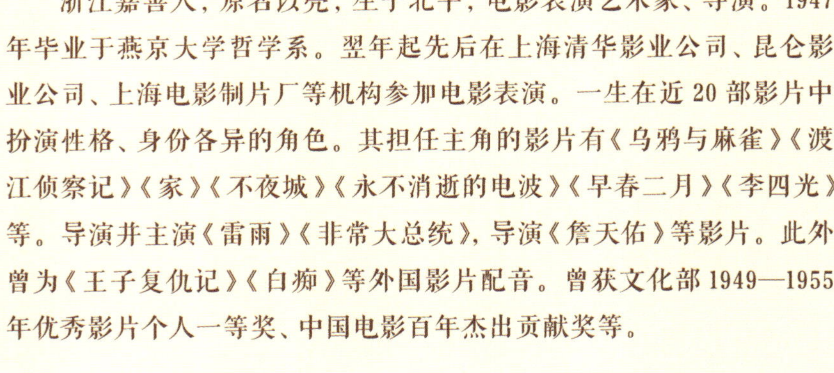

浙江嘉善人，原名以亮，生于北平，电影表演艺术家、导演。1947年毕业于燕京大学哲学系。翌年起先后在上海清华影业公司、昆仑影业公司、上海电影制片厂等机构参加电影表演。一生在近20部影片中扮演性格、身份各异的角色。其担任主角的影片有《乌鸦与麻雀》《渡江侦察记》《家》《不夜城》《永不消逝的电波》《早春二月》《李四光》等。导演并主演《雷雨》《非常大总统》，导演《詹天佑》等影片。此外曾为《王子复仇记》《白痴》等外国影片配音。曾获文化部1949—1955年优秀影片个人一等奖、中国电影百年杰出贡献奖等。

孙道临
（1921—2007）

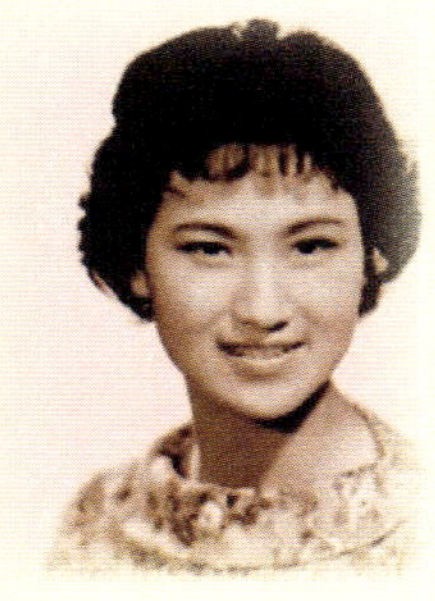

生于浙江绍兴，越剧表演艺术家。表演上以善于描摹人物神态、传达内心感情著称。曾任中国戏剧家协会理事、上海越剧院红楼剧团团长等职务。唱腔平易质朴、流畅自然，早年曾受支兰芳、小白玉梅、王杏花的影响，后在长期艺术实践中，博采众长、融会贯通，形成自己的唱腔风格，被誉为“王派”。戏路宽广，创造了各种不同的舞台形象，主要作品有《红楼梦》《春香传》《追鱼》《则天皇帝》《西园记》《孟丽君》等。

王文娟
（1926—　）

琴瑟和鸣

孙道临、王文娟恋爱时，常在深夜绕着武康路、华山路、湖南路、淮海路散步。从王文娟的“枕流”公寓到孙道临的“密丹”公寓，再从“密丹”公寓到“枕流”公寓，难舍难分的“十八相送”是两人恋爱时的保留节目。月光下，那一叶叶梧桐树影见证了两人矢志不渝的爱情。

1964年，女儿孙庆原出生。翌年，孙道临、王文娟将“枕流”和“密丹”两处寓所置换到武康大楼四楼。二十平方米左右的客厅中最醒目的要数那几座摆满了各类书籍的书架了。朝南有一扇全透明的落地景观窗，窗外的阳台上孙道临亲手栽种的绿植郁郁葱葱，与马路对面宋庆龄旧居成林的绿树连绵成一整片怡人的绿，为这对伉俪在喧嚣的尘世中开辟了一方雅静的艺术构思空间。

20世纪60年代初，王文娟因声带小结在华东医院动了手术，嗓子易沙哑。每次晚上演出回到家，她总能欣喜地在水果盘中发现上好的鲜梨，那是孙道临心疼因演唱了整晚而喉干舌燥的妻子，特意精心准备的。

为了帮助妻子克服因声带动过手术引发的喉音较重的问题，研修过声乐且拥有丰富舞台经验的孙道临如果在家，必然会自告奋勇地为妻子弹琴练声彩排，并结合具体情境分析人物的内心世界，诚恳地提出建议供妻子参考，携手攀登艺术高峰。

一天，他帮助王文娟练唱《沉香扇·书房会》选段。王文娟以柔美委婉的音色唱到“今日里夫妻书房会”时，孙道临轻轻停下了弹琴的手，凝视爱妻的双眸深情地说：“文娟，这句要唱出患难夫妻的复杂感情，抑扬顿挫，在‘夫妻’两字上逐渐扬高去。”说罢便试唱起来。夫唱妇随，夫妻两人将共渡难关、不离不弃的自身经历深深融入其中，情浓韵醇的唱腔果然更深沉感人，久久萦绕在温馨的艺术“忘归”小巢中。孙道临还向妻子介绍了程砚秋和荀慧生以唱腔传神的特点，帮助王文娟掌握以气带情、以情带声的演唱方法。这位电影表演艺术家在与妻子的切磋交流中，对越剧表演艺术也日益精通、如数家珍。

四十载光阴荏苒，夫妻两人流连艺术天地的“忘归”小巢始终和美温馨，见证着孙道临、王文娟这对艺术伉俪相濡以沫的深情与对于艺术执着不懈的追求。

建筑简介：淮海中路1836—1858号武康大楼

孙道临、王文娟寓所位于淮海中路1836—1858号武康大楼，旧称东美特公寓，又称诺曼底公寓，建于1924年，由法商万国储蓄会投资兴建，为著名建筑师邬达克早期作品，占地面积930平方米。建筑为八层钢筋混凝土结构，外形略具法国文艺复兴风格。建筑为外廊式公寓，采用古典三段式划分，一至二层处理成基座，底层对应商铺功能，沿街为连续的券廊，水泥仿石墙面饰券心石；二层平券，窗间墙上部设双联的巴洛克样式巨大支托，上承第三层的外廊，具有浓郁的古典风格。1945年抗战胜利后，孔二小姐孔令伟（孔祥熙的二女儿）买下整栋公寓的产权。1953年改名为武康大楼，许多文艺界名人在此安家。孙道临、王文娟夫妇的寓所原先就是孔二小姐的住处。1994年2月15日上海市人民政府公布其为市优秀历史建筑。

SUN Daolin and WANG Wenjuan

SUN Daolin (1921–2007), a film performance artist and director, has his ancestral family from Jiashan in Zhejiang province. Born in Beijing, he had a former name of Yiliang. In 1947 he graduated from the Philosophy Department of Yenching University. From the next year, he successively acted in films produced in Shanghai Tsinghua Film Company, Kunlun Film Company, and Shanghai Film Studio. In his lifetime he acted in nearly 20 films as roles of different personalities and identities. The films in which he starred include *The Crow and the Sparrow, Reconnaissance across the Yangtze River, Family, Ever-bright City, The Eternal Wave, Threshold of Spring*, and *LI Siguang*. He directed and starred in *Thunderstorm* and *Extraordinary President*, and also directed films like *ZHAN Tianyou*. In addition he dubbed foreign films such as *Hamlet* and *The Idiot*. He won the first prize for excellent films issued by the Ministry of Culture during 1949–1955 and the award for outstanding contribution to Chinese film in 100 years.

WANG Wenjuan (1926–), born in Shaoxing in Zhejiang province, was a performing artist of Yue Opera. Her performance featured the depiction of the spirit and manner of characters and the expression of their inner feelings. She once served as director of China Theatre Association and head of the Red Chamber Troupe of Shanghai Yue Opera House. Her aria was characterized by being simple, plain, natural and smooth. In early years, she was influenced by some well-known artists in this field. In her later long-term artistic practice, she absorbed widely from others and digested it to form her own style of singing, becoming known as the “WANG Style”. She created a wide range of different stage images. Her main works include *A Dream of Red Chamber, Empress Chung, Snakefish, Empress WU, The Story of Western Garden* and *Eternal Happiness*.

Harmony of Husband and Wife

When SUN Daolin and WANG Wenjuan fell in love, they often walked in the midnight along the Wukang Road, Huashan Road, Hunan Road and Huaihai Road. From her apartment to his and then from his to hers, they found it hard to part from each other. In the moonlight, the shadows of phoenix tree leafs witnessed their dedicated love.

孙道临、王文娟 1962 年结婚照
Wedding photo of SUN Daolin and WANG Wenjuan (1962).

In 1964, their daughter was born. In the following year, they replaced their two apartments by the fourth floor in Wukang Building. In the living room about twenty square meters, the most eye-catching were the bookshelves filled with all kinds of books. Facing south is a transparent French window of landscape. On the balcony outside of the window the lush plants planted by SUN form a whole piece of pleasant stretch of green together with the green trees in the former residence of SONG Qingling across the road. All this opened up an elegant and secret space of artistic conception for the couple in the hustle and bustle of the earthly world.

At the beginning of the 1960s, the wife had a surgery for vocal illness, and her voice was apt to be hoarse. Each night when she was back home after performance, she was always delighted to find a dish of fresh pear on the fruit plate. It was specially prepared by the husband, since he had deep love for her while she had sung all night and dried her throat.

In order to help his wife overcome a guttural sound caused by vocal operation, the husband, who had training in vocal music and also had rich stage experience, would inevitably volunteer to play the piano for his wife to practice voice or for a rehearsal. In addition, he would analyze the inner world of the characters in specific contexts and give hearty suggestions for her reference. In this way the couple explored artistic creation hand in hand.

One day, he helped his wife sing an excerpt from the opera *Eaglewood Fan: Meeting in the Study*. In a soft, mild and marvelous tone color, the wife sang, "today the husband and wife meet in the study", when the husband gently stopped playing the piano and looked into her eyes, saying with deep emotions, "darling, this sentence reflects complex feelings of husband and wife in difficulty, which should be represented with rise and fall of tone, i.e. rising gradually at the words 'husband' and 'wife'." At this remark, he started to have a try to be followed by the wife. The husband and wife sang into the opera their personal experiences of weathering the hard times and never leaving without another. The sound of strong affection and mellow charm was really more moving indeed, lingering long in the warm artistic home. The husband also introduced to her the vivid characteristics of two famous masters of Beijing operas, helping her get a good command over the singing method to express love with breath and fuse emotion into sound. Increasingly this film artist also became proficient in and familiar with the Yue Opera in the exchange with his wife.

Forty years went by, and the small nest for the husband and wife to linger in the world of art was always beautiful and warm, witnessing both the deep love between husband and wife who had helped one another in difficult time and also their persistent pursuit of art.

The apartment of SUN Daolin and WANG Wenjuan is located in Wukang Building at No. 1836–1858 on Middle Huaihai Road, formerly known as East Meite Apartment and also known as Normandy Apartments. Founded in 1924 by the International Savings Society, a French business, this building is an early works of Ladislaus Edward Hudec, a famous architect, which covers an area of 930 square meters. It has eight stories of reinforced concrete structure with an appearance of French Renaissance style. As an apartment with outside corridor, it adopts the classical division of three sections with the first and second floors as the foundation. The first floor serves the function of shops. A continuous arched corridor runs along the street and the stone walls imitated with cement are decorated with keystones. The second floor is directly on the arched corridor; over the wall between windows are set twofold large supports of baroque style, which bears the balconies on the third floor. All these reflect a rich classical style. After the victory of the War against Japanese Invasion in 1945, KONG Lingwei, the second daughter of KONG Xiangxi, bought the property right of the whole apartment. After the founding of the New China it was renamed as the Wukang Building and many celebrities in the literary and art circles once lived here. The apartment of SUN and WANG was once the residence of Miss KONG, the second daughter of the finance minister. On February 15, 1994, it became a Heritage Architecture issued by the Shanghai Municipal People's Government.

孙道临、王文娟 （刘为民画） SUN Daolin and WANG Wenjuan （By LIU Weimin）

师陀
（1910—1988）

河南杞县人，原名王长简，常用笔名师陀、芦焚，作家、剧作家。1921年高中毕业后赴北平谋生。1931年开始发表作品。1936年出版第一本短篇小说集《谷》，同年从北平到上海，后长期在上海居住。1941年后，任苏联上海广播电台文学编辑、上海戏剧学校教员、上海文化电影制片公司特约编辑等。中华人民共和国成立后，历任上海出版公司总编辑、上海电影剧本创作所编剧。1957年后为中国作家协会上海分会专业作家。20世纪60年代后，专注于历史小说和历史剧的创作。代表作品有剧本《大马戏团》和《夜店》（与柯灵合作）。另著有短篇小说集《春梦》《芦焚短篇小说选集》，长篇小说《结婚》《马兰》《历史无情》和剧本《西门豹》等。

《大马戏团》常演不衰

作为一个剧作家，师陀最成功的作品无疑是创作于20世纪40年代的《大马戏团》（根据俄国作家安德列耶夫的《吃耳光的人》改编）和《夜店》（与柯灵合作，根据高尔基的《底层》改编）。这两部剧作，师陀采用了“改译”的方法，堪称典范，奠定了其在中国现代戏剧史上的地位。

1942年10月，《大马戏团》在上海首演，由黄佐临导演。这是师陀写的第一个话剧剧本。改译本同原著差异甚大：作者抽去原著的主角，一个无足轻重的小丑——吃耳光的人，仅保留其他主要人物、人物关系和故事轮廓，也隐去了原著中那种灰暗沉重的色调。剧本描写流动马戏团中的一个恋爱悲剧。马戏团团主的妻子盖三爷以火一般的热情追求马戏团男演员小铳，小铳却嫌弃她，一心爱着女演员翠宝。翠宝的养父慕容天锡是一个“死不要脸又死要面子”的无耻之徒，他要将翠宝卖给黄大少爷做妾。在慕容天锡强迫翠宝和黄大少爷定亲之夜，小铳和翠宝双双饮毒酒自杀。盖三爷疯狂地放火烧了马戏团篷帐，酿成一场毁灭性的悲剧。

改译剧是跨文化对话的产物，是中外戏剧文化的混合体，师陀巧妙地对原作进行了中国化。剧作揭示了旧中国马戏艺人的悲惨命运，这是他对贫困生活的感受和正义人格的反映，为底层人物谱写哀歌，却充满着传奇、讽刺和寓意。

话剧皇帝石挥在剧中出演慕容天锡，这是一个十足的坏蛋，而又伪装成绅士、上等人。石挥从自己所熟悉的生活中吸收了不同人的特性、习惯甚至语调来塑造这个形象。逼真的表演左右着观众的情绪，演出结束，观众仍迟迟不肯离去。在剧场的大厅里，观众还不断议论着石挥的表演细节。那天，京剧大师梅兰芳也来看戏，并给此戏很高的评价。

《大马戏团》在上海演出盛况空前，连演40天，共77场，轰动上海。由此，师陀名声大振。

建筑简介：武康路280弄35号

师陀旧居位于武康路280弄35号，为里弄住宅。房屋为二层砖木结构，承重墙体采用黏土青砖、柴泥砌筑，纸筋石灰内粉刷。房屋建筑平面近似矩形。外立面为涂料饰面，主屋面为机制平瓦双坡屋面，北侧原露台区域为平屋面。一层入户房间为厨房间，穿过厨房为楼梯间区域，木楼梯，木扶手；楼梯间南侧分布两间房屋；一层半北侧区域为亭子间，二层南侧为房间。

SHI Tuo

SHI Tuo (1910–1988), native of Qixian county in Henan province, had a former name of WANG Changjian with such commonly used pen names as SHI Tuo and LU Fen, and is known as writer and playwright. After graduating from high school in 1921, he went to Beijing to make a living. In 1931 he began to have works published. In 1936 he got published his first short story collection *Valley*. In the same year he left Beijing for Shanghai, where he lived for a long time. After 1941, he served as literary editor of a Soviet Union radio station in Shanghai, teacher of Shanghai Drama School, and special editor of Shanghai Culture Film Studio. After the founding of the People's Republic of China, he served in succession as editor-in-chief of Shanghai Publishing Company and script writer of Shanghai Film Script Studio. After 1957 he became a professional writer of the Shanghai branch of China Writers Association. After the 1960s, he focused on the creation of historical novels and dramas. His representative works include such scripts as *The Greatest Show on Earth* and *Nightclub* (co-author with KE Ling). In addition he published short story collections including *Spring Dream* and *An Anthology of Short Stories by LU Fen*, as well as novels such as *Marriage*, *MA Lan*, *Ruthless History* and the script *XIMEN Bao*.

The Greatest Show on Earth in Full Swing

As a playwright, SHI Tuo's most successful work is undoubtedly *The Greatest Show on Earth* created in the 1940s (adapted according to *He Who Gets Slapped* by the Russian writer Leonid Andreyev) and *Nightclub* (co-authored with KE Ling and adapted according to Gorky's *The Lower Depths*). In these two plays, SHI Tuo adopted the method of "adaptation", which deserved the reputation of model and made his fame in the history of modern Chinese drama.

In October 1942, the drama *The Greatest Show on Earth* had its debut in Shanghai with HUANG Zuolin as its director. This was the first drama script he wrote. The adapted version was quite different from the original. The author took away the original protagonist, an insignificant clown—a person who got slapped, and only preserved other major characters, relations between characters and story outline, while concealing the gray and heavy tone in the original. The script describes a love tragedy in a mobile circus. Lord GAI, wife of the circus leader, courts the circus actor Little Pistol with fire-like enthusiasm while the latter despises

20 世纪 40 年代的师陀
SHI Tuo in the 1940s.

her and loves the actress Green Gold. But MURONG Tianci, her adoptive father, is an impudent person who is "extremely shameless and also dead determined to save face" and sells Green Gold to Master HUANG as his concubine. At the night when MURONG forced his adopted daughter to be engaged with the master, both Little Pistol and Green Gold committed suicide by drinking poison. Lord GAI was crazy and set fire to the tent of the circus only to create a devastating tragedy.

The adapted drama is the product of cross-cultural dialogue and a mixture of Chinese and foreign drama cultures. SHI Tuo cleverly sinicized the original. The play reveals the tragic fate of the circus artists in old China, which stands for his feelings of poverty and a reflection of a just personality. He created a lament for the people at the bottom of the society, which is nevertheless filled with legend, irony and moral message.

SHI Hui, the drama emperor, played the role MURONG, who was an unmitigated scoundrel and disguised as a fine gentleman from the upper class. SHI Hui absorbed from life familiar to him characteristics, habits and even tone of different people in order to shape the image. His lifelike performance dominated the audience's emotions. At the end of performance, the audience was still reluctant to leave. In the hall of the theater, the audience was still talking about the details of his performance. That day, MEI Lanfang, the master of Beijing Opera, also came to watch the performance and made a high evaluation of the drama.

The performance of *The Greatest Show on Earth* in Shanghai was unprecedented, which was played consecutively for 40 days and for a total of 77 times. A sensation was made in Shanghai. Thus SHI Tuo rose to fame vigorously.

The former residence of SHI Tuo is located at No. 35 in Alley 280 on Wukang Road, which is a residence in an alley. The building has two floors with a structure of brick and wood. The bearing walls adopt black clay bricks with mud masonry and inner whitewash of paper strip mixed lime mortar. The building plane is approximately rectangular. The facade has a paint finish and the main roof has double slopes covered with flat tiles. The original terrace at the north side has a flat roof. The room at the entrance on the first floor is for kitchen, which leads to the staircase with wooden steps and handrails. At the south side of the staircase are two houses. At the north side on the first and half floors is a garret and at the south side on the second floor are rooms.

师陀 （钱定华画） SHI Tuo （By QIAN Dinghua）

庄俊
（1888—1990）

原籍浙江宁波，生于上海。1909 年毕业于南洋中学。1910 年公费留学美国伊利诺伊大学建筑工程系。1914 年毕业回国，任教于北京清华预备学校（清华大学前身）。1925 年开设庄俊建筑师事务所。1927 年与范文照等建筑师发起成立上海建筑师学会（第二年改为中国建筑师学会）并任会长。1950 年春，庄俊应中央人民政府之邀北上建设首都，关闭自己已开设 25 年之久的建筑师事务所，组建了一支 50 余人的技术队伍赴京工作，加入交通部华北建筑工程公司，任总工程师。1953 年初，建筑工程部成立，在华北建筑工程公司的基础上，建立中央建筑设计院，被任命为总工程师。建筑作品有上海金城银行、中南银行、大陆商场、汉金城银行、大陆银行等。20 世纪 90 年代，庄俊获中国建筑学会授予的“建筑泰斗荣誉证书”。晚年著书立说，著有《英汉对照建筑工程名词汇编》等书籍。

开创中国人自己的建筑天地

1923 年，庄俊在欧美考察建筑时，深感中国建筑界全然由洋人掌控，毕业于建筑设计专业的中国人往往只能充当外国人的助理，这使他下决心回国后要开创中国人自己的建筑天地。1924 年，他辞去在清华大学的职务回到上海，在克服重重阻碍后，在租界开办庄俊建筑师事务所（在此之前也仅有“华海建筑师事务所”为中国人所设立）。该所承接的第一项业务是设计坐落于江西中路汉口路的上海金城银行大楼，此大楼于 1926 年 1 月底落成，其设计体现了欧洲文艺复兴时期的建筑艺术以及 20 世纪初的建筑水平，证明了中国人也能设计出有着高度艺术水准的现代化大型建筑。

在他的激励下，一大批中国建筑师自己开设的事务所，如雨后春笋般纷纷崛起于上海，这打破了洋商建筑师垄断中国建筑设计行业的局面。但当时中国建筑师面临的障碍依然强大，如租界的歧视与干扰等，为了齐心协力与洋商抗衡，庄俊于 1927 年发起组织了由数十名建筑师参加的“中国建筑师学会”（初名“上海建筑师学会”），其宗旨为“团结建筑师，交流技术，维护建筑师的合法权利”，并吸收学生会员、出版刊物。他担任首任会长，订立了“诫约”：不与同行争夺业务、不准不合理地降低设计工费、不得向任何方面收受额外费用等，这既增强了国内建筑师的凝聚力，又有助于提高他们的职业素养。

庄俊身体力行，恪守诫约，抵制不良风气。有一次，一位营造商为了表达对他的谢意，赠送他一件皮桶子。他将礼物退回，并诚挚地规劝营造商，使那位先生感动不已。对于子女，庄俊严格教育道：“我愿我的子孙后代，无分男女，都要树立勤劳刻苦的精神，舍己为群的风格，朝气蓬勃，保持气节，稳步前进，忠诚老实，为祖国服务，使我国成为最伟大、最富强的国家之一。”

建筑简介：复兴西路45号

庄俊旧居位于复兴西路45号，由他本人设计，建于1921年，为独立式花园住宅，占地面积306平方米。建筑为三层砖混结构，占地狭长，整体平面呈“L”形，由南北衔接的两套单元组成。北套住宅临街，大门内为甬道式庭院，南部建有较大花园。淡黄色水泥砂浆外墙，墙角以清水红砖砌筑成齿状隅石造型。南立面装饰相对丰富，阳台围栏镶嵌方形绿釉花窗，中央列置深绿色的陶瓷宝瓶栏杆，窗下设置带花窗的混凝土花箱，窗楣及花箱皆以橘黄色涂料勾边，加之淡黄墙面和绿釉栏杆的衬托，显得立面雅致且明亮欢快。

ZHUANG Jun

ZHUANG Jun (1888–1990) has his ancestral family from Ningbo in Zhejiang province and was born in Shanghai. In 1909 he graduated from Nanyang High school. In 1910 he went to study abroad at public expense in the Department of Architecture Engineering of University of Illinois. In 1914 he graduated and came back to teach in Tsinghua Preparatory School (predecessor of Tsinghua University) in Beijing. In 1925, he founded ZHUANG Jun Architects. In 1927 he co-founded with other architects including FAN Wenzhao the Shanghai Institute of Architects (renamed as China Institute of Architects) and served as its president. In the spring of 1950, he went to the north at the invitation of the Central People's Government to build the capital. In the case, he closed down his architectural affairs office which existed for 25 years and set up a team of more than 50 technical staff to work in Beijing. In addition he joined the North China Construction Engineering Corporation of Ministry of Transport and served as Chief Engineer. In early 1953, the Ministry of Construction Engineering was established and the Central Institute of Architectural Design was founded on the basis of the North China Construction Corporation. He was appointed as chief engineer. His architectural works included KinCheng Bank of Shanghai, China & South Sea Bank, Continental Shopping Mall, Han KinCheng Bank and Continental Bank. In the 1990s, he won the "honorary certificate of construction master" awarded by Architectural Society of China. In his later years he wrote books and authored books including *English-Chinese Dictionary of Construction Engineering* and others.

Creating a World of Chinese Construction

When he went to Europe and the United States to make an on-the-spot observation of buildings in 1923, he had a deep understanding that the field of Chinese construction was entirely controlled by foreigners and the Chinese people who graduated from the major of architectural design could only act as assistants of foreigners. This made him determined to create a world of construction by Chinese themselves after returning home. In 1924, he resigned from the position of Tsinghua University and went back to Shanghai. After overcoming obstacles, he founded the ZHUANG Jun Architects in the settlement (previously there was only "Huahai Architects" established by the Chinese people). The first undertaking of his firm was to design the building of KinCheng

庄俊（右一）全家合影
A family photo of ZHUANG Jun (first from right).

Bank at the crossroad of Middle Jiangxi Road and Hankou Road, which was completed at the end of January 1926. Its design reflected the architectural art of the European Renaissance and the building level of the early 20th century and proved that the Chinese people could also design modern large-scale constructions with a high degree of artistic content.

With his encouragement, a large number of Chinese architects set up their own firms, which rose in Shanghai like mushrooms and ended the situation that foreign business architects monopolize China's architectural design industry. But at that time the obstacles faced by Chinese architects were still strong, including the discrimination and interference from the settlement. In order to work together to compete with foreign businesses, he initiated the organization "China Institute of Architects" ("Shanghai Institute of Architects" at first) which dozens of architects participated in. Its purpose was "to unite architects, exchange technology, safeguard the legitimate rights of architects", absorb student members and publish journals. He served as the first president and set the "commandments"—do not compete for business with peers; do not unreasonably reduce the design costs; and do not charge additional costs in any aspect. This not only enhanced the cohesion of domestic architects, but helped improve their professionalism as well.

He set an example personally to abide by the commandments and resist unhealthy practice. Once a builder presented him with fur lining to show his gratitude. He returned the gift and sincerely gave advice to the builder, which left the gentleman deeply moved. For his children, he gave them strict instructions, "I would like my future generations, no distinction between male and female, must set up the spirit of hard work, the style of self-sacrifice for others. You must be full of vigor and maintain integrity to make steady progress and keep loyal and trustworthy to serve the motherland so that China will become one of the greatest and most powerful countries."

The former residence of ZHUANG Jun is located at No. 45 on West Fuxing Road and was designed by himself. Built in 1921, it is an independent garden house which covers an area of 306 square meters with a three-story structure of brick and concrete. The building covers a long and narrow area and the overall plane is L-shaped. It is composed of two units connected from north to south. The residence at the north side faces the street and inside the gate is the corridor courtyard; a large garden was built in the south. Its walls have light yellow cement mortar and the corners have water red bricks to form odontoid masonry. The facade decorations in the south are relatively rich. The balcony rails are inlaid with lattice windows of square green glaze; in the middle of the balconies are installed dark green rails of ceramic bottles; under the windows there are concrete boxes with lattice windows; window lintels and lattice boxes are fringed with orange coating. Foiled with pale yellow walls and green glazed rails, the facade looks elegant, bright and cheerful.

庄俊 （杨宏富画） ZHUANG Jun （By YANG Hongfu）

朱恒清
（1902—1986）

祖籍无锡，人称“钢铁大王”。1920 年到上海当学徒，经过多年打拼后在北苏州路开设了自己的“恒馀铁号”。1940 年，朱恒清携手几十家大小铁号，成立了茂兴钢铁股份有限公司。随着实力的增加，朱恒清买下各小股东手里的股份，最后他的股份接近 90%，成为上海当时最大的私营钢厂老板。1955 年，茂兴钢铁厂成为公私合营企业。翌年，茂兴钢铁厂等 10 家企业合并，组建成上海第八钢铁厂。

“肉烂了，也要烂在汤里”

朱恒清祖辈家境殷实，至太平天国时，世代居住的无锡荣巷镇朱家巷村子被大火烧毁，由此败落。朱恒清出生后不久，母亲离世，由二姑抚养。童年时他的祖父离开无锡前往上海打工，这或许给年幼的朱恒清留下些许印象，他 18 岁时也走上了到上海谋生的奋斗之路。

经亲戚介绍，他在一家由无锡人开办，名为“源椿号”的五金店当学徒，学成之后，产生自立门户之念。他虽目不识丁，但自学了足以和洋人打交道的英语会话。1930 年，他自己的五金店“恒馀铁号”开业，并逐步扩大规模，发展为北苏州路 608 至 620 号沿街店面。在经营五金店的过程中，他越来越感到受制于洋人，于是决心创办自己的钢铁厂。1940 年，他联合几十家五金店创立茂兴钢铁股份有限公司，厂址设于长寿路 111 号，事务所位于北苏州路 670 号。钢铁厂以轧铁、生产竹钢为主，工人 90 多人，月产量达 300 余吨，向交通部属下津浦、京沪、浙赣等铁路局，江苏省工部局以及大型建筑公司、纱厂、五金店等供货。朱恒清担任厂长，又向诸多小股东收购股份，最终他持股接近 90%，成为当时上海最大的私有钢厂厂主。

朱恒清精明且心细，“肉烂了，也要烂在汤里”是他的口头禅。他善于和洋人谈生意，往往在餐桌筵席间便做成订购几艘废旧洋轮以拆取钢板的生意。但他也有失手的时候：一次向外国公司订一批 40 英尺长竹节钢时，把“forty”说成了“fourteen”，致使每根钢材短了足足 26 英尺，他急中生智，陆续出售给需要短钢材的建筑商，补救了纰漏。他喜欢购买地皮，认为“水淹不掉、火烧不掉”，购买五原路原意大利俱乐部所在地皮并非以居住为首要目的，而是为了以此作抵押申请更多贷款办厂且能出租赚租金。

上海沦陷后，面对想要吞并钢铁厂的日本人，他坚决拒斥对方要求，起初把厂租给别人，后来干脆关闭厂房。阴谋无法得逞的日本人在 1942 年诬陷他与重庆方面有生意往来，将他逮捕入狱。两周后，他的妻子托关系花了两根金条方才把他赎出。

建筑简介：五原路283号

朱恒清旧居位于五原路283号。据朱文琪（朱恒清长女）介绍：1948年朱恒清在五原路283号占地四亩的原意大利俱乐部废墟上盖起了一座马蹄形四层楼房。他凭借手中的钢铁，竟然投入了600吨作为这个房子的骨架，其坚固程度可想而知。该建筑南面为主楼，西面为厨房大菜间，北面为汽车间。主楼底楼分东、中、西三间房，之间均有活动移门隔开，拉开来俨然是个漂亮的标准舞厅，房屋高，屋内明亮。屋外有一大花园、两个网球场，园内是一片绿油油的草地，中间植有几棵香樟，两旁为瓜子黄杨和冬青，看上去十分淡雅。1949年元宵节他们全家人搬入。20世纪50年代，该建筑被作为武警上海市总队摩托车三中队营房。1982年归还原屋主，使用至今。

ZHU Hengqing

ZHU Hengqing (1902–1986) has his ancestral family from Wuxi in Jiangsu province. As the owner of the largest private steel factory in Shanghai, he was known as the "Iron and Steel King". In 1920, he went to Shanghai to become an apprentice. After years of hard work on the North Suzhou Road, he founded Hengyu Iron Company of his own. In 1940, he joined together dozens of iron and steel companies to establish Maoxing Iron and Steel Company Limited. With the increase of strength, he bought the shares of small shareholders, for which his shares finally approached 90% of the total, and he became owner of the largest private steel company in Shanghai. In 1955, Maoxing Iron and Steel Company became a public-private joint venture. In the following year, ten companies including Maoxing Iron and Steel merged into Shanghai Eighth Iron and Steel Plant.

"Rotten meat must stay in the soup"

ZHU Hengqing has a well-off ancestral family. During the time of the Taiping Heavenly Kingdom, a fire destroyed the ZHU Alley village at RONG Alley Town in Wuxi where generations lived a life. Thus his family collapsed ever since. Shortly after his birth, his mother passed away and he was raised by his second aunt. In his childhood his grandfather left Wuxi for Shanghai to do work for others, which might leave an impression on the young kid. Subsequently at the age of 18 he also went to Shanghai to set foot on a road of struggle for a living.

With the introduction of his relatives, he worked as an apprentice in a hardware shop called "Yuanchun Shop" run by a person from Wuxi. After the completion of his learning, an idea crossed his mind to run an independent shop. Though illiterate, he taught himself English enough to negotiate with foreigners. In 1930, his own hardware store "Hengyu Iron Company" was set up, which gradually expanded its scale to develop into a store along the street from No. 608 to 620 on North Suzhou Road. In the process of

朱恒清(后排右二)全家合影
A family photo of ZHU Hengqing (second from right, back row).

operating the hardware store, he increasingly felt the status of being subject to foreigners so that he determined to set up his own steel plant. In 1940, he united dozens of hardware stores to co-found Maoxing Iron and Steel Company Limited, which was located at No. 111 on Changshou Road, and its office was located at No. 670 on North Suzhou Road. The plant focused on rolling iron and the production of bamboo steel with over 90 workers and a production volume of over 300 tons of steel per month. It supplied steel to railway bureaus under the Ministry of Transportation, Jiangsu Provincial Bureau of Industry as well as large construction companies, cotton mills and hardware stores. As director of the plant, he also purchased shares from many small shareholders and ultimately his shares amounted to nearly 90% of the total, so that he became the owner of the largest private steel factory in Shanghai.

He was smart and cautious and that "rotten meat must stay in the soup" was his pet phrase. He was adept at talking business with foreigners, often deciding a business at table or at banquet where he placed an order for a few used foreign ships to dismantle the steel plates. But there were also times when he played below par. Once he ordered 40-foot long bamboo steels from a foreign company while he mispronounced "forty" as "fourteen", resulting in the shortage of 26 feet in length for each. Fortunately he had quick wits to sell these steels to architectures in need of short steels, managing to remedy the careless mistake. Moreover he had a liking for land property business, believing that "land is safe from flood and fire". His purchase of the land on Wuyuan Road which was the seat of the "Italian Club" was primarily not for the purpose of residence, but for the purpose of applying for more loans based on mortgage of the land to set up factories or to put out to lease for rentals.

After the fall of Shanghai, he firmly rejected the requirements in the face of the Japanese invaders who conspired to annex his iron plant. In the beginning he rented his factory buildings to others and later simply closed it up. When the Japanese aggressors failed in the conspiracy, they framed a case against him in 1942 that he had business dealings with the Chongqing government so that he was arrested and imprisoned. Two weeks later, his wife resorted to their connections and spent two gold bars to succeed in redeeming him.

The former residence of ZHU Hengqing is located at No. 283 on Wuyuan Road. According to the description of his eldest daughter, he had a horseshoe-shaped four-story building completed at No. 283 on Wuyuan Road in 1948, which covered an area of four acres occupied formerly by the Italian club. With steel at hand, he even bestowed 600 tons of steel on the skeleton of the building which resulted in its unimaginable solidity. In the south of the building is its main part; in the west is the kitchen; in the north are garages. At the bottom floor the main building has three rooms in the east, the middle and the west, which are separated with sliding doors. Removing these sliding doors, a beautiful standard ballroom will be ready since the ceiling is high and rooms are bright. Outside there is a big garden and two tennis courts. In the garden is a green lawn with a few camphor trees in the middle and some box trees and holly on both sides. Naturally it looks quietly elegant. In 1949, the whole family moved into the building on the Lantern Festival. In 1950s the building was used as the barracks for the third motorcycle squadron of Shanghai Armed Police Corps. In 1982, it was returned to the original owner for use up to today.

朱恒清 （吴耀明画）　ZHU Hengqing （By WU Yaoming）

江寒汀
（1903—1963）

江苏常熟人，名上渔，字寒汀，花鸟画家、艺术教育家。16岁学习花鸟画，28岁开始专业绘画，后任教于上海美术专科学校。中华人民共和国成立后为上海中国画院首聘画师。擅长工笔及写意花鸟，亦精金石。其花鸟画深得古代名家画法，技法十分娴熟，双钩廓填和没骨写生尤得精髓，画风近华岩、任颐等，构图稳健，笔墨老到，格调清雅，无论家禽还是野鸟，均能描绘得栩栩如生、神形俱备。画作早年清隽秀丽、高雅静美；晚年趋向豪放苍劲、气息酣畅。1960年应周恩来总理邀请为人民大会堂绘制巨幅《红梅图》。传世名作有《百鸟图》《百卉册》《百兽图》等。出版有《江寒汀百兽图》《当代名画家江寒汀》《江寒汀百兽图画册》等。

寒汀笔下鸟，天下到处飞

江寒汀、唐云、张大壮和陆抑非，被誉为近代海上花鸟画的“四大名旦”，而江寒汀尤以描绘各类禽鸟著称。他悉心研究历代花鸟画家的技法，上溯宋元诸家，下至明清画坛方家。据他女儿江圣行回忆，父亲深入研究宋元以来各派名家花鸟画技法的同时，注重写生，两者互为参悟，经过消化，成为自己的技法。

养鸟是江寒汀平时最大的爱好。江圣行记得童年时，父亲有空便带她一起去五马路（现在的广东路）鸟市街，那里出售各种各样的飞禽、鸟食、鸟笼等。几乎每家店主都与父亲很熟，每当有新品种的鸟，他们总先给父亲看，有时甚至还向父亲请教鸟的名称、特性等。

有一天，她又随父亲去鸟市街。那时正值春天，到处是一笼笼的黄嘴绿毛的幼雏。忽见一家店里有几只长尾巴的鸟，江寒汀停住脚步，观察了好一会儿，便和店主攀谈了起来。她不耐烦了，就自顾自朝前走，结果发现找不到父亲了，便大哭起来。一家店主的儿子一看是江寒汀的女儿，便陪她一路返回找到父亲。谁知江寒汀居然还在津津有味地谈论那长尾巴的鸟，丝毫没发觉自己最喜欢的小女儿走失了。那天，江寒汀将这长尾巴的鸟买回了家。他精心调配食物，用煮熟的鸡蛋黄拌粟米后亲自喂养，还用小刷子轻轻地刷洗鸟尾上的羽毛。长尾巴鸟渐渐长大，只要一见江寒汀便叫个不停，叫声悦耳动听。这只长尾巴鸟就是唐山鹊。

上海画院成立后，为了让画家对禽鸟有更多的感性认识，院部特地在画院的一角建了个高大的铁笼，里面有各种禽鸟。江寒汀毫不吝惜，将家中的几十种鸟，包括那只他最喜欢的唐山鹊，一并送入这个禽鸟天地。每天，江寒汀与吴湖帆、来楚生、张大壮、张聿光等大画家们主动承担起喂养任务。不过这些禽鸟没有辜负画家的厚爱，努力当好“模特”，让画家们尽情描绘。近水楼台先得月，画家们相继创作出一批可爱的花鸟画作品。其中包括江寒汀的传世作品——二十米长卷《百鸟图》。

建筑简介：五原路248号

江寒汀旧居位于五原路248号，新式里弄住宅。建筑为三层砖木结构，采用青砖和石灰砂浆砌筑墙体。一层设有架空层，建筑平面近似矩形。房屋外立面形式简洁，白色水泥拉毛墙面，局部窗边为清水砖外墙面，机制小瓦缓坡屋盖。南立面设有阳台，钢筋混凝土悬挑板结构。一层入口位于房屋北侧，入口门厅及走道地面为水磨石饰面，白色涂料粉刷墙面，木结构双跑楼梯，木踏板，木栏板，一梯两户。二层南侧设有阳台、居住房间，中部为客厅、厨卫。室内走道及房间楼面基本为硬木长条地板。房屋南侧有庭院。

JIANG Hanting

JIANG Hanting (1903–1963) has his ancestral family from Changshu in Jiangsu province. With a personal name of Shangyu and a courtesy name of Hanting, he is known as a flower-and-bird painter and an art educator. He began to learn flower-and-bird painting at the age of 16 and commenced professional painting at the age of 28. Later he served as a teacher in Shanghai Academy of Fine Arts. He was one of the first painters employed by Shanghai Chinese Painting Academy after the founding of the People's Republic of China. He was not only good at traditional Chinese realistic and freehand flower-and-bird painting, but also expert in epigraphic painting. His flower-and-bird paintings absorbed the essence of skills from ancient masters. In addition, he was particularly versed in double-stroke contour-filling and boneless sketching so that his painting style was similar to that of HUA Yan and REN Yi. His painting is characterized by moderate composition, skillful control of color and elegant style. Either poultry or wild birds could be painted vivid and true to life in his works. In his early stage of paintings, beauty and purity could be discerned while freedom and vigor could be seen in the late stage of his paintings. In 1960, at the invitation of Premier ZHOU Enlai, he finished a huge painting of *Red Plum* to be displayed in the Great Hall of the People. Some of his well-known masterworks include *All the Birds*, *All the Pretty Flowers*, *All the Wild Animals* and so on. He also published such painting albums as *All the Wild Animals by JIANG Hanting*, *JIANG Hanting—A Famous Contemporary Painter* and *The Album of Wild Animals by JIANG Hanting* and so on.

Birds in his Paintings Fly across the Country

JIANG Hanting, TANG Yun, ZHANG Dazhuang and LU Yifei were honored as "Four Famous Painters" of modern bird-and-flower painting in Shanghai. JIANG Hanting was especially known nationwide for his depiction of all kinds of birds. He devoted himself to learning techniques from different schools of bird-and-flower painting of all dynasties, from Song and Yuan Dynasties to Ming and Qing Dynasties. According to the memory of his daughter JIANG Shengxing, he made an in-depth study of different bird-and-flower painting techniques of different schools; meanwhile, he attached importance to painting from life. He could absorb a lot

江寒汀在作画
JIANG Hanting at painting.

from both approaches and shape his style painting style.

Aviculture is one of his favorite hobbies in his spare time. His daughter could still remember that in her childhood her father took her to the birds' market on Wuma Road (now Guangdong Road) whenever he was free, where a variety of birds, bird food, birdcages were sold. Almost every shopkeeper was familiar with her father. When having a new breed of birds, they always invited her father to take a look and even consulted him about the names and features of these birds.

On a spring day, she went to the birds' market with his father where nestlings with yellow beaks and green feathers could be found everywhere in the cages. Suddenly, at the sight of a few birds with long tails in one shop, her father stopped, observed the birds for a long time and then talked with the shopkeeper. She grew impatient and went ahead by herself. However, after a while she could not find her father and burst into crying. The son of a shopkeeper saw her and knew who she was, so he took her all the way back to find her father. Surprisingly, he was still talking about those birds with apparent delight and even didn't realize the absence of his favorite daughter. After buying the bird home that day, he carefully chose and made food and fed it himself with food mixed with cooked egg yolk and corns. Besides, he gently scrubbed feathers of the bird's tail with a small brush. As the bird gradually grew up, every time it saw him, it couldn't stop its pleasant chirping. This bird was called Tangshan Magpie.

After the establishment of Shanghai Chinese Painting Academy, the Academy authorities specifically made a tall steel cage with a variety of birds in it at one corner to enable the artists to have more perceptual knowledge of birds. He was generous enough to bring dozens of birds from his home to this birds' world, including his favorite Tangshan Magpie. Together with WU Hufan, LAI Chusheng, ZHANG Dazhuang, ZHANG Yuguang and other famous painters, he volunteered to take up the task of feeding the birds. Of course, these birds did not fail to live up to the painters' love and strived to be good "models" so that painters could enjoy painting them. Just as the saying goes, a waterfront pavilion gets the moonlight first. The advantage of living in such a favorable situation enabled the painters to create a number of lovely bird-and-flower painting works in succession. Among them is his popular 20-meter scroll masterpiece *All the Birds*.

The former residence of JIANG Hanting is located at No. 248 on Wuyuan Road. This building boasts itself a new style alley residence. It is of a three-storied structure of brick and wood with walls made of black brick and lime mortar. The first floor has the open space and the building plane is approximately rectangular. The outside facade of the building is concise with white napped walls and partially around the window are simple bricks. The roof has gentle slopes covered with small tiles made by machines. At the front of the south, there are balconies with a reinforced concrete structure. One entrance is located at the north of the house. The entrance porch and the path are decorated with terrazzo, the exterior walls are coated with white cement and the double staircases are made of wood. The stairs enjoy wood grating and wood handrail. At the stairs are two households. At the south of the second floor, there are balconies and bedrooms and in the center are the living rooms, a kitchen and a toilet. Indoor walkways and the floor of the room are mainly of the hardwood stripes. There is a courtyard on the south of the house.

江寒汀 （钱定华画） JIANG Hanting （By QIAN Dinghua）

汤晓丹
（1910—2012）

福建华安人，电影导演艺术家。童年时侨居印度尼西亚。10岁随父回国。1928年在厦门集美农林专科学校学习时，因参加学生运动被开除学籍。后到上海，1931年进入天一影片公司任布景师。1933年拍摄了处女作《白金龙》，自此走上导演之路。而后拍摄了抗日影片《上海火线后》《小广东》《民族的吼声》，及揭露国民党腐败统治的《天堂春梦》等。中华人民共和国成立后，加入上海电影制片厂。一生导演电影近50部，有“银幕将军”和“战争片之父”之誉。由其执导的影片《渡江侦察记》《南征北战》《红日》《难忘的战斗》《南昌起义》等，成为中国战争题材影片的经典。1984年获第四届金鸡奖最佳导演奖。2004年获中国电影金鸡奖终身成就奖。

蓝为洁
（1926—2014）

四川重庆人，电影剪辑师。1944年，高中毕业后进入重庆中国电影制片厂，后与导演汤晓丹结为伉俪。1946年，随厂迁回上海。1952年在上海翻译片组任剪辑。1957年后，调入江南电影制片厂，后并入上海电影制片厂。一生参与过300多部电影的剪辑，有“南方第一剪”之称，曾剪辑出《巴山夜雨》《城南旧事》《苦恼人的笑》《南昌起义》《廖仲恺》等多部经典影片。1984年退休后，为全国数十家电视台、电影厂剪辑过《徐悲鸿》《传奇夫人》《杨家将》等近千部（集）电视剧和多部电影。1993年起，在报上开设专栏，并出版多部专著，记录下中国影人和中国影史的点点滴滴。

“三个艺术家，一个保姆”

蓝为洁与汤晓丹相识于20世纪40年代，彼时，刚刚高中毕业的蓝为洁是中影厂一名职员，汤晓丹是从香港逃难到后方的“金牌导演”。两人相识、相爱，婚后不到三年，在上海有了两个儿子。蓝为洁曾回忆，一日三餐、一家四口，全靠她这个“磨心”人物操劳。

蓝为洁不仅是非常成功的职业女性，也是一位伟大的家庭主妇。她相夫教子，操持家务，使四口之家成为非常成功的艺术之家：丈夫汤晓丹导演过《南征北战》《红日》等战争大片，被誉为“战争片之父”；大儿子汤沐黎和小儿子汤沐海，分别是蜚声中外的油画家和指挥家。

蓝为洁因此被称为“银幕将军”汤晓丹导演的夫人，画家汤沐黎、指挥家汤沐海的母亲。父子两代都是大艺术家，蓝为洁曾自豪地说：“我家出了三个艺术家，一个保姆。”保姆说的是她自己。

“可爱的老太太”，是电影圈很多人提到蓝为洁脱口而出的评价。不仅因为她从不以“大师”自居，更因心直口快，一生都给人率直、有个性的川妹子印象。

蓝为洁晚年好写书，写对儿子的培养，写对“汤爷爷”的照料，而她自己却是电影剪辑大家，诚如她所言：“我们的家庭是很奇怪的组合，我的脾气说来就来，想到什么说什么；‘汤爷爷’不一样，他修养很好，就像一块橡皮，用针扎下去，拔出来看不到孔。我们的家庭之所以能有一点成绩，离不开汤晓丹的宽容和体谅。”

2012年年初，汤晓丹以102岁高龄辞世。两年后，曾说过“我们不要把离别看作是悲伤的……”的蓝为洁追随而去。相濡以沫66年的银幕伉俪，终于在天堂相会。

建筑简介：泰安路10弄1号

汤晓丹、蓝为洁旧居位于泰安路10弄1号，一栋三层三开间石库门房子。建筑为砖混结构，红瓦双坡顶，外墙作水泥仿石抹层，层间有腰檐；细棂木窗外设木质硬百叶，仅窗裙做简单装饰。底层南向有入口处庭院，入内即为堂屋，东、西两侧为厢房；二、三层中部均设有内阳台，三层北向有晾衣晒台。此处原是中国电影制片厂上海办事处的职工宿舍，1946年电影厂厂长为照顾汤晓丹一家生活，腾出了10弄1号三楼一间电影厂杂物间给他住，没有抽水马桶和自来水，汤晓丹却甘之如饴，一家人一住就是七年。

TANG Xiaodan and LAN Weijie

TANG Xiaodan (1910–2012) has his ancestral family from Hua'an in Fujian Province and is known as a film direction artist. In his childhood he migrated to Indonesia and lived there. When he was 10 years old, he came back to China together with his father. When he studied in the Xiamen-based Jimei Agriculture and Forestry College, he was expelled from school in 1928 due to his participation in the students' movement. After that he went to Shanghai and then he served in Tianyi Film Studio and became a setting decorator in 1931. In 1933, he produced his first film *The White-golden Dragon* and embarked on the road to be a director since then. Later he produced the resisting-Japanese films including *Shanghai under Fire*, *Little Boy from Guangdong*, *Roar of the People* as well as the film *Dreaming In Paradise*, which exposed the corrupted rule of the KMT. After the founding of the People's Republic of China, he joined the Shanghai Film Studio. In his lifetime he directed nearly 50 films and was reputed as both "General of the Screen" and "Father of War Film" . Films directed by him include *Reconnaissance after Crossing the Yangtze River*, *Fighting North and South*, *The Red Sun*, *Unforgettable Battle* and *Nanchang Uprising*, which all became the classics of war films in China. In 1984, he was awarded the Golden Rooster Award for Best Director and in 2004 he won the Golden Rooster Award for Lifelong Achievement.

LAN Weijie (1926–2014) has her ancestral family from Chongqing in Sichuan province and was known as a film editor. In 1944, after graduating from high school, she entered China Film Studio in Chongqing and later got married to director TANG Xiaodan. In 1946, she moved back to Shanghai with the studio. In 1952, she became the film editor of Shanghai translation film group. After 1957, she was transferred to the South Film Studio which was merged into the Shanghai Film Studio. She edited over 300 films in her life and was reputed as "the First Editor in the South". She edited quite many classical films such as *Evening Rain at Mount Ba*, *My Memories of Old Beijing*, *Troubled Laughter*, *Nanchang Uprising*, *LIAO Zhongkai* and so on. After her retirement in 1984, she edited nearly one thousand television series and many films for dozens of television stations and film studios, the former including *XU Beihong*, *Legendary Lady* and *Generals of the Yang Family*. Since 1993, she launched special columns for herself in newspapers and published many monographs which recorded abundant details of Chinese filmmakers and Chinese film history.

"Three Artists and One Nanny"

LAN Weijie and TANG Xiaodan got to know each other in the 1940s. At that time, she was the staff of the Central Film Studio

汤晓丹全家合影
TANG Xiaodan and his whole family.

and just graduated from high school while he was the "Gold Director" who fled from Hong Kong to the rear. They met with each other and then fell in love with each other. Within less than three years after their marriage they had two sons in Shanghai. She once recalled that the whole family of four members relied on her labor for three meals a day.

She was not only a successful professional woman, but also a great housewife. She helped her husband and taught their children. She ran her house well and made the family of four a successful home of art. Her husband directed such large-scale war films such as *Fighting North and South*, and *The Red Sun*, known as the "Father of War Film", and her first son TANG Muli and the younger son TANG Muhai were famous oil painter and music conductor well-known both at home and in the world.

Therefore she was known as wife of the director and "General of the Screen" and mother of a painter and a conductor. Both father and sons being great artists, she said proudly that "My family breeds the three artists and one nanny." Nanny meant to refer to herself.

"A lovely old lady"—this was what escaped from the lips of many people in the film circle when they made any comment on her. This was not only because she never viewed herself as a "master", but also because her straightforwardness impressed people with the image of Sichuan girls who have the reputation of being enthusiastic and frank.

She took to writing books in her old years, writing about the training of sons or about her taking care of "Grandfather TANG", while she was a great master of film editing. Once she said, "Our family is a very strange combination. My temper is changeable, saying whatever I think. In contrast, 'Grandpa TANG' is quite different with a good command of accomplishment, just like a piece of rubber which you can't find any hole on the surface after pricking with a needle. Thanks to his tolerance and understanding, our family has been able to have a little success."

In the early 2012, the husband bid a forever farewell to the world at the age of 102. Two years later, the wife followed him, who once said, "We do not regard the parting as sadness...". This screen couple who had been married for 66 years finally had a gathering in heaven again.

The former residence of TANG Xiaodan and LAN Weijie lies at No.1 in Alley 10 on Tai'an Road, which is a three-story house with a style of stone gate and with a width of three rooms. The building is of a structure of bricks and concrete. The roof has double slopes covered with red tiles and the exterior walls have imitated stone surface of cement. Between floors, there are belt eaves; the wooden hard shutters are set outside the wood windows with thin lattices and only the window curtains have simple decorations. At the south side of the ground floor, there is a courtyard at the entrance and inside it is the main room. At the east and west sides are wing rooms; the second and third floors are equipped with balconies and at the north side on the third floor there is a drying veranda. Here it was formerly the dormitory for staff members working in Shanghai office of China Film Studio. In 1946, in order to favor the whole family of TANG, the director of the film factory had a utility room emptied on the third floor at No.1 in Alley 10 for him. The house did not have toilet and tap water. Though the living conditions were so humble, he enjoyed it and the family stayed here for seven years.

汤晓丹 （忻秉勇画）　　TANG Xiaodan （By XIN Bingyong）

达式常
（1940—　）

原籍江苏南京，生于上海，电影表演艺术家。1962年毕业于上海电影专科学校，同年入上海电影制片厂任演员。先后在《兄妹探宝》《年青的一代》《难忘的战斗》《曙光》《人到中年》《燕归来》《谭嗣同》《T省的八四、八五年》《地狱·天堂》《站直啰，别趴下》等影片中饰演主角或重要角色。1981年获第四届《大众电影》百花奖最佳男演员奖。1983年主演电视剧《走进暴风雨》，获《大众电视》金鹰奖最佳男主角奖。为日本电视剧《蔷薇海峡》男主角川岛俊夫配音，1986年获第四届《大众电视》金鹰奖最佳男演员配音奖。曾获上海首届文学艺术奖电影优秀表演奖、1987年中国电影表演艺术学会奖、1994年宝钢高雅艺术奖。是中国电影家协会理事，上海电影家协会理事，中国电影表演艺术学会理事、副理事长。

纯洁的爱

达式常与妻子王文皓的相爱相守始于就读上海电影专科学校的青葱岁月。

王文皓从小失去父母，寄养教师家中，尤感亲人般的嘘寒问暖弥足珍贵；达式常家境贫困，父母重病，使他较同龄人更懂得付出关爱。他们同病相怜而又志趣相投，互相照应、彼此依靠。王文皓曾患肺病，又因用嗓过度而损伤了声带，在她人生中最痛苦艰难的时期，达式常经常陪伴她，给予她慰藉。

当时他们各自听到好友的劝说——“她身体差，可能成为你演艺事业的包袱”“他一贫如洗，你的身体需要物质条件更好的男同志照顾”……他们不为所动，欣然结婚了，充满喜悦地布置6.8平方米的小房间——一张床、一个方桌、一把椅子、从集体宿舍搬来的被子、朋友送的一对枕套，构成了他们新婚的家当。两碗阳春面是他们“婚宴”的主食，达式常幽默而自豪地说：“我们的婚宴名字叫‘同甘共苦’，我们永远不会忘记。”

他们从未忘记他们的誓言。夫妇俩生活拮据，省吃俭用。达式常工作外出时，王文皓常常连荤菜都舍不得吃。没有衣柜，也鲜少购置新衣，她努力帮助偿还达式常因父亲的病所负的债务，还挑起了家务活的担子。达式常感念恩情，不论到何处，都将妻子和女儿的照片珍藏于上衣口袋中。

达式常接到剧本，常征求王文皓的意见，倾听她对角色的细致分析。“无论演什么电影，我心中只有我的妻子。我怎么也不会动心的，王文皓有多美，有多善良。”达式常坚定于对妻子的忠诚，而通情达理的妻子对他抱以充分信任——“在戏中你该爱就爱，该恋就恋。”达式常感恩地说：“我扮演的每个角色，都有她一份心血、一份功劳。”

建筑简介：永福路147弄33号

达式常寓所位于永福路147弄33号。20世纪初这里人烟稀少，多为菜地，法租界越界筑路后，开始建独院式别墅，但直至解放后还夹杂着简屋和空地。20世纪80年代为解决住宅困难，见缝插针建了33号一幢六层公房，配套有煤卫设施。

DA Shichang

DA Shichang (1940–), born in Shanghai, has his ancestral family from Nanjing in Jiangsu province, and he is known as a film performance artist. In 1962 he graduated from Shanghai Film Academy and entered into Shanghai Film Studio in the same year to work as an actor. Successively he played leading or important roles in such films as *Go Prospecting, The Younger Generation, Unforgettable Battle, Dawn, Men of a Certain Age, Swallows Return, TAN Sitong, 1984 and 1985 in T Province, Hell-Heaven and Stand Straight*. In 1981 he won the Fourth Popular Movie Hundred Flowers Award for Best Actor. In 1983 he starred the TV series *Getting into the Storm*, which won him the Public TV Golden Eagle Award for Best Actor in a Leading Role. He dubbed for Kawashima Toshio, the chief actor of the Japanese TV series *Rose Straits*, which won him the Fourth Public TV Golden Eagle Award for Best Voice in 1986. Also he once won the First Shanghai Literature and Art Award for Outstanding Film Performance, China Film Society of Performing Art Award in 1987, and Baogang Elegant Art Award in 1994. In addition, he is director of China Film Association, director of Shanghai Film Association, and director and vice president of China Film Society of Performing Art.

Pure Love

The love between him and his wife WANG Wenhao began in the green years when they were at Shanghai Film Academy.

The wife lost her parents in her childhood and therefore she was fostered by one of her teachers. In this case she especially cherished the values of warm blessing from loved ones. The husband came from a poor family and his parents were seriously ill so that he knew more than his peers to give love. They were sympathetic for and congenial to one another and they took care of and relied on each other. The wife once suffered from lung disease and experienced overuse of her throat, so her vocal cords were hurt. During the most painful and difficult period in her life, her husband stayed in her company and comforted her.

At that time they each heard persuasion from good friends, who said that "she is in poor health condition and may be the burden of your career" or "he is penniless, but you need better material conditions and care from better husband"... In spite of this, they were not swayed and got married cheerfully, arranging with heart full of joy a small room of 6.8 square meters—a bed, a square table, a

达式常与王文皓
DA Shichang and WANG Wenhao.

chair, a quilt taken back from the dormitory, a pair of pillowcases from a friend—all these constituted the possessions for their new marriage. Two bowls of plain noodles were the main food for their "wedding feast". The husband said with humor and pride, "Our wedding is called 'sharing the happiness and woe', which we will never forget."

Never did the couple forget their vows. They lived in low water and lived frugally. When the husband was out at work, the wife was often reluctant to have meat or fish. With no wardrobe, they also rarely bought new clothes. Moreover, she made every effort to help pay off the debts because of his father's disease. Also she shouldered the burden of housework. With her love and kindness in heart, he cherished the photos of his wife and daughter in the coat pocket wherever he went.

When he received a script, he asked for views from his wife, listening to her careful analysis of the role. "No matter what film it is, I have only my wife in my heart. I could never be tempted, since my wife is the best and most beautiful." Clearly he was firmly loyal to his wife and the sensible wife also had full confidence in him, saying, "In the film you love one where you should." He replied gratefully, "Each role I played has her bit of painstaking efforts and contribution."

The apartment of DA Shichang is located at No. 33 in Alley 147 on Yongfu Road. In the early 20th century, this place was sparsely populated and was mostly vegetable field. After the French Settlement crossed the border to build road, the building of an independent courtyard-style villa was started. But until after the liberation it was still mixed with simple houses and open spaces. In 1980s, to solve the housing difficulties, a six-story building was completed for public housing in making use of every bit of space. It was supported with gas and sanitary facilities.

达式常 （桑麟康画） DA Shichang （By SANG Linkang）

严裕棠
（1880—1958）

生于上海，号光藻。1902年与人合办大隆铁工厂，1907年后独资经营。同时与英、日商人合作经营房地产，获取高利。1925年租办苏纶纱厂。1927年建立光裕公司，总管大隆、苏纶两厂，自任总经理，同年由于杜月笙的支持，买进苏纶厂，逐渐发展成棉铁联营企业，1937年，总资本已达50万元法币。上海沦陷后，企业为日军强占。1938年，开办上海泰利制造机器有限公司，聘美商为董事长。1940年以出让大隆为条件收回苏纶等企业，并从事五金、地产等商业经营。抗战结束后，赎回所有企业。1948年去台湾，1958年11月在台湾病故。

大隆机器厂诞生记

1902年，严裕棠与人合伙各出资2500两，租赁杨树浦太和街梅家弄两间平房作为临时厂房，招收7个熟练工、4个学徒，与益泰轧花厂及德商老湖丝厂建立业务关系，从事一些简单而零星的修理。后通过叔父所在的洋行，从国外订购了8部机床、1部牛头刨床、1部龙门刨床、一套二十匹马力引擎设备。临时厂房已不够用，便向父亲租赁在平凉路的12间平房，大隆机器厂得以创立。当时上海仅有15家机器厂家，主要业务是为抵达上海的外国船舶供应小配件和提供零星修理服务，竞争不算激烈。

严裕棠精通如何与洋人打交道，比竞争对手更善于招揽生意，渐渐地，大隆机器厂在外国商船中树立起口碑，规模也不断发展壮大，又置备了两条小拖轮，并承接船舶以外的厂家机件修配业务。

1906年，因意见分歧，合伙人退出资金，大隆机器厂遂由严裕棠独资经营。严裕棠同时从事地产投资，购进杨树浦等地若干地产，并营造光裕里，从中获得丰厚利润，以此对大隆厂进一步扩充，例如为国内纺织企业配零件、试制纺织机械。当时国内厂家惯用进口设备，对国产的不敢轻易尝试。为打开销路，严裕棠决定试水农业机械，开辟广大农村市场。小柴油机引擎、戽水机、碾米机、磨粉机等应运而生，1922年成功试制我国第一部自制小型拖拉机。这些农业机械深受江浙两省农村用户欢迎，而一战的爆发使机械进口受阻，大隆厂业务量遂与日俱增。

严裕棠懂得识人用人，当他发现一家倒闭的纺织机器厂总工程师意志顽强地从失败中吸取经验教训，以求发奋图强、全面改进生产过程、提高机器质量时，毅然将他聘入大隆厂担任总工程师，使大隆厂面貌焕然一新。

建筑简介：武康路212号

严裕棠旧居位于武康路212号，是一幢并不引人注意的花园别墅。进入大门，在花园深处矗立着一幢亮丽的英国式乡村别墅。建筑立面朝东，屋面陡峭，铺盖红瓦，东边屋顶为壁炉烟囱。建筑外墙为白色粉墙，木构架外露，色彩对比十分鲜艳。二层有宽大的阳台，底层为联排落地门窗。整幢别墅在四周花木的簇拥下显得十分幽静典雅。1937年，严裕棠从虹口搬到这里居住。1949年后，此处长期由他的儿媳钱小铮女士居住。

YAN Yutang

YAN Yutang (1880–1958), born in Shanghai, has a courtesy name of Guangzao. In 1902 he co-founded with others the Dalong Iron Factory, which he independently operated after 1907. At the same time he cooperated with British and Japanese businessmen to engage in real estate for high profit. In 1925 he started the Sulun Cotton Factory on the basis of lease. In 1927 he founded the Guangyu Company to include the above two factories and he himself served as the general manager. In the same year and with the support by DU Yuesheng, he bought the Sulun Factory and gradually developed a joint enterprise of cotton and iron. In 1937, the total capital of the enterprise had reached half million yuan of legal money. After the fall of Shanghai, the enterprise was occupied with force by Japanese invaders. In 1938, he started Shanghai Taili Manufacturing Machine Company and employed an American businessman to serve as chairman. In 1940 he used the transferring of the Dalong Iron Factory as the precondition in order to take back his enterprises including Sulun and he also started such businesses as hardware and real estate. After the War of Resistance against Japanese Aggression, he redeemed all his enterprises. In 1948 he went to Taiwan and died of illness in November 1958.

The Birth of Dalong Machine Factory

In 1902, YAN Yutang partnered with another person and each invested 2,500 taels of silver to found a factory. They rented two single-storied houses as a temporary place for the factory and recruited seven skilled workers and four apprentices. In addition they established business relationship with Yitai Cotton Ginning Factory and the Old Lake Silk Factory, a German business, to do some simple and fragmentary repairs. Later by means of a foreign business where his uncle worked, he ordered from abroad 8 machines, 2 shaping machines and an engine of 20 horsepower. Now the temporary two houses for the factory were not enough. Then he rented from his father 12 single-storied houses so that the Dalong Machine Factory was founded. At that time, there were only 15 machine manufacturers in Shanghai and their main business was to supply small parts and fragmentary repair services for foreign ships which arrived in Shanghai. Therefore, the competition was not fierce.

YAN was proficient in dealing with foreigners so that he was better at getting business than his competitors. Gradually, the Dalong Machine Factory established a reputation among foreign merchants and its scale continued to grow. Later it purchased two small tugboats and undertook parts repair business besides repairs of ships.

In 1906, due to the differences of opinions, the partner took back his investment and YAN ran the factory on the basis of

严裕棠创建的大隆机器厂厂房
The Dalong Machine Factory founded by YAN Yutang.

independent capital. At the same time, he was also engaged in real estate investment, purchasing some pieces of land and getting handsome profits, so that he could further expand the factory to include such businesses as supply of parts for domestic textile enterprises and trial production of textile machinery. At that time, manufacturers in China were fond of using imported equipment and were unwilling to try domestic products. In order to enhance sales, he decided to have a try in making agricultural machinery to open up the vast rural market. Small diesel engines, scooping machine, rice milling machines and flour grinding machine emerged at the right moment. In 1922 he successfully produced China's first self-made small tractor. These agricultural machines were welcomed by rural users. When the import of machinery was blocked due to the First World War, the business of the Dalong Machine Factory increased accordingly day by day.

YAN also knew the importance of employees. When he found that the chief engineer in a collapsed factory of textile machinery drew lessons from failures, worked with determination to improve production process and improve the quality of machines, he resolutely hired the engineer as the chief engineer so that his factory took on a new outlook.

The former residence of YAN Yutang is located at No. 212 on Wukang Road. It is a garden villa not so noticeable. In the depth of the garden stands a beautiful countryside villa of British style. Its front faces east. The steep roof is covered with red tiles, and on the east of the roof is a fireplace chimney. The building has white exterior walls and its wooden frame is exposed with striking contrast of colors. The second floor has a large balcony and the ground floor enjoys French doors and windows in a row. The whole villa, surrounded by flowers and trees, it is very quiet and elegant. After the outbreak of the War of Resistance, YAN moved away from Hongkou district to live here. In 1949, it was the residence of his daughter-in-law for a long period of time.

严裕棠 （杨宏富画） YAN Yutang （By YANG Hongfu）

何世桢
（1894—1972）

安徽望江人，字思毅。毕业于东吴大学，曾参加五四运动，任上海学联会会长，由此结识孙中山，并加入国民党。后留学美国密歇根大学，获法学博士学位。回国后，任东吴大学法科教授，上海大学教务长。1923年，任第三届国际律师协会中国代表。1924年，任国民党“一大”上海代表，同年创办持志大学并任校长。五卅运动中，被宋庆龄指定为后援会法律组副主任。抗日战争时期是打入日伪内部的国民党地下工作者。中华人民共和国成立前夕，何世桢断然拒绝王宠惠赴台邀请，坚持留在大陆。

民族气节

1939年4月，汪精卫由日本特务秘密护送至上海组织伪中央政府。何世桢不愿与卖国求荣的汉奸为伍，关闭了自己的法律事务所，携家眷住进高邮路68号这栋独立式花园住宅。8月，汪精卫召开伪国民党第六次全国代表大会前，曾威逼利诱何世桢参加大会并担任主席团成员。何世桢义正词严地拒绝参加，不料汪精卫仍在会上将何世桢列入中央委员名单并擅自在报纸上散播假新闻。义愤填膺的何世桢立即登报阐述自己的政治立场，澄清诬陷。汪伪政权的阴谋没有得逞，便以卑鄙的手段进行报复。汪伪特工总部以持志学院暨附中拒绝向政府登记为名，于1939年9月13日派出大批特务砸毁学校、劫走公章。坚贞不屈的何世桢为了坚持民族气节、维护师生安全，毅然宣布持志大学及附中停办，获得学校师生的一致支持。

汪精卫仍不肯罢休，1942年11月，他令说客力邀何世桢出任伪司法院长，何世桢又坚辞不受。恼羞成怒的汪精卫气急败坏，令“76号”特工绑架了何世桢年仅四岁的儿子，将他劫持到一艘船上。经何世桢多位朋友四方奔走营救，在吴淞口整整漂泊了56天的孩子终于得以回家，然而心灵受到了巨大创伤。

由持志大学学生、中共地下党上海市负责人之一徐明诚牵线，何世桢结识了潘汉年。在何世桢的帮助下，中共地下党在汪伪政府的中央储备银行建立了一个透支户，名义上组织的公司其实是新四军抗日后勤供应站。何世桢秉承国共联合抗日的宗旨，冒险接受潘汉年领导的中共地下组织以重庆地下组织名义秘密设立电台的重任，既通重庆，又通延安。当时电台负责人刘人寿带领几位工作人员长期隐蔽在何世桢高邮路寓所三楼，夜以继日地进行艰辛的情报工作。何世桢的家成了中共地下党的一个重要情报基地，潘汉年曾亲赴何宅讨论工作。

何世桢在动荡的年代以拳拳爱国心坚守民族气节，不畏强暴，为抗战胜利作出了贡献。

建筑简介：高邮路68号

何世桢旧居位于高邮路68号，建于1927年，为西式独立式花园住宅。建筑南立面左右对称，外观形式庄重大气，属于比较典型的西方新古典主义建筑。中段突出的科林斯式圆柱和壁柱通高两层，形成气派的门廊和露台。此外，栏杆扶手和窗套的几何图形、入口两边壁柱顶部的浮雕、正立面及墙隅的白色石材贴面，又处处呈现出该住宅古典传统气息中的风格混搭。抗日战争及解放战争时期，何世桢的住宅曾是中共地下组织情报工作的重要基地，电台设在三楼。20世纪50年代由上海市政工会上海电力公司分会购入。20世纪80年代初在原有房屋上加层。

HE Shizhen

HE Shizhen (1894–1972) has a courtesy name of Siyi and has ancestral family from Wangjiang in Anhui province. He graduated from Soochow University. Once he participated in the May 4th Movement and acted as the president of the Shanghai Students' Federation, which made it possible for him to get acquainted with Sun Yat-sen and joined the KMT. Later on he went to study at University of Michigan in the United States and received a doctorate degree of law. After returning home, he worked in succession as a law professor at Soochow University and the provost at Shanghai University. In 1923, he acted as the Chinese representative in the Third International Bar Association. In 1924, he was elected as the Shanghai representatives of the First Congress of the KMT. In the same year he founded Chizhi University and assumed the post of its president. In the course of the May 30th Movement, SONG Qingling appointed him as the deputy director of the legal group. During the War against Japanese Invasion he was an underground worker of the KMT infiltrating into the Japanese puppet government. On the eve of the founding of the People's Republic of China, he resolutely rebuffed the invitation to go to Taiwan and remained in the mainland.

National Integrity

In April 1939, WANG Jingwei was secretly escorted to Shanghai by Japanese secret agents to organize the puppet central government. HE Shizhen, unwilling to associate himself with traitors who sought after glory by betraying the country, closed his law office and brought his family to live in this independent garden residence at No. 68 on Gaoyou Road. In August, WANG once forced and enticed him to attend the Congress and serve as a member of the presidium before holding the Sixth National Congress of the puppet KMT. Speaking with justice, he refused to participate. Out of his expectation, WANG still included his name in the list of the members of the puppet Central Committee and scattered false news in newspapers. Filled with indignation, he immediately published in newspapers to express his political stance and clarify the mud slinging. In this case, the puppet government failed to actualize its plot and then it resorted to vicious means to take revenge. In the name of the pretext that the Chizhi University and its affiliated high

何世桢创办的持志大学
Chizhi University founded by HE Shizhen.

school refused to register with the government, the spy headquarters of the puppet government sent a large number of spies on September 13, 1939 to smash schools and rob the official seals. In order to persevere in national integrity and guarantee the safety of teachers and students, he resolutely declared to close the university and the high school, which won him the support of all the teachers and students.

The puppet government still did not give up. In November 1942, WANG ordered lobbyists to invite him to serve as the president of the judicial committee, but he sternly refused the invitation. Enraged and exasperated, WANG ordered spies from "No. 76" to kidnap his son only at the age of four and hijacked him onto a ship. With the rushing about of his friends for rescue, the kid who floated at Wusong Estuary for 56 days finally got back home. However, his son was tremendously hurt in his heart.

Thanks to the work of a go-between who was a student from Chizhi University and also one of the leaders of the underground Communist Party in Shanghai, he got to know Pan Hannian, brother-in-law of the student. With the help of HE, the underground Communist Party established an overdraft account in the Central Reserve Bank of the puppet government. In its name a company was organized which was actually a resisting-Japanese logistics supply station of the New Fourth Army. Upholding the purpose of joint resistance by the two parties against the Japanese invasion, HE ran the risk to take up the important task that the CPC underground organization under the leadership of PAN Hannian set up a secret telegram station in the name of the KMT underground organization, which contacted both Chongqing and Yan'an. At that time the underground station staff members hid themselves on the third floor in his apartment on Gaoyou Road, painstakingly working day and night for information. The apartment had become an important intelligence base of the underground Communist Party and PAN Hannian once visited it in person to discuss work with HE.

In the turbulent years, HE adhered to national integrity with his sincere patriotism against brute forces and made his contribution to the victory of the War against Japanese Invasion.

The former residence of HE Shizhen is located at No. 68 on Gaoyou Road. First built in 1927, it is an independent garden residence of western style. The south facade of the building is symmetrical and its appearance is solemn and confident, a building of the typical Western neoclassical architecture. The Corinthian column and the pilasters projected in the middle rise along the two stories and serve to form the splendid porch and balcony. In addition, the geometric figures on the railings and window frames, the relief at the top of the columns on both sides of the entrance, the white stone veneers on the facade and the wall corners—all these present the stylistic mix of the building with a classic and traditional flavor. During the War against Japanese Invasion and the War of Liberation, the residence was once an important base of the underground Communist Party and the telegraph station was located on the third floor. In 1950s it was purchased by the Shanghai Municipal Labor Union and the branch of the Shanghai Power Company. In the early 1980s more floors were added on the original.

何世桢 （吴耀明画） HE Shizhen （By WU Yaoming）

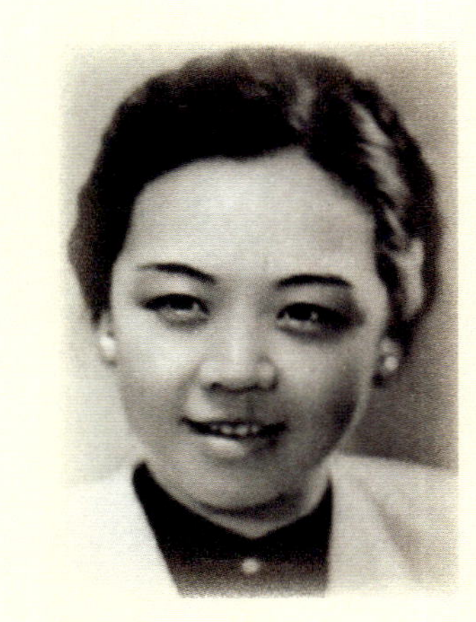

吴茵
（1909—1991）

祖籍江苏吴县，生于天津，原名杨瑛，电影表演艺术家。13岁来到上海。1934年参加影片《新女性》的拍摄，自此从影，改名为吴茵。一生出演电影、话剧各约50部，其中有《压岁钱》《十字街头》《八千里路云和月》《一江春水向东流》《万家灯火》《希望在人间》《乌鸦与麻雀》《三毛流浪记》《这不是误会》《落山风》和《夜上海》《残雾》《大地回春》等。表演真实，以饰演老年妇女而享誉影坛，有"东方第一老太"之称。尤其在《一江春水向东流》中塑造的张母和在《万家灯火》中塑造的智清母亲的形象，给观众留下深刻印象。1955年以《乌鸦与麻雀》中的精湛表演获文化部颁发的演员一等奖。1991年获电影表演艺术学会特别荣誉奖。

"东方第一老太"

自 1934 年吴茵正式从影后，先后参加拍摄了《火的洗礼》《青年中国》《塞上风云》等影片，并主演了《卢沟桥之战》《夜上海》《芳草天涯》《大地回春》《忠王李秀成》等 30 多部话剧，特别是在《残雾》和《大地回春》中，成功地塑造了两个各具风采的老太婆形象，受到当时报纸杂志的热烈追捧。

抗战胜利后，昆仑影业公司相继推出《一江春水向东流》《万家灯火》《希望在人间》《乌鸦与麻雀》等影片。导演蔡楚生、郑君里等将影片中的老年妇女主角锁定为吴茵。《一江春水向东流》里的张母，《万家灯火》里的智清母亲，《乌鸦与麻雀》中的萧太太，吴茵演得活灵活现，各具风采，"东方第一老太" 的称号呼之欲出。

1982 年，与观众阔别了 18 年之后，吴茵重新出山，在影片《这不是误会》里扮演了一个乐观风趣的刘奶奶，这是她一生中饰演的第 70 个"老太"。1985 年 9 月吴茵离休后，又相继在电影《男人的世界》和《落山风》中扮演角色。

1990 年的夏天，南昌电影研究所的张刚导演来到上海请 81 岁高龄的吴茵参演由他导演和主演的第 12 部"阿满喜剧"《面目全非》。

拍戏在大热天，小农舍里只有两个小电扇。吴茵腿不好，大部分戏都坐着拍，但最后有一场阿满别母进城的戏，吴茵坚持要站在门口送儿子、孙女进城，说："只有这样才能让阿满走得放心，也会让观众相信瞎眼奶奶的身体好着呢！"吴茵忍着疼，扶着门框，凭着感觉"遥望"远去的儿子和孙女。不仅是戏里的儿孙，所有在场的人都被感动了。

影片进入后期制作阶段，吴茵坚持要自己配音，说这样才真实。有一段戏因镜头组接的关系，口型很难找准。吴茵说，口型不对，感情会走样。于是一遍遍重配，直到她认为满意为止。

《面目全非》中的阿满妈，戏份不多，但吴茵却以她的敬业精神和精湛演技依然给观众留下深刻的印象，为"东方第一老太"画上了圆满的句号。

建筑简介：淮海中路1842—1858号武康大楼

吴茵旧居位于淮海中路1842—1858号武康大楼，旧称东美特公寓，又称诺曼底公寓，建于1924年，万国储蓄会投资建造，克利洋行邬达克设计，高30米，占地面积1580平方米，建筑面积9755平方米，属法国文艺复兴式建筑风格的公寓住宅，是上海最早的外廊式公寓建筑。建筑为八层钢筋混凝土结构，平面依楔状地形布置，楼身狭长似船。其前部为骑楼，骑楼形式为连续券廊。立面作横三段划分，第一、二层处理成基座，连续半圆券廊，水泥仿石墙面。三层挑出长阳台，四至七层挑出小阳台。一、二层水泥墙面，三至七层为清水红墙外砖。顶层由连续的挑出阳台和女儿墙构成双重檐部水平线脚。1930年，又在该楼东侧再建五层混合结构新武康大楼1幢，建筑面积1700平方米。底层为商店，二至五层为住宅。1945年抗战结束后多为国民政府官员居住。1953年改名为武康大楼，许多文艺界名人在此安家。1994年2月15日上海市人民政府公布其为市优秀历史建筑。

WU Yin

WU Yin (1909–1991) has her ancestral family from Wu County in Jiangsu province. Born in Tianjin, she had a former name of YANG Ying and was known as film performance artist. At the age of thirteen, she came to Shanghai. In 1934 she participated in the film *New Women*, engaging herself in the field of film since then and renaming as WU Yin. In her lifetime she performed in some 50 films and 50 dramas respectively, including *Lucky Money, Crossroads, Eight Thousand Li of Cloud and Moon, A Spring River Flows East, Myriad of Lights, Hope in the World, Crow and Sparrow, The Winter of Three Hairs, This is Not a Misunderstanding, Amid the Howling Wind, The Longest Night in Shanghai, Remnant Fog and Spring Again*. Her performance was true to life and was renowned for her roles of elderly women, hence her fame of "the Oriental First Granny". In particular, her role of the images Granny ZHANG in *A Spring River Flows East* and mother of Zhiqing in *Myriad of Lights* left a deep impression on the audience. In 1955 her superb performance in *Crow and Sparrow* won her the first prize for actors and actresses issued by the Ministry of Culture. In 1991 she won the special honor award by the Film Performing Arts Society.

"Oriental First Granny"

After she officially engaged herself in the field of film since 1934, she successively participated in films such as *A Baptism by Fire, Young China and Storm on the Border* and starred in the performance of over 30 dramas including *The Battle at Lugou Bridge, The Longest Night in Shanghai, Fragrant Grass at Horizon, Spring Again* and *LI Xiucheng as a Loyal Prince*. Particularly in *Remnant Fog* and *Spring Again*, she successfully created two images of old granny, which was well received by newspapers and magazines at that time.

After the victory of the War of Resistance against Japanese Invasion, the Kunlun Film Company successively launched such films as *A Spring River Flows East, Myriad of Lights, Hope in the World, Crow and Sparrow* and others. Directors like CAI Chusheng and ZHENG Junli fixed on WU Yin leading roles of elderly women in films. Granny ZHANG in *A Spring River Flows East*, and Madame XIAO in *Crow and Sparrow* were performed in a lifelike way by her and each had her unique style. "The Oriental First Granny" seemed ready to come out at any call.

After a long absence of 18 years from the audience, she came back in 1982 and played the role of an optimistic and humorous

1948年，吴茵（左）与上官云珠出演影片《万家灯火》
WU Yin (left) and SHANGGUAN Yunzhu performed in *Myriad of Lights* in 1948.

Granny LIU in the film *This is Not a Misunderstanding*, which was the 70th granny she played in her lifetime. After retiring with honors in September 1985, she still performed roles in succession in the films like *The World of Men* and *Amid the Howling Wind*.

In the summer of 1990, the director ZHANG Gang from Nanchang Film Research Institute came to Shanghai and invited her at the age of 81 to participate in *Beyond Recognition*, the twelfth of "Comedy of a Man" directed and starred by him.

The shooting was made on hot days while there were only two small fans in the small farmhouse. Her legs were not in good health condition and she sat down for most of her performance, but in the end there was a scene where A Man bid adieu to his mother. She insisted on standing at the door to see off her son and granddaughter to get into the city, explaining, "Only in this way could enable A Man to leave reassured and allow the audience to believe that the blind granny is in good health condition!" Tolerating the pains, she leaned on the door frame and "looked into the distance" with the sense at her son and granddaughter disappearing afar. Both the son and granddaughter in the play and all people present were moved.

When the film got into the stage of post-production, she insisted that she dubbed on her own so that the result could be true to life. Because of the editing of scenes in one part of the film, it was hard to match the voice with mouth. She believed that feelings could be deformed if the shape of mouth was incorrect. So she dubbed time and again until she was satisfied.

The mother of A Man in *Beyond Recognition* did not have much part in the film, but she still left a deep impression on the audience with her professional dedication and consummate acting, drawing a satisfactory conclusion for "the Oriental First Granny".

The former residence of WU Yin is located in Wukang Building at No. 1842—1858 on Middle Huaihai Road, formerly known as East Meite Apartment and also known as Normandy Apartments. Founded in 1924 by the International Savings Society and designed by Ladislaus Edward Hudec from R. A. Curry Company, the building is 30 meters in height and covers an area of 1,580 square meters with a construction area of 9,755 square meters. It is an apartment of French Renaissance style and is the earliest apartment building with outside corridor in Shanghai. With eight stories of reinforced concrete structure, it has a wedge-shaped layout and its body part at once long and narrow like a boat. Its front is of an arcade, which takes on the form of continuous arched corridors. The facade adopts the horizontal division of three sections with the first and second floors as the foundation, which have continuous semicircular arched corridors and wall surface of cement imitation stone. At the third floor long balconies are projected and from fourth to seventh floors small balconies are protruded. Wall surfaces from the first to the second floor are of cement and those from the third to seventh floors are of exposed red brickwork. At the top floor continuous projected balconies and parapets constitute the horizontal architrave of double eaves. In 1930, a new Wukang Building of a five-story mixed structure was constructed to its east side with a construction area of 1,700 square meters. The bottom floor is for stores and floors from the second to the fifth are for residence. After the end of the War in 1945, it was mostly occupied by national government officials. After the liberation it was renamed as Wukang Building and many literary celebrities once lived here. On February 15, 1994, it became a Heritage Architecture issued by the Shanghai Municipal People's Government.

吴茵 （钱定华画）　WU Yin （By QIAN Dinghua）

吴强
（1910—1990）

江苏涟水人，原名汪大同。1933 年参加左翼作家联盟。1938 年参加新四军。1949 年后曾任华东军区政治部文化部副部长、上海文艺工作委员会秘书长、上海作家协会副主席等。1933 年开始发表作品。著有长篇小说《红日》《堡垒》（上部），散文集《咆哮的烟苇港》，中篇小说集《养马的人》，小说散文集《心潮集》，报告文学《淮海前线纪事》等。1952 年转业至地方，先后任华东文学艺术联合会党组成员和中国作家协会上海分会副主席、中国作家协会理事等。1990 年病逝于上海。

《红日》的创作过程

1947 年 5 月 10 日，孟良崮战役结束的第二天上午，时任苏中军区政治部副部长的吴强，亲眼目睹溃败的国民党军七十四师师长张灵甫的尸体被解放军战士从山上抬下来的一幕，萌生写作想法，“不知是什么缘故，笔下写不成，心里却老是想写，有时候，竟打起腹稿来，仿佛着了迷似的”（《红日》自序）。

经过反复构思人物、情节以及忙里偷闲的写作，20 世纪 50 年代初，吴强完成了《红日》的 8 万余字故事梗概与人物简表，“透过这些血火斗争的史迹，描写、雕塑人物，既可以有所依托，又能够同时得到两个效果：写了光彩的战斗历程，又写了人物”（《红日》自序）。

他阅读大量中外军事名著，搜集资料、修改草稿。“在写作过程里，我感觉文学赋予我的创作上的自由权利，我是充分享受和使用了的。史实不但没有限制和束缚我，反而支持和方便了我，使我能够沿着一条轨道，比较顺利地走完了这一段写作路程……睡到深夜，忽然梦中醒来，想起了一个什么情节，或者对已经写好的字句，觉得需要进行补充、修改，便从床上披衣而起，扭亮了灯，又临时写了一点……”（《红日》自序）。

他每天伏案五六个小时，奋笔疾书，常常不完成六千字的既定任务就废寝忘食，错过开饭时间则以饼干、馒头充饥，全然沉浸于创作，忘却了华发早生、形容憔悴。初稿完成当天，他扛不住了，住院输液。半个月后刚稍有恢复，就急着写第二稿，字斟句酌持续四个月，近乎虚脱。

功夫不负有心人，《红日》自诞生以来，先后被译成英、法、俄、日、德等十多种文字。拿到第一笔版税，他为一位急需钢琴的作曲家买了一架钢琴，为一位收藏家挚友买了一幅心爱的画。

建筑简介：复兴西路34号

吴强旧居位于复兴西路34号卫乐公寓，原名卫乐精舍，建于1934年，赉安洋行设计，占地面积1720平方米，建筑面积3797平方米，汽车间附屋802平方米，属现代点式建筑风格的公寓住宅。建筑为十三层钢筋混凝土结构，两翼跌落一层，立面对称，竖三段布置，中间凸出，设一串挑出的半圆阳台为构图中心，两边为卧入式阳台形成竖向线条；水泥砂浆外墙，立面中部竖线条及突出的半圆阳台为暗红色粉刷，其余部分为浅黄色粉刷，山墙顶部及南侧有重复线条装饰，楼前有小花园。解放后，吕蒙与黄准夫妇、陈鲤庭、吴强、赖少其、峻青、王西彦等一批文化人在此居住。1994年2月15日上海市人民政府公布其为市优秀历史建筑。

WU Qiang

WU Qiang (1910–1990) has his ancestral family from Lianshui in Jiangsu province and has a former name of WANG Datong. In 1933 he participated in the Left-Wing Writers Union, and in 1938 he joined the New Fourth Army. After 1949, he once served as vice minister of the political and cultural department of the East China Military Region, secretary-general of the Shanghai Literature and Art Work Committee and vice chairman of the Shanghai Writers Association. Since 1933 he began to have works published. He got published such works as novels including *The Red Sun* and *The Fortress (I)*; prose collection *The Roaring of the Smoky Reed Port*, collection of novellas *Horsemen*; collection of stories and prose *Collection of Surging Thoughts*, documentary literature *Huaihai Frontline Chronicle*. In 1952, he moved to local places and served successively as Party member of the East China Federation of Literary and Art Circles and vice chairman of Shanghai branch of Chinese Writers Association and director of Chinese Writers Association. In 1990 he died in Shanghai.

The Process of the Creation of *The Red Sun*

On May 10, 1947, it was the next morning at the end of the Menglianggu Battle, when WU Qiang served as deputy minister of the political department of the Middle Jiangsu Military District. There he witnessed the defeat of the KMT army and the body of ZHANG Lingfu, commander of the Seventy-four Division, was carried down from the mountain by the PLA soldiers. The idea of writing crossed his mind—"I do not know why I wanted to write while writing with a pen was beyond my ability. Sometimes, I was actually writing a draft in my mind as if I was fascinated with it."

In the early 1950s, he completed the outline of the story and the table of characters with over 80 thousand words for *The Red Sun* after repeated planning of characters and plot and finding time for writing. "Through the historical traces of the struggle with

《红日》电影剧照
A film photo of *The Red Sun*.

blood and fires, characters are described and molded. A kind of spiritual support can be found in addition to two effects achieved: depiction of a glorious course of fighting and delineation of characters."

He read a large number of Chinese and foreign military masterpieces in order to collect information and modify the draft. "In the process of writing, I felt the right of freedom in literary creation which I fully enjoyed and used. The historical facts did not restrict or bind me. Rather they were supporting me and convenient for me, enabling me to march along one track and smoothly finish the course of writing... Sometimes it was late at night, but I might suddenly wake up from a dream and had a plot in my mind or felt it better to supplement or modify what had been written. In this case I might put on clothes, get up from the bed, switch on the light and write a little for a moment."

He spent five or six hours every day writing books. Often he forgot to have meals or had sleepless nights if he did not complete the given task of six thousand words. When he missed meals, he used to have biscuits or bread to allay his hunger, completely immersed in creation and forgetting his age and haggard expression. On the day when the first draft was completed, he could not stand any longer and went to hospital. Half a month later when he had just a little bit recovered, he was in a rush to write the second draft. After refining on wording for four months, he almost collapsed.

Hard work paid off. After the birth of *The Red Sun*, it had been translated into over ten languages, including English, French, Russian, Japanese, German and others. But when he got the first royalties, he bought a piano for a composer who was in great need of it and bought a beloved painting for a collector who was his friend.

The former residence of WU Qiang is located at Willow Apartment at No. 34 on West Fuxing Road, formerly known as Willow Court. Designed by Leonard-Veysseyre-Kruze Architects and built in 1934, it covers an area of 1, 720 square meters with a construction area of 3, 797 square meters and attached rooms of 802 square meters for garage. It is an apartment house of point construction and modern architectural style. The building has thirteen floors with a reinforced concrete structure. Its facade is symmetrical with three sections with the middle standing out and the two wings being one floor lower than the middle. A series of projected semi-circular balconies form the center of the composition. At both sides the receding balconies form vertical lines; exterior walls are coated with cement mortar; the vertical lines and prominent semi-circular balconies in the middle section have color of dark red, and the remaining parts are of light yellow. At the top and south side of the gable repeated lines are used for decoration. In addition, a small garden is in front of the building. After the liberation, a number of cultural people once lived here. On February 15, 1994, it became a Heritage Architecture issued by the Shanghai Municipal People's Government.

吴强 （钱定华画）　　WU Qiang （By QIAN Dinghua）

应云卫
（1904—1967）

祖籍浙江慈溪，出生于上海，字雨辰，号扬震，中国早期话剧、电影导演和戏剧活动家。1930 年 8 月加入中国左翼戏剧家联盟，在上海从事左翼戏剧电影运动。1933 年导演话剧《怒吼吧！中国》。1934 年加入电通影业公司，导演电影《桃李劫》《梅萝香》等。次年任南京国立戏剧学校教务长。抗日战争时期，先后发起组织中华全国戏剧界抗敌协会、中华剧艺社，任上海救亡演剧队第三、四队总队长，执导《保卫卢沟桥》等剧和电影《塞上风云》。中华人民共和国成立后曾任江南电影制片厂厂长、上海市电影局顾问、中国电影协会上海分会副主席等。先后导演了《妇女春秋》《周信芳舞台艺术》《武松》等故事片和戏曲片。

为戏下跪

应云卫在其 30 多年的艺术生涯中，所导演的话剧和电影在 80 部以上。他的一生就是一部中国戏剧春秋史。为了戏，他曾两度给人下跪。

1943 年 2 月 24 日，中华剧艺社在国泰大戏院演出《复活》，场内座无虚席。正当准备敲锣开幕时，导演陈鲤庭却发现台上摆放的沙发不像俄罗斯贵族家庭陈设，当即下令“马上换沙发”。换沙发谈何容易，当时在重庆城根本难觅俄罗斯贵族沙发。而作风严谨、追求艺术真实的陈鲤庭坚持己见：“不换沙发就不准开幕！”

开幕时间已过，满场观众开始躁动，演员们着急地来劝导演开幕。可陈导仍抓住大幕，固执不允。正相持不下，任中华剧艺社社长的应云卫快步上台，“咚”的一声，双膝跪在陈鲤庭面前，连声说：“鲤庭，我求你了，饶我这一次吧！”应云卫这一惊人举动，弄得陈鲤庭不知所措。舞台监督辛汉文急中生智，乘势敲锣将大幕拉开，《复活》终于开演。

1943 年 7 月 12 日，在中共南方局的安排下，中华剧艺社赴成都，在川西坝子掀起了一场演剧热潮。然而，剧作家陈白尘此时却怒不可遏。他暗地作调查，认为剧团里的浪费和贪污现象触目惊心，将矛头直指社长应云卫。面对突如其来的兴师问罪，应云卫无言以对，双膝下跪，怆然叹道：“这个团长我不干了，交给你吧！”陈白尘见状，只好说：“你留下，我走。”他回到重庆向阳翰笙作了汇报。不料，阳翰笙却告诉说：“云卫过去的生活与你我不同，他本来是外国轮船公司的高级职员，月入千金，后来下海演话剧。为解决演出经费和演职员吃饭问题，把家中值钱的东西都卖光了。这回他辞去中影厂的高薪待遇，前来主持中艺，这难能可贵啊。”一番话，让陈白尘如梦初醒，追到乐山，愧色满面地向应云卫表示歉意。

剧作家夏衍、于伶、宋之的以应云卫为原型，创作了话剧《戏剧春秋》。这出戏轰动剧坛，载入了中国话剧史册。

建筑简介：淮海中路1842—1858号武康大楼

应云卫旧居位于淮海中路1842—1858号武康大楼，旧称东美特公寓，又称诺曼底公寓，建于1924年，万国储蓄会投资建造，克利洋行邬达克设计，高30米，占地面积1580平方米，建筑面积9755平方米，属法国文艺复兴式建筑风格的公寓住宅，是上海最早的外廊式公寓建筑。建筑为八层钢筋混凝土结构，平面依楔状地形布置，楼身狭长似船。其前部为骑楼，骑楼形式为连续券廊。立面作横三段划分，第一、二层处理成基座，连续半圆券廊，水泥仿石墙面。三层挑出长阳台，四至七层挑出小阳台。一、二层水泥墙面，三至七层为清水红墙外砖。顶层由连续的挑出阳台和女儿墙构成双重檐部水平线脚。1930年，又在该楼东侧再建五层混合结构新武康大楼1幢，建筑面积1700平方米。底层为商店，二至五层为住宅。1945年抗战结束后多为国民政府官员居住。1953年改名为武康大楼，许多文艺界名人在此安家。1994年2月15日上海市人民政府公布其为市优秀历史建筑。

YING Yunwei

YING Yunwei (1904–1967) has his ancestral family from Cixi in Zhejiang province. Born in Shanghai, he has a courtesy name of Yuchen and a style name of Yangzhen and was known as director of drama and film and theatre activist in early China. In August 1930 he joined China Left-Wing Dramatists Union and engaged himself in the left-wing drama and film movement in Shanghai. In 1933 he directed the drama *Roar! China*. In 1934 he joined Diantong Film Company, directing films including *Plunder of Peach and Plum, MEI Luoxiang* and others. In the following year he served as provost of Nanjing National Drama School. During the War against Japanese Invasion, he launched organizations including China National Resisting-enemy Theater Association and Chinese Drama Society. He served the general team commander of the third and fourth teams of Shanghai Salvation Theater, and directed such dramas as *Defending the Lugou Bridge* and others, and the film *Storm on the Border*. After the founding of the PRC, he once served as factory director of Jiangnan Film Studio, consultant of Shanghai Film Administration, and vice president of the Shanghai Branch of China Film Association. Successively he directed the feature films and opera films including *The Age of Women, The Stage Art of ZHOU Xinfang, WU Song* and others.

Stooping for Drama

In his 30 years of artistic career, YING Yunwei directed over 80 dramas and films. His lifetime is a history of Chinese drama. For the sake of performance, he once knelt down twice to others, which has become a much-told story to this day.

On February 24, 1943, the Chinese Drama Society put on *Resurrection* in Cathay Theater, in which all seats were occupied. Just at the moment for the opening gongs, the director CHEN Liting found that the sofa placed on the stage was unlike the furnishings in a Russian aristocratic family and immediately ordered that “the sofa be exchanged immediately”. It was easier said than done to replace it, since it was difficult to find a Russian aristocratic sofa in the city of Chongqing. With his rigorous style and the pursuit of artistic truth, CHEN Liting insisted on his own opinion, “No change, no opening allowed!”

The opening time had passed. The audience began to be restless while the actors and actresses were anxious to persuade the

戏剧协社部分社员合影（左一为应云卫）
A group photo of some members of the Drama Xie Society (YING Yunwei at first from left).

director for the opening. But Director CHEN still caught hold of the huge curtain, too stubborn to leave his grip. During this deadlock, YING as president of the Chinese Drama Society quickly came to the stage. At a sound of "thud", he knelt down in front of the director and repeatedly said, "Liting, I beg you! Spare me this time!" His amazing move left the director at a loss about what to do. Stage supervisor XIN Hanwen had quick wits in an emergency to strike the gong and withdraw the curtain. The drama *Resurrection* was finally on.

On July 12, 1943, under the arrangement of the Southern Bureau of the CPC, the Chinese Drama Society went to Chengdu to set off a craze of drama at Bazi in the west of Sichuan province. However, the playwright CHEN Baichen was furious beyond control at this time. He made secret investigation and believed that waste and corruption of the troupe was horrifying and directed the spearhead of his attack against the president YING Yunwei. Faced with the sudden denunciation, YING was speechless, kneeling down on his knees and sighing sadly, "I quit the post of president and give it you!" Seeing this, the playwright had to say, "You stay and I leave." He returned to Chongqing and made a report to YANG Hansheng. Unexpectedly, the latter told him, "The past life of YING is different from yours and mine. He was a senior staff of a foreign shipping company with a high monthly income. Later he became a professional actor. To solve the problems of the performance and life expenses of the crew, he sold out all valuable objects at home. This time he resigned from the post of high salary in China Film Studio to come to preside over the Chinese Drama Society. How commendable this is!" His words awaked CHEN. Dogging the society to Leshan, he apologized to YING with his face full of sense of shame.

With YING Yunwei as the prototype, playwrights including XIA Yan, YU Ling and SONG Zhidi, co-created a drama *The Age of Drama*, which was sensational in the field of theater and went down in the history of Chinese drama.

The former residence of YING Yunwei is located in Wukang Building at No. 1842-1858 on Middle Huaihai Road, formerly known as East Meite Apartment and also known as Normandy Apartments. Founded in 1924 by the International Savings Society and designed by Ladislaus Edward Hudec from R. A. Curry Company, the building is 30 meters in height and covers an area of 1,580 square meters with a construction area of 9,755 square meters. It is an apartment of French Renaissance style and is the earliest apartment building with outside corridor in Shanghai. With eight stories of reinforced concrete structure, it has a wedge-shaped layout and its body part at once long and narrow like a boat. Its front is of an arcade, which takes on the form of continuous arched corridors. The facade adopts the horizontal division of three sections with the first and second floors as the foundation, which have continuous semicircular arched corridors and wall surface of cement imitation stone. At the third floor long balconies are projected and from fourth to seventh floors small balconies are protruded. Wall surfaces from the first to the second floor are of cement and those from the third to seventh floors are of exposed red brickwork. At the top floor continuous projected balconies and parapets constitute the horizontal architrave of double eaves. In 1930, a new Wukang Building of a five-story mixed structure was constructed to its east side with a construction area of 1,700 square meters. The bottom floor is for stores and floors from the second to the fifth are for residence. After the end of the War in 1945, it was mostly occupied by national government officials. After the liberation it was renamed as Wukang Building and many literary celebrities once lived here. On February 15, 1994, it became a Heritage Architecture issued by the Shanghai Municipal People's Government.

应云卫 （钱定华画） YING Yunwei （By QIAN Dinghua）

张伐
（1919—2001）

祖籍山东，原名张大民，国家一级演员。1936年到上海，入君毅中学学习，后考入上海华光戏剧学校。1940年入上海剧艺社任演员，相继加入上海职业剧团、苦干剧团、上海艺术剧团任演员，先后参加《蜕变》《阿Q正传》《文天祥》《夜店》《雷雨》等话剧的演出和电影《乱世风光》的拍摄。1947年起在文华影业公司、启明影片公司、中电二厂参演《母与子》《太太万岁》《夜店》《平步青云》《鸡鸣早看天》《街头巷尾》《喜迎春》等影片。中华人民共和国成立后任上海电影制片厂演员，在《翠岗红旗》《伟大的起点》《幸福》《龙须沟》《枯木逢春》《黄浦江的故事》《金沙江畔》《家庭问题》《子夜》《最后的太阳》等20余部影片中饰演主角或重要角色。为第三、四届中国电影协会理事。荣获国家文化部优秀影片创作个人奖及第四届中国电影表演艺术学会“金凤凰奖”特别荣誉奖，被授予“从事电影工作五十年——中国电影家”荣誉称号。

一点都不含糊

电影《红日》根据吴强同名小说改编，取材于1947年闻名中外的孟良崮之战，拍摄于1961至1963年。张伐塑造的军长沈振新，脱胎于解放战争中的真实人物——华东野战军第六纵队司令员王必成。

《红日》剧组为再现孟良崮战役激烈壮观的场面，远赴孟良崮进行实地拍摄。剧组住在一所破旧的小学校里，高低不平的课桌拼接成“床”，睡在上面，皮肉极易被夹在拼接的缝隙里，烙下一道道血印子。张伐瘦削的身躯躺在坚硬的课桌上，可谓“骨头碰木头”，一觉醒来浑身都疼，但他没有丝毫怨言。由于饰演主角，戏份较多，张伐常比别人早起一两个小时，细致地化完妆就潜心钻研表演艺术。

张伐精益求精地对待表演创作，从沈振新这一角色的身份和特定环境设计动作、细节、语言及节奏，通过行为动作、眼神手势、心理活动来表现角色的基本特征。张伐在文学本和分镜头本的字里行间，写满了自己对人物、场景、情境的分析。正如曾受张伐悉心指导的仲星火所言：“他创作态度非常严肃认真，很用功。剧本中的每句台词边上都写上自己的表演设计，写得密密麻麻的，一点都不含糊。”

拍摄《红日》时有一段时间恰逢酷暑时节，气温常高达40度，但由于摄制的是冬季戏，张伐还得穿着厚厚的大棉衣、裹着绑腿布，汗水常常浸透了他的衣服。而且《红日》拍的是宽窄两个银幕，每个镜头都要拍两次，这意味着演员须反复受罪。张伐的衣服湿了又干，干了又湿，却仍镇定自若、全心全意地塑造沈振新这一制定战术沉着冷静、有勇有谋的指挥员形象。他的表演沉稳、质朴、自然，铿锵有力的嗓音字字掷地作金石声，传神展现了在敌强我弱的困境中，为赢得最后的胜利而废寝忘食的解放军指挥员谨慎果敢、正气凛然的气魄与风采，成为银幕中永恒的经典。

建筑简介：永福路147弄35号

张伐曾居住于永福路147弄35号。永福路147弄原是永福路（旧名古神父路）上的曹家巷，20世纪初这里人烟稀少，多为菜地，法租界越界筑路后，开始建独院式别墅。35号为假三层老房子，类似三开间石库门，两厢一厅。

ZHANG Fa

ZHANG Fa (1919–2001) has his ancestral family from Shandong, and he had a former name of ZHANG Damin, an actor at the national level. In 1936 he arrived at Shanghai and entered into Junyi High School. Later he studied in Shanghai Huaguang Drama School. In 1940, he entered Shanghai Drama Art Society and worked as a performer. Later he joined troupes one after another, including Shanghai Professional Troupe, Working Hard Troupe and Shanghai Art Troupe to work as an actor and successively participated in drama performance such as *Transformation, Ah Q, WEN Tianxiang, Nightclub* and *Thunderstorm* and performance in the film *Gone with the Wind*. Since 1947, he had worked in Wenhua Film Company, Qiming Film Company, the Second Factory of China Film Studio and participated in the performance of the films such as *Mother and Son, Long Live the Wife, Nightclub, Imagination, Looking at Weather When Rooster Crows, Our Neighbor, Happy to Greet Spring* and others. After the founding of the People's Republic of China, he worked as actor in Shanghai Film Studio and performed leading or important roles in over 20 films which include *Red Flag on the Cuigang Mountain, The Great Beginning, Happiness, The Dragon Canal, Withered Trees Revive, The Story of the Huangpu River, Along the Jinsha River, Family Problems, Midnight* and *The Sunset*. He was director of the third and fourth sessions of China Film Association. Also he won individual award of outstanding film creation of the Ministry of Culture as well as special honor award of Golden Phoenix Award of the fourth session of China Film Performance Art Academy. In addition, he was awarded the honorary title of "film work for 50 years—China Film Artist".

Nothing Unclear

The film *The Red Sun* was adapted according to the novel of the same title by WU Qiang, which drew the materials from the

张伐在话剧《大马戏团》中饰小铳
ZHANG Fa played the role of Little Chong in the modern drama *The Greatest Show on Earth*.

famous battle at Menglianggu in 1947, and was produced from 1961 to 1963. The leading role of SHEN Zhenxin, commander performed by ZHANG Fa, was born out of a real person in the War of Liberation—WANG Bicheng, commander of the sixth column of East China Field Army.

In order to reproduce the fierce and spectacular scenes of the battle, the crew members of the film covered a long distance to go to Menglianggu for field shooting. They lived in a dilapidated primary school, making use of the uneven desks to make "beds". When they slept on them, the skin and flesh could be easily caught in the rifts, leaving strips of bloodstain. ZHANG was rawboned. When he lay on the hard desks, "his bones touched the wood." After waking up, he was all pains, but he did not complain at all. As the leading role, he had more scenes than others. Accordingly he had to get up one or two hours earlier. After finishing meticulous makeup, he used to do painstaking researches on performance art.

He always endeavored to do still better in performing creation and designed movements, details, speech and rhythm according to the identity and specific environment of the role of SHEN Zhenxin, representing the basic characteristics of the role through behavior, action, eye expression, gestures and psychological activities. He filled the lines of the literary text and shooting script with his own analysis of the characters, scenes and situation. As ZHONG Xinghuo, to whom ZHANG Fa had given careful guidance, once put it, "His creation attitude is very serious and he is also hard-working. Beside each line of the script are densely written his own performance designs. Nothing is unclear."

The production of *The Red Sun* coincided with a period of hot season and the temperature was often as high as 40 degrees. But the time in the story of the film was winter so that ZHANG Fa had to wear a thick coat and wrapped leggings and sweat often soaked his clothes. In addition, *The Red Sun* was produced in two versions: wide screen and narrow screen. In this case each motion picture must be shot twice, which meant that actors had to suffer time and again. His clothes changed from wet to dry, and back from dry to wet. Still he kept composed and wholeheartedly devoted himself to the shaping of the image of a commander, who was calm, courageous and conscientious in his development of tactics. His performance was calm, modest and natural. Moreover his sonorous and powerful voice rang with force and clarity with each word. All this vividly exhibited the cautious and courageous, upright and awe-inspiring boldness and style of the PLA commander who lost sleep and forgot to have food in order to win the final victory in the predicament that the enemy was strong while the PLA army was weak. Consequently the film had become an eternal classic on the screen.

ZHANG Fa once lived at No. 35 in Alley 147 on Yongfu Road, which was originally CAO Alley on Yongfu Road (old name of Ancient Priest Road). It was sparsely populated in the early 20th century and most parts were fields of vegetable. After the French settlement crossed border to build roads, the building of an independent villa was initiated. No. 35 in the alley is a nominally three-storied old house, which is similar to the three-bay Stone Warehouse Gate and enjoys two rooms and one hall.

张伐 （钱定华画）

ZHANG Fa （By QIAN Dinghua）

张澜
（1872—1955）

四川南充人，字表方。清末秀才。辛亥革命前参加立宪派，为四川保路同志会领导人之一。1917年秋任四川省省长。1919年五四运动后，赞助青年学生赴法勤工俭学。1925年创办成都大学，自任校长。四一二反革命政变后，曾掩护和营救共产党员。1935年国民党势力入四川，曾一度附和国民党，任四川安抚委员会委员长。抗战时期，任四川建设委员会川北办事处主任，被聘为国民参政会参政员，参加抗日民主运动。1939年与黄炎培等人发起组织统一建国同志会。“皖南事变”后组成中国民主政团同盟，被推为主席。1944年中国民主政团同盟改名为中国民主同盟，继任主席。抗战胜利后，反对蒋介石发动内战，拒绝参加国民大会。1949年参加中国人民政治协商会议第一届全体会议。中华人民共和国成立后，历任中央人民政府副主席，第一届全国人大常委会委员、副委员长，第一届政协常委、副主席。1955年2月9日在北京病逝。

从虹桥疗养院脱险

张澜是中国民主同盟主席。抗战期间，他积极主张民主政治，赞成中国共产党建立民主联合政府的主张。抗战胜利后，以他为首的民盟提出反对独裁、要求民主、反对内战、要求和平的政治主张，在李公朴、闻一多、杜斌丞等优秀民盟成员被国民党杀害的情况下，仍然坚持反对国民党召开国民大会。

1947年10月17日，国民政府内政部宣布，民盟是非法团体。几天后，民盟中央常委扩大会议在永嘉路集益里8号张澜住处举行，被迫宣布解散民盟。张澜表示，杀头我是不怕的，我之所以这样做，完全是为了全体盟员的身家性命。至于我个人的一切，早已置之度外。

1948年1月，遭到国民党镇压的民盟成员在香港召开一届三中全会，决定将总部迁往香港，恢复民盟活动，并宣布与中国共产党合作，为彻底摧毁国民党政府，建立民主、和平、独立、统一的中国而奋斗。张澜委派沈钧儒去香港参加了这些活动，并带去了他筹集到的全部款项。但是，从四川赶到上海的女儿发现，一身重病的张澜，这时候连吃饭的钱都没有了。解放战争三大战役结束，国民党败局已定，国民党元老张群要求张澜出面调解国共矛盾。张澜表示，现在是革命与反革命之争，我站在共产党这一边，不再做调解人了。

正当张澜的处境越来越危险之际，上海虹桥疗养院院长丁惠康将他和民盟的另一位领导人罗隆基接到了院中。国民党军警不肯放松，疗养院副院长郑定竹挺身而出：“张先生患尿道感染和齿槽脓漏，罗先生患活动性肺结核和糖尿病，都病重不能离院。”并以性命担保，总算保护二人躲过一劫。后在中共上海地下党的策划和国民党要员杨虎的保护下，张澜和罗隆基才脱离虎口。

建筑简介：淮海中路966号5号楼

上海虹桥疗养院旧址位于淮海中路966号5号楼，建于1938年。建筑为假四层砖混结构，装饰艺术派风格，布局对称，立面强调垂直线条，构图以左右两块前出墙体把整个立面分成五段。中间入口拱形门洞，挑出弓形雨厦。红瓦折脊式屋顶开棚式老虎窗。赭色面砖外墙，窗框、窗间墙遍饰水泥几何形图案。全部疗养室朝南布置，并设特大阳台，且从低到高的楼层呈阶梯形层叠。解放战争期间，张澜、罗隆基被国民党特务软禁于上海虹桥疗养院，后获中共上海地下党营救。宋庆龄曾借用虹桥疗养院，作为中国福利会夏令营儿童健康营、儿童剧团、幼儿园达8年之久。1956年2月，虹桥疗养院成为上海市首家改私为公的医院。1958年，虹桥疗养院与怡和医院合并为淮海医院。1961年，更名为上海市徐汇区中心医院。现为徐汇区中心医院办公楼。

ZHANG Lan

ZHANG Lan (1872–1955) has his ancestral family from Nanchong in Sichuan province. He has a courtesy name of Biaofang and was a scholar in the late Qing Dynasty. He joined the constitutionalist school before the Revolution of 1911, and was one of the leaders of the Railway Protection League in Sichuan province. In the autumn of 1917, he took up the post of the governor of Sichuan province. After the May Fourth Movement in 1919, he supported young students to go to France to pursue studies in the work-study program. In 1925, he founded Chengdu University and served as its president. After the April 12 Counter-revolutionary Coup, he once shielded and rescued members of the Communist Party of China. Later, when the KMT forces entered Sichuan province in 1935, he had once affiliated himself to them and served as chairman of Sichuan Pacification Committee. During the War against Japanese Invasion, he was the office director of the Northern Sichuan Branch of the Sichuan Construction Committee and was recruited as member of the National Political Council, participating in the democratic movements against Japanese invasion. In 1939, he initiated the United Founding Society together with HUANG Yanpei and others. After the "Southern Anhui Incident", he organized the China Democratic Political Group League and was elected its chairman, which was renamed the China Democratic League in 1944 and continued to serve as chairman. After the victory of the War against Japanese Invasion, he was opposed to the civil war waged by JIANG Jieshi and refused to attend the National Assembly. In 1949, he took part in the first plenary session of the CPPCC. After the founding of the People's Republic of China, he served successively as vice chairman of the Central People's Government, member and vice chairman of the first session of the standing committee of the National People's Congress, and member and vice chairman of the first session of the CPPCC standing committee. On February 9, 1955, he departed of illness in Beijing.

Escaping from Danger in Hongqiao Sanatorium

ZHANG Lan was chairman of the China Democratic League. During the War against Japanese Invasion, he actively advocated democracy and stood by the proposition of establishing coalition government put forward by the CPC. After the victory of the War, he headed the China Democratic League to raise the proposition of opposing dictatorship and civil war and demanding democracy

张澜在出席全国政协一届一次会议时签到
ZHANG Lan was signing at the first meeting of the first session of the CPPCC.

and peace. Under the circumstance that many outstanding members such as LI Gongpu, WEN Yiduo and DU Bincheng were murdered by the KMT, he still insisted on his opposition to the KMT National Assembly.

On 17 October, 1947, the KMT Ministry of Internal Affairs outlawed the China Democratic League. A few days later, an enlarged meeting of the Central Committee of the China Democratic League was held at the residence of ZHANG Lan, which was at No. 8, on Jiyi Alley on Yongjia Road. But they were forced to declare the dissolution of the China Democratic League. At the meeting, ZHANG Lan said that such decision was totally for the sake of life of all members. As for himself, everything was put out of consideration.

In January 1948, members of the party, repressed by the KMT, convened the Third Plenary Session of the First Central Committee in Hong Kong. They decided to relocate their headquarters to Hong Kong and resume the activities of the China Democratic League. In addition, they announced that they would cooperate with the Communist Party of China to completely destroy the KMT government and struggle for democracy, peace, independence and unity of the new China. He commissioned SHEN Junru to participate in these activities in Hong Kong and brought all the money he had raised. However, when his daughter reached Shanghai from Sichuan, she found that he was in poor health condition and even couldn't afford any food. After the three decisive campaigns in the War of Liberation, the defeat of the KMT was predetermined. Then ZHANG Qun, senior statesman of the KMT, asked him to mediate the contradiction between the KMT and the CPC. He replied that he stood on the side of the Communist Party of China in the struggle between the revolution and counter-revolution and he would no longer be the mediator.

When he was in increasingly great danger, DING Huikang, president of Shanghai Hongqiao Sanatorium offered admission to him and LUO Longji, another leader of the China Democratic League. Still the KMT military guards did not give away, when ZHENG Dingzhu, vice president of the Sanatorium, stepped forward bravely, saying, "Mr. ZHANG has suffered from urethral infection and alveolar septic leak and Mr. LUO has been attacked by active tuberculosis and diabetes. Both of them are so seriously ill that neither of them should be discharged." Besides, he even swore they couldn't leave the sanatorium on his own life, which helped the two manage to escape the arrest. Later, thanks to the plan of the underground party of the CPC in Shanghai and the protection from YANG Hu, a key figure of the KMT, they finally escaped from being arrested.

The former site of Shanghai Hongqiao Sanatorium is located in Building No. 5 at No. 966 on Middle Huaihai Road, which was built in 1938. This building is nominally four-storied structure of brick and concrete with the stylistic characteristic of decorative arts. Its layout is symmetrical and the façade emphasizes vertical lines, which is divided into five sections by the left and right prominent walls in the composition. The middle entrance has an arched door with a bow-shaped canopy. On the roof with red tiles and folding ridge there is a shelf-type dormer. The building has exterior walls of ochre brick, window frames and the walls between windows are decorated with cement geometrical patterns. All treatment rooms face south with especially large balconies, which form stair-type from the lower floors to the higher floors. During the War of Liberation, ZHANG Lan and LUO Longji were under house arrest by secret agents of the KMT in Hongqiao Sanatorium and then rescued by the CPC underground organization in Shanghai. SONG Qingling once borrowed the sanatorium for the children's health camp of the summer camp, the children's troupe and kindergarten of the China Welfare Institute for eight years. In February 1956, Hongqiao Sanatorium became the first hospital which changed its ownership from a privately-owned hospital to a state-owned one in Shanghai. In 1958, Hongqiao Sanatorium and Yihe hospital merged into the Huaihai Hospital. In 1961, it changed its name to Shanghai Xuhui Central Hospital. Now the former building is used as the office of Xuhui Central Hospital.

张澜 （杨宏富画）

ZHANG Lan （By YANG Hongfu）

张翼
（1909—1983）

浙江慈溪人，生于上海，原名张雨亭。早年当过水手、店员。1925年起，先后进入海峰影片公司、暨南影片公司任演员，连续拍摄《风尘剑侠》《荒山奇僧》等七十余部神怪武侠片，成为中国早期电影中当红的"武侠明星"。因他扮演的多为劫富济贫的好汉，雄姿英武，故有"影坛雄狮"的美称。1934年加入联华影业公司，拍摄了《体育皇后》《大路》《狼山喋血记》等10部影片。在《大路》中，他以自己固有的"雄狮"般的体魄和刚健、坚毅的性格，塑造了一个筑路工人的形象。抗日战争时期，曾在香港艺联，上海民华、艺华、光华等影片公司拍摄的《孔夫子》《中国罗宾汉》等影片中饰演重要角色。抗战胜利后，进入昆仑影业公司，参加了《丽人行》《锦绣山河》《幸福狂想曲》《大地回春》等影片的演出。中华人民共和国成立后，作为上海电影制片厂演员，先后参演了《宋景诗》《林冲》等二十余部影片，留下了令人难忘的黑旗军首领和花和尚鲁智深等银幕形象。一生参加拍摄影片一百二十余部。

王老德风采

张翼在1955年摄制的影片《母亲》中饰演王老德。为传神地展现这位工人领袖的风采，张翼倾注了许多心血。

仅念过小学的张翼特意购买了一本汉语词典及一系列文学作品和文艺理论书籍，在繁忙的工作间隙一字一句认真研读，为提升表演艺术以至废寝忘食。

因早年当过水手，攀爬搬运、惊涛骇浪练就了张翼宽厚的身躯、有力的双臂及坚韧刚强的性格。他对工人阶级怀有深厚的感情，自学文化知识之余，主动前往工厂与工人们交流谈心并参与劳动实践，藉此深入体验生活、积累创作素材，并将点点滴滴的感悟融入表演中。

张翼为王老德这一独特角色精心设计了符合工人身份并富有鲜明时代气息的服装。他那双粗壮有力的双手干起针线活儿来却十分灵巧，他一针一线、全神贯注地将新服装"做旧"，使角色更丰满真实。当他穿上亲手加工的演出服装时，逼真的工人形象闪耀着劳动焕发的熠熠光彩，颇具生活气息。

在拍摄《母亲》期间，张翼哮喘病发作，每次呼吸都伴随着粗重的气喘声。由于当时拍戏是同期录音，为保障录音质量，他艰难地屏住呼吸说台词。其中有一段戏，在一个长镜头里包含很多台词，和张翼搭戏的主演张瑞芳担心他憋不过气，就加快语速说台词。张翼敏锐地察觉后，微笑着劝慰张瑞芳说："你用不着管我，你该怎么演就怎么演，我们不能让戏受损失。"这个长镜头摄录完成后，深受哮喘折磨的张翼已憋得双颊通红，良久才喘过气来。唯恐影响拍摄进度，张翼隐瞒着自己的病情坚持拍戏，功夫不负有心人，他成功塑造了坚毅、果敢的工人领袖王老德这一艺术形象。

建筑简介：武康路376号

张翼旧居位于武康路376号，建于1928年，占地面积约600平方米。建筑为新古典主义风格的花园住宅，三层砖混结构，清水红砖外墙，人字坡红瓦屋顶。主立面三段式划分，左右结构布局完全对称，局部有欧洲古典元素。南面底层为塔斯干柱廊，二层内阳台为简化的爱奥尼克券柱结构，建筑主入口门楣具巴洛克风格。建筑内部用材考究，制作精良，整体保存较好，多数室内装饰和卫浴设备仍在使用。早年为民国外交部长郭泰祺私宅，解放后一度作为超声波仪表厂和长江计算机厂的办公用房，现为民居。

ZHANG Yi

ZHANG Yi (1909–1983) has his ancestral family from Cixi in Zhejiang province. Born in Shanghai, he had a former name of ZHANG Yuting. In the early years he worked as a sailor and clerk. Since 1925, he successively entered Haifeng Film Company and Jinan Film Company to work as actor, and continuously participated in over 70 fantasy martial arts films including *Swordsman*, *A Strange Monk in the Wild Mountain* and others, he became a popular "martial arts star" in the early Chinese film. Because most roles he played were majestic heroes who robbed the rich to feed the poor, he was reputed as "film lion". In 1934, he joined Lianhua Film Company and played roles in 10 films including *Queen of Sports*, *The Big Road*, *The Wolf Hill* and others. In *The Big Road*, he shaped the image of a road construction worker with his inherent lion-like physique as well as a strong and perseverant character. During the War against Japanese Invasion, he played important roles in films such as *Confucius*, *The Chinese Robin Hood* and others produced by such companies as Hong Kong Administrative Art Circle Federation, Shanghai Minhua Film Company, Shanghai Yihua Film Company and Shanghai Guanghua Film Company. After the victory of the Resisting-Japanese War, he entered Kunlun Film Company and participated in the performance of films like *Three Women*, *The Beautiful Rivers and Mountains*, *Happiness Rhapsody*, *Spring Again* and other films. After the founding of the PRC, he acted as actor in Shanghai Film Studio and performed in over 20 films such as *SONG Jingshi*, *LIN Chong* and others, leaving unforgettable screen images of the Black Flag Army leader and ritual-breaking monk LU Zhishen. In his lifetime, he participated in the performance of over 120 films.

The Style of WANG Laode

ZHANG Yi played the role of WANG Laode in the film *Mother* produced in 1955. In order to vividly demonstrate the style of the worker leader, he devoted a lot of effort.

With an education of only primary school, he specially bought a Chinese dictionary, a series of literary works and books on literary and artistic theories, and made a serious study of them word by word and sentence by sentence between his busy work. To enhance his performing arts, he even spent sleepless nights.

As a sailor in the early years with climbing and transporting in addition to stormy waves, he procured broad and thick body,

青年张翼
ZHANG Yi in youth.

powerful arms and strong tough character. He had deep feelings for the working class. In his spare time of self-studing, he took initiative to go to factories to talk with workers and participate in labor practice. In this way he got rich experience of life, accumulated materials for creation and incorporated the sentiment and understanding into his performance.

For the unique role of WANG Laode, he designed with great care the clothes in line with the identity of workers and with rich flavor of the times. Sturdy as his hands were, he was so smart in needlework that he made the new costume "old" stitch by stitch, which made the role more fleshy and more trustful. When he put on the performance costume processed by himself, the lifelike image of workers shined with gleaming gloss of labor, which radiated with a strong flavor of life.

During the production of the film *Mother*, he was attacked by asthma, each breath being accompanied by heavy sound. At that time recording was done in the same period together with the film production. In order to ensure the recording quality, he struggled to hold his breath when uttering his lines. In one the scenes which contained many lines in a full-length shot, the leading actress ZHANG Ruifang who played with him worried that he could not hold back his breath so that she speed up in her lines. After finding this, he smiled and persuaded her, saying, "You do not need to care about me and just perform in your own way. We can not bear any loss in the performance." After the completion of this recording, he was deeply afflicted by asthma and his cheeks flushed for suppression of breath. A long time passed until he could gasp again. For fear of affecting the progress of the film production, he concealed his illness and persisted in film performance. Hard work pays off. He successfully molded the artistic image of the worker leader WANG Laode who was equipped with perseverance, determination and courage.

The former residence of ZHANG Yi is located at No. 376 on Wukang Road. Built in 1928, it covers an area of about 600 square meters. As a garden house of the neo-classical style, it has a three-story structure of brick and concrete with outer walls of water red bricks and a herringbone-shaped roof covered with red tiles. The main facade has three sections and the structure of left and right sides is completely symmetrical with European classical elements at local parts. At the bottom of the south are the Tasman colonnades, the inner balconies at the second floor are of simplified structure of the Ionic columns. Its main entrance has a lintel with the Baroque style. Its interiors adopt elegant materials and are well produced. The overall structure is well preserved and most of the interior decorations and bathrooms are still in use. It was once the private residence of GUO Taiqi, minister of foreign affairs during the early Republic of China. After the liberation it was once used as factory offices of the Ultrasonic Instrument Factory and the Yangtze River Computer Factory. Now it is a residence of civil citizens.

张翼 （陆小弟、陆旻画） ZHANG Yi （By LU Xiaodi and LU Min）

张元济
（1867—1959）

浙江海盐人，字菊生。光绪进士。曾任刑部主事、总署章京。中日甲午战争后，参加维新变法运动。1897年在上海首创通艺学堂，博采西学书籍，发行维新报刊。1898年6月受光绪帝召见。戊戌政变时被革职。后在上海致力于文化出版业，主持商务印书馆。曾校印百衲本《二十四史》，影印《四部丛刊》等。中华人民共和国成立后参加中国人民政治协商会议，当选为全国人民代表大会代表。著有《校史随笔》《涵芬楼烬余书录》等。

铮铮铁骨存文脉

1941年太平洋战争打响后，上海商务发行所和各工厂都被查封，被抄走书籍460万册、铅字50多吨。张元济在风雨飘摇中仍坚守商务印书馆苦撑危局，他不向日伪当局注册，更严词拒绝日伪的“合资”“合作”要求，只印刷一些旧版书籍勉强维持营业。虽然入不敷出，家庭经济每况愈下，甚至不得不变卖家藏的善本书籍以维持生计，但张元济始终不忘自己是一名堂堂正正的中国人，坚决不向日伪政权屈服妥协。

1942年初，两个日本军官驱车前往沙发花园张元济寓所，取出名片求见。张元济以民族气节为重，置个人安危于度外，接过名片就大义凛然地在背面写下“两国交兵，不便接谈”八个大字，让家人将名片退还日本军官，坚辞不见。

在日伪占领时期，张元济与叶景葵等志同道合者痛惜动乱年代古籍破坏和流失严重，创办了合众图书馆，意为“合众人之长”。张元济诚邀青年学者顾廷龙主持合众图书馆的工作。1949年5月17日，解放上海的号角声越来越嘹亮，一支国民党军队企图强占合众图书馆。张元济不顾生命危险，以衰迈之躯，坐镇图书馆大门，拼命阻挡国民党军官兵进入，并在第三天以大无畏的精神亲赴国民党军官办公室，不卑不亢地与之面对面交谈。交谈后，张元济安慰顾廷龙：“你放心，我看此人心不在焉，语无伦次，恐怕想溜。”果然，这天深夜，此国民党军官见大势已去，便带领部队撤离图书馆溜走了。忐忑不安的合众图书馆全体人员终于长长地舒了一口气，馆内珍贵的历史文献藏书在张元济的舍身庇护下得以保全。

建筑简介：淮海中路1285弄

张元济旧居位于淮海中路1285弄上方花园，占地面积26634平方米，建筑面积13674平方米。原为英籍犹太人沙发的私家花园，1933年浙江兴业银行购买后建造，马海洋行设计，至1941年共建成74幢三层砖木结构花园住宅，仍名沙发花园。建筑群为行列式布局，有独立式、两户联立式、多户联立式等户型，既有装饰简洁的现代式，也有缓坡筒瓦的西班牙式。栅门、窗栅、阳台、栏杆都用铸铁精制而成，室内宽敞明亮，硬木打蜡地板，各种生活设施一应俱全，园中布有草坪、喷水池和小别墅。张元济于1939—1959年间在上方花园24号居住；被誉为“中国现代会计之父”的潘序伦曾在16号居住。20世纪50年代，沙发花园改名为上方花园，寓有幽静美好之意，由张元济题名。1992年6月1日上海市人民政府公布其为市文物保护单位。1994年2月15日上海市人民政府公布其为市优秀历史建筑。

ZHANG Yuanji

ZHANG Yuanji (1867–1959) has a courtesy name of Jusheng and has his ancestral family from Haiyan County in Zhejiang province. A *jinshi* during the reign of Emperor Guangxu, he once served as principal of the office of the Ministry of Punishments and clerk of the General Administration. After the Sino-Japanese War in 1894, he participated in the Hundred Days' Reform. In 1897 he founded the Liberal Arts School in Shanghai, broadly buying and publishing Western books and issuing newspapers of reform. In June 1898, he was summoned by the emperor. During the 1898 Coup D'état, he was dismissed. Later he dedicated himself to the publishing industry in Shanghai, taking charge of the Commercial Press. Once he proofread and printed the *Twenty-Four Histories* based on the collection of various editions and photocopied the *Four Series*. After the founding of the New China, he participated in CPPCC and was elected as member of the National People's Congress. He was the author of such works as *Essays of Proofreading History Books* and *A Catalogue of Books from Hanfen Building after Fire*.

Unyielding in Protecting Ancient Books

In 1941 the Pacific War started. The sale office and factories of Shanghai Commercial Press was closed down, and 4.6 million copies of books and more than 50 tons of types were taken away. In such a difficult situation, ZHANG still adhered to the Commercial Press on the verge of crisis. Moreover he didn't get registered in the Japanese puppet authority and sternly refused the request of "joint venture" and "cooperation" from the puppet. Therefore only some old versions of book were reprinted to manage the business of the press. Although the ends could not be met and his family financial condition went from bad to worse to the extent that he had to sell rare books in order to maintain his livelihood, he always remembered that he was an honest and upright Chinese and was determined not to yield to the Japanese puppet government.

抗战中的商务印书馆
The Commercial Press during the War of Resistence.

At the beginning of 1942, two Japanese officers drove to his apartment in the Sofa Garden and took out the name card for an interview. Cherishing national integrity and putting aside personal safety, he took the card and righteously wrote on the back that "it is inconvenient for interview in war time". He returned the card to the Japanese officers and refused to see them.

During the Japanese occupation, he and some friends deplored the serious destruction and loss of ancient books in the turbulent years so that they founded the United Library, meaning "uniting the strength of all people". He invited a young scholar to manage the work of the library. On May 17, 1949, the horn of the liberation of Shanghai sounded louder and clearer. A group of KMT soldiers attempted to forcibly occupy the library. Regardless of the danger of life and his old age, he personally guarded the gate of the library and desperately stopped the KMT army officer and soldiers from entering. Moreover, on the third day he fearlessly went to the office of the KMT army to talk with the officer face to face, being neither haughty nor humble. After talking, he consoled the library manager, saying, "Take it easy. I see he is absent-minded and he speaks incoherently. So I guess they will slip away." Exactly. That night, seeing that nothing much could be done about it, the KMT officer led the troops out of the library. All the staff members of the library finally sighed a long sigh of relief after being uneasy for some time. All the valuable historical collections of books in the library were well saved from damage under his protection.

The former residence of ZHANG Yuanji is situated in the Shangfang Garden in Alley 1285 on Middle Huaihai Road, which covers an area of 26,634 square meters and a construction area of 13,674 square meters. It was formerly the private garden of Sofa, a British Jew, which was designed by Moorhead & Halse and was built in 1933 by Zhejiang Industrial Bank. Up to 1941, a total of 74 garden residences of three-storied structure of brick and wood were built, it still taking the name of the Sofa Garden. The building complex has a layout of lines and rows and different types of house, including independent type, two-house type and multiple-house type and embracing modern style with simple decoration and Spanish style as well as gentle slopes and pantile. The fence gate, window grilles, balconies and railings are all made of cast iron. The inside is both bright and spacious and the floor is of waxed hardwood. In addition, all living facilities are available. Moreover there are lawns, fountains and small villa in the Garden. From 1939 to 1959, ZHANG lived in the Shangfang Garden at No. 24. PAN Xulun, known as "the father of Chinese modern accounting", once lived at No. 16. In the 1950s, the Sofa Garden was renamed as the Shangfang Garden, with the meaning of being quiet and beautiful. The title was written by ZHANG Yuanji. It became a Cultural Relics Protection Unit and a Heritage Architecture issued respectively on June 1, 1992 and on February 15, 1994 by the Shanghai Municipal People's Government.

张元济 （忻秉勇画）

ZHANG Yuanji （By XIN Bingyong）

张乐平
（1910—1992）

祖籍浙江海盐，漫画大师。1925年到上海当学徒。1935年起创作系列长篇连环漫画《三毛》，以三毛这一典型形象深刻表现了旧中国流浪儿童的苦难生活，揭露了不合理的社会制度，表达了对美好未来的向往。1937年参加抗日漫画宣传队直至抗战胜利。1946年，《三毛从军记》在上海《申报》连载。1947年，另一部传世之作《三毛流浪记》在《大公报》上连载。中华人民共和国成立后，历任中国美术家协会上海分会、解放日报社、少年儿童出版社专业画家。1985年任《漫画世界》主编。其作品原稿已毫无保留地捐献给了国家：《三毛流浪记》原稿共234组由中国美术馆收藏；《三毛从军记》原稿共114组由上海美术馆收藏；其余592幅（组）原稿捐赠给家乡浙江海盐；《三毛翻身记》原稿捐赠给中国少年儿童基金会。

"三毛"的生日之谜

漫画大师张乐平用了半个多世纪塑造的经典艺术形象——那翘鼻、噘嘴、额上飘着三根头发的可爱"三毛"，影响了几代中国人。他画笔下的"三毛"，就如同一个真实存在的历史人物，述说着人世间的喜怒哀乐，传递着人生的感慨和对美好未来的向往。

"三毛"是如何诞生的？后人知之甚少。由于各种原因，甚至连大师本人也记忆有误。张乐平当初画"三毛"时，还是个20多岁的青年漫画家。据他自己回忆，第一幅"三毛"漫画诞生于1935年春夏之交，发表在上海《小晨报》上。但据查证，《小晨报》创刊于1935年9月12号，显然日期有误。《小晨报》并非"三毛"诞生的"摇篮"。

张乐平的子女们知道父亲的作品主要发表在报刊上，但要寻觅散见于中华人民共和国成立前多种报刊上的漫画，这无异于"沙里淘金"。为此，从1991年起，小儿子张慰军来到上海图书馆徐家汇藏书楼，开始艰苦的查寻。1998年后，大儿子张融融带领上海三毛形象发展有限公司员工在上海图书馆近代文献阅览室，几乎查遍了馆藏20世纪三四十年代所有报刊。在找出一百余幅"三毛"漫画的同时，最有价值的发现是改写了"三毛"的生日和诞生地。

经从众多的报刊档案资料中查悉，张乐平创作的"三毛"，最早见于《晨报》副刊《图画晨报》，时为1935年7月28日。据了解，当天因为发表连环漫画《王先生》的漫画家叶浅予生病，张乐平便以两幅"三毛"漫画补《王先生》之缺。至此，这位开中国一代漫画新风的"三毛"问世了。

张融融说，父亲最初设计的形象是光头男孩，秃脑袋虽然有趣但在造型上较为单调。他对此仔细琢磨推敲，而突发灵感，在光头上加了三笔，人物的形象立刻变得鲜活起来。

就这样，在"三毛"之父张乐平的精心打造和培育下，"三毛"茁壮成长。"三毛"系列漫画册成为我国印数最多、最畅销的儿童读物之一。仅《三毛流浪记》总印数就早已超过一千万册，而且被译成多种外文版本在国外发行。

建筑简介：五原路288弄3号

张乐平旧居位于五原路288弄3号，建于20世纪30年代，占地面积261平方米，其中建筑占地面积192平方米。建筑为近代独立式花园住宅，砖混结构两层两开间，机平瓦坡顶，有出檐。外立面简洁，仅入口处有几何形装饰线脚，阳台栏杆为铁艺。2016年，经过修缮的张乐平旧居已对公众开放，一楼展出了“三毛”故事和张乐平的创作，二楼复原了张乐平先生居住时的原貌。1950年6月至1992年9月张乐平在此居住。

ZHANG Leping

ZHANG Leping (1910–1992) has his ancestral family from Haiyan in Zhejiang province and is known as a master of caricature. In 1925, he went to Shanghai and served his apprenticeship there. Since 1935, he began to create the series of comic books *Three Hairs*. The typical image of *Three Hairs* demonstrates the miserable life of the homeless children in old China, exposes the unreasonable social system and expresses the public's strong desire for a better future. In 1937 he participated in the cartoon publicity team against Japanese invasion until the victory of the war. In 1946, his works *Three Hairs Joins the Army* was serialized in Shanghai *Shenbao*. In 1947, another masterpiece *The Winter of Three Hairs* was serialized in *Ta-kung Daily*. After the founding of the People's Republic of China, he became a professional painter of Shanghai Branch of the China Artists Association, Liberation Daily and Juvenile and Children's Publishing House. In 1985 he served as editor of *Comic World*. All his original manuscripts have been donated to the country without reservation, including 234 groups of works *The Winter of Three Hairs* collected by the National Art Museum of China, 114 groups of works *Three Hairs Joins the Army* collected by the Shanghai Museum of Art, and the remaining 592 groups of manuscripts donated to his hometown Haiyan County of Zhejiang province. The original manuscripts of *Three Hairs Gaining Freedom* have been contributed to the China Children and Teenagers' Fund.

The Riddle of Creating "Three Hairs"

ZHANG Leping, a master of caricature, has spent over half a century shaping the classic image of "Three Hairs" with a tip-tilted nose, sucking mouth and three lovely hairs floating on the forehead, which has influenced generations of Chinese people. The "Three Hairs" under his brush is just like a real historical figure, telling about all the sufferings and happiness of the world, passing on the understandings of life and longing for a better future.

How did the character of "Three Hairs" come into being? People knew very little about it and even the master himself couldn't remember it clearly. When he painted the "Three Hairs", he was still a young cartoonist in his 20s. According to his own memories, the first cartoon of "Three Hairs" was drawn in 1935 at the transitional season between spring and summer and was published in *Little Morning News* in Shanghai. However, *Little Morning News* was founded in September 12, 1935. Obviously there was something wrong with the date. The *Little Morning News* is not the cradle where "Three Hairs" was born.

张乐平
ZHANG Leping.

His children know that their father's works were mainly published in the press. However, to find comics scattered in a variety of newspapers before the founding of People's Republic of China is something like "finding gold in the sands". Therefore, the youngest son ZHANG Weijun came to Xujiahui Collection Building of Shanghai Library and started his hard search. After 1998, ZHANG Rongrong, the eldest son, led employees of Shanghai Three Hairs Image Development Company Ltd. to search nearly all the newspapers and periodicals of the 1930s and 1940s in Modern Literature Reading Room of Shanghai Library. While finding a hundred pieces of "Three Hairs" comics, the most valuable discovery is the rewriting of the birthday and birthplace of "Three Hairs".

After searching numerous newspaper and magazine archives, the "Three Hairs" created by Mr. ZHANG first appeared in *Picture Morning Newspaper*, the supplement of *Morning Newspaper* and the time was July 28, 1935. The story goes like this. That day the cartoonist YE Qianyu, who published comic serials *Mr. WANG*, fell ill and ZHANG Leping used two cartoons "Three Hairs" to make up the vacancy. At this point, "Three Hairs" came out, which inaugurated a new generation of the Chinese caricature.

ZHANG Rongrong said that the initial design of the image was a bald boy from his father's perspective. Interesting as the bald head was, it was monotonous in shape. After detailed considerations, it suddenly dawned on him that the image of the character could immediately become alive by adding three strokes on the bald head.

As a result, the image of "Three Hairs" grew sturdily under the elaboration and nurturing of Mr. ZHANG Leping who is regarded as the father of "Three Hairs". The series of comic books of "Three Hairs" became one of the most printed and best-selling children's books. The total copies of *The Winter of Three Hairs* have reached over 10 million, and it was published abroad with various editions in foreign languages.

The former residence of ZHANG Leping is located at No. 3 in Alley 288 on Wuyuan Road. Built in 1930s, it covers an area of 261 square meters with a construction area of 192 square meters. This building boasts itself an independent garden house in modern times, which is of a structure of brick and concrete with two stories and a width of two rooms. It has a roof covered with flat tiles manufactured by machines. A concise facade has architrave of geometric patterns and balcony railings of iron art only at the entrance. After renovation, the former residence of ZHANG Leping has been open to the public in 2016. The story of "Three Hairs" and works of ZHANG Leping can be accessible on the first floor. Meanwhile, the original architecture appearance during his living here has been restored on the second floor. From June 1950 to September 1992, ZHANG Leping lived here.

张乐平 （王荻画） ZHANG Leping （By WANG Di）

张织云
（1904—1975）

广东番禺人，原名张阿善。1923年进入大中华影业公司，翌年在该公司拍摄的第一部影片《人心》中饰演女主角而成名。此后，相继在大中华、明星、民新等影片公司任演员，主演了《战功》《可怜的闺女》《新人的家庭》《空谷兰》等影片，以端庄而不失妩媚的形象，令众多影迷为之倾倒，因而声名大振。1925年在上海新世界游艺场主持的“电影皇后”选举中位居榜首，成为中国电影史上第一位“电影皇后”。又因在影片《玉洁冰清》中饰演女主角孔素贞，被誉为“悲剧圣手”。后一度沉寂影坛，1935年复出，在新华影业公司拍摄的《新桃花扇》中扮演角色，但因国语不佳，不受欢迎。后移居香港，曾参加粤语片拍摄。1975年在香港去世。

中国第一位“电影皇后”的悲剧人生

张织云出生三个月后失去了父亲，随养母和几个姐姐在上海艰难度日，初中未毕业已辍学。她进入电影圈源于一个意外：1923年刚成立不久的大中华影业公司在《申报》刊登广告招募女演员，让应聘者将照片、简历投至报社信箱，一时之间信件纷至沓来。报名截止之后，工作人员失望地发现信箱里的一万多张照片都毫不引人注目。此后一个消息不胫而走——一名记者曾私自取走部分照片。经过大中华电影公司创办者出面交涉，记者终于答应归还照片，其中便有张织云母亲寄出的其女儿的照片。张织云虽貌不惊人，但在这峰回路转之下被与众不同的光芒笼罩，经过电影公司的包装宣传，她首次演戏便主演了《人心》，后又主演了《战功》等影片。

她在表演上悟性不足，与她合作过的导演张石川曾说过：“张织云由于受教育程度不高，初入影坛又仅谙粤语，指导她在开麦拉前表演，非常吃力……不过她谦抑虚心，所以后来也成为一颗红星。”除了勤能补拙磨炼出了她细腻真挚的表演风格外，摄影师卜万苍精心选取她最美的画面也为她增色不少，此后他们擦出了爱情火花，一次次珠联璧合的演绎与拍摄，成就了她令人动容的荧幕形象。

然而好景不长，有情人没能成为眷属，名利场是横亘在他们之间的隔阂。她坦言：“物质的诱惑，就渐渐环绕了我，我因经历浅薄，学识不足，不知不觉向物质享受递了降书。”其养母更是推波助澜，对卜万苍说道：“我可以补贴你三百块大洋，但是张织云是回不去了。”张织云接受了商人唐季珊的虚情假意，最终遭遇了一场失败的婚姻。

她痛苦地回忆道：“我的‘黄金时代’已随青春消逝了……离婚后，我的精神，又几次地遭受了莫大的打击。”这位中国第一位“电影皇后”悔悟已晚，最终她在贫病交加中离开人世。

建筑简介：新乐路100弄8号

张织云旧居位于新乐路（原名为亨利路）100弄永利村8号。永利村建于1938年，单面行列式布置44幢，总建筑面积8902平方米，属新式里弄。建筑为砖木混合结构，三层，两幢连体，平面方形，立面对称，中间以一竖墙分隔，无阳台，相邻两个号码的主入口均设有方形雨厦。沿街住宅以褐色毛面砖贴墙，作竖直隔离装饰之用。弄堂主入口三层通高壁柱直达檐口。缓坡屋顶，挑檐较小，方窗，水泥砂浆外墙。永利村素有“影人村”之称，20世纪二三十年代，“影帝”“影后”们云集于此。

ZHANG Zhiyun

ZHANG Zhiyun (1904–1975) has her ancestral family from Panyu in Guangdong province with a former name of ZHANG Ashan. In 1923 she entered Greater China Film Company. In the following year she rose to fame for her performance as the heroine in the company's first film *The Will of the People*. Since then, she worked as actress consecutively in Greater China Film Company, Star Film Company, Minxin Film Company, starring in such films as *Amid the Battle of Musketry, A Sincerely Pity Girl, Suspects of Couple, Orchid in an Empty Valley* and others. Her dignified and yet charming image on the screen found many film fans greatly fascinated, so her reputation was considerably boosted. In 1925 she topped the list in the election of "Movie Queen" hosted in Shanghai New World Amusement Park and became the first in the history of the Chinese film. Then she was reputed as "Tragedy Sage" for her starring the leading female role KONG Suzhen in the film *Why Not Her*. Later she became silent for a period of time in the circle of film. In 1935, she made a comeback, performing a role *The New Peach Blossom Fan* produced by Xinhua Film Company. But for her poor Mandarin, the film was unpopular. After moving to Hong Kong, she once participated in the production of film in Cantonese. In 1975, she passed away in Hong Kong.

The Tragic Life of China's First "Movie Queen"

ZHANG Zhiyun lost her father when she was three months' old and lived a hard life together with her foster mother and several sisters in Shanghai. She dropped out of school before she graduated from junior high school. She entered the film circle by accident. In 1923, the Greater China Film Company which was just established advertised in *Shanghai Newspaper* to recruit actresses. Candidates were asked to send their photos and resumes to the newspaper mailbox. All of a sudden letters came in a throng. After the deadline, the staff was disappointed to find none of the more than 10,000 photos in the mailbox compelling. Then a message spread that a reporter had privately taken away some photos. After the founder of Greater China Film Company came forward to negotiate, the reporter finally agreed to return the photos, among which there was the photo of ZHANG Zhiyun that her mother sent off for her. Her appearance was ordinary, but after all those twists and turns, and with the packaging and publicity of the film company, her first

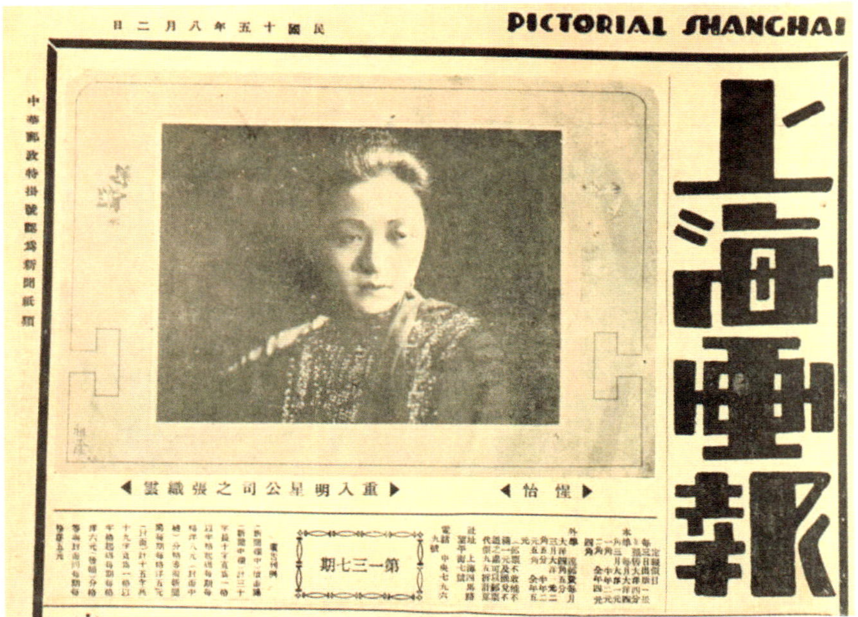

民國十五年八月二日

PICTORIAL SHANGHAI

上海畫報

中華郵政特掛號認為新聞紙類

重入明星公司之張織雲

第一三七期

1926 年 8 月 2 日《上海画报》头版报道张织云重入明星公司
On August 2nd, 1926, *Shanghai Pictorial* reported on the front page the return of ZHANG Zhiyun into the Star Film Company.

acting started from her starring in *The Will of the People* and later in *Amid the Battle of Musketry* and others.

Her power of understanding was not enough in performance. ZHANG Shichuan, a director who had worked with her, once said, "ZHANG Zhiyun had a low level of education and she could only speak Cantonese at the beginning of her experience in the circle of film, it was very hard to guide her to perform in front of the camera…but she was modest and had an open mind, so later she became a star." Practice makes perfect. Diligence helped mold a delicate and sincere performance style. In addition, the cameraman BU Wancang carefully selected her most beautiful pictures which graced her performance considerably. Later on the spark of love was ignited between them. After perfect cooperation in interpretation and shooting time and again, her moving screen image was accomplished.

However, this did not last long. Lovers were not finally united in a family. The vanity fair was the gap which lay between them. She frankly admitted, "The temptation of material gradually surrounded me. Because my experience was not rich and also because of the lack of knowledge, I unwittingly surrendered to material comforts." Her foster mother aggravated the situation by saying to BU Wancang, "I can compensate you with three hundred yuan, but she could never go back to you." ZHANG accepted the hypocritical show of affection of a businessman and ultimately suffered a failed marriage.

She painfully recalled, "My 'golden age' has gone with the youth... After the divorce, my spirit further suffered severe blows for several times." The Chinese first "Movie Queen" repented too late and left the world in poverty and sickness in the end.

The former residence of ZHANG Zhiyun is located at No. 8 in Yongli Village in Alley 100 on Xinle Road (formerly Henry Road). The Yongli Village was built in 1938. As a new style alley, it has a one-sided layout of rows with 44 buildings, and with a total construction area of 8,902 square meters. The buildings have a mixed structure of brick and wood. Each having three stories, two buildings are connected. The horizontal plane is a square while the longitudinal one is symmetrical. The middle has a vertical wall to separate the two buildings, which have no balcony. The main entrances of two adjacent numbers are equipped with a square canopy. Residences along the street have walls with brown napped bricks for the purpose of decoration and vertical separation. The main entrance of the alley has high pilasters with a height of three stories reaching directly to cornices. The roof has gentle slopes with smaller eaves. Windows are square and exterior walls have cement mortar. The Yongli Village is known as the "Filmmakers Village". In the 1920s and 1930s, "Movie Kings" and "Movie Queens" gathered here in crowds.

张织云 （钱定华画）　　ZHANG Zhiyun （By QIAN Dinghua）

张强辛
（1948— ）

浙江萧山人。1964年进入上海工艺美术学校，师从申石伽、曹简楼。1969年毕业后至甘肃祁连山煤矿工作。1976年转入安徽马鞍山铁路局工作。1980年回上海。参加历年美术展览，发表作品二百余件，曾获中宣部优秀作品奖。2000年任上海书画院执行院长。为上海美术家协会理事，国家一级美术师，民进市委委员及艺术委员会副主任。

梅花香自苦寒来

1969年，21岁的张强辛从上海工艺美校毕业后，来到了甘肃祁连山的煤矿工作。在奇峰高插天、西走接嘉峪、凝素无青云的祁连山，这位身高不到1.70米、体重不足60公斤的年轻人，每天早晨6点就要起床，戴上安全帽，手持手杖和矿灯去挖煤，工作任务就是一铲一铲把煤铲到矿车上。从矿口到矿井深处每天还要往返14公里的路。日常生活也非常艰苦，日常吃的是土豆、白菜，每个月里只有3天能吃上荤菜。在这样艰苦的环境中，每天晚上，当其他人入睡之后，张强辛却坚持绘画、读诗词、练书法，从不放松。

7年后，张强辛即将离开煤矿时深有感触地说："放眼窑洞外，逶迤三百里莽莽群峰，丹青纵横，迎寒风赏飞雪。登大通河峭壁咆哮，领略长河落日，大漠孤烟苍茫景观。空山无人，水流花开，西北高原浑厚撲茂之气。"艰辛的矿工生活不仅使他领略了大自然的博大精深，也造就了他数十年绘画的风格。

1983年的一天，张强辛去拜访87岁高龄的王个簃先生，个老指着刚完成的六尺整张"秋光图"上题的"一片秋光无限好"来考考张强辛。张强辛犹豫了一下，说道："八怪李复堂句子是一片秋光万古青，就差后三字，意境却大不一样。"个老不禁叫好，对后生嘉许有加，当即以"墨梅图"相赠，以示勉励。

1986年7月，张强辛的恩师申石伽在成都饭店（今天的美辰饭店）办80岁寿宴。张强辛、蔡天雄等弟子都赶来为老师祝寿，十年间足不出户的申石伽先生给每位弟子送了张画。席间，张强辛面对恩师，端起酒杯连饮三杯为老师祝寿，并动情地说："投之以桃，报之以李。老师，我不会忘了您的谆谆教诲。"老师见学生如此豪爽、动情，深深地被打动了，便送对联一副"酒胆逞强惊四座，画笔含辛动八方"。张强辛如获至宝，直至现在还把老师的这副对联挂在自己的书房，作为座右铭和人生的鼓励。

2000年，52岁的张强辛担任上海书画院执行院长。他在《墨淡烟浓——张强辛水墨作品选》序中写写道："问学求益，孜孜于跬步之寸进，不求躐等。竟之乎重铸之千锤，不务空想。宁复重攀高巅而假舆马以驰途。"

建筑简介：永福路49弄14号

张强辛寓所位于永福路49弄14号。建筑为多层住宅公寓，四层砌体结构，建筑平面呈矩形。淡黄色涂料外立面，南立面设有阳台，混凝土悬挑板结构，镂空水泥栏板。一层入口位于房屋北侧，钢筋混凝土双跑楼梯，一梯四户，白色涂料内墙面。楼梯间位于中部，两侧各有两户，北侧设有走廊。各层平面布局相似。

ZHANG Qiangxin

ZHANG Qiangxin (1948–) has his ancestral family from Xiaoshan in Zhejiang province. In 1964 he entered the Shanghai Arts and Crafts Academy, learning from Mr. SHEN Shijia and Mr. CAO Jianlou. After graduation in 1969 he went to work at the Qilian Mountain Coal Mine in Gansu province. In 1976 he was transferred to work in Maanshan Railway Administration in Anhui province. In 1980 he went back to Shanghai. Once he won award for outstanding works issued by the CPC Publicity Department, participated in art exhibition over the past years and published more than 200 pieces of works. In 2000, he was the Executive Director of Shanghai Painting and Calligraphy Academy. Also he was director of the Shanghai Artists Association, national first-grade artist, member of the municipal Party committee of the China Association for Promoting Democracy and deputy director of its Arts Committee.

The Fragrance of Plum Blossoms Sharpens in the Bitter Cold.

In 1969, ZHANG Qiangxin graduated from the Shanghai Arts and Crafts Academy at the age of 21 and went to work at the Qilian Mountain Coal Mine in Gansu province. In the Qilian Mountains where peculiar peaks soar high into the sky, extending westward to meet the Jiayuguan Pass and enjoying clean sky without black clouds, this young person with a height of less than 1.7 meters and a weight of less than 60 kg got up at 6 o'clock every morning. After putting on a helmet, he held a cane and a cap-lamp to go to dig coal and his task was to get coal up to bogie trucks shovel by shovel. From the mine mouth to the depths he traveled back and forth for 14 km every day. His life was also very hard, potatoes and cabbage were his daily food and he could only have meat three times a month. In such a difficult situation, he still insisted on painting, reading poetry and practicing calligraphy every night when other people fell asleep and he never slackened.

Seven years later when he was about to leave the coal mine, he said with deep feelings, "Looking out of the cave-house into the distance, I galloped across paintings with three hundred miles of vast mountains meandering, braving against the cold wind and appreciating the flying snow. Climbing up to the cliff at Datong River, I roared and enjoyed the sunset along the river as well as the great landscape of vast desert and solitary smoke. Empty mountains had no human trace, water flowed and flowers blossomed—all these things formed the simplicity, vigorousness and luxuriance of the Northwest Plateau". Hard life at coal mines not only enabled

张强辛（左三）参与公益活动
ZHANG Qiangxin (third from left) in a public welfare activity.

him to appreciate the profoundness of nature, but also helped create his painting style within decades of time.

One day in 1983, he paid a visit to Mr. WANG Geyi at the age of 87, who pointed to a newly completed painting "Autumn Light" on a whole piece of paper with a length of two meters and with a title of "An autumn with Extreme Splendor" to ask for his comment. Hesitating for a moment, he said, "LI Futang, one of the Eight Eccentric Artists of Yangzhou, made a statement of 'An Autumn with Forever Greenness'. Differ in two words but differ greatly in artistic conceptions." Mr. WANG could not help but praise him and gave him a painting "Ink Plum" as a gift to show his encouragement.

In July 1986, his teacher SHEN Shijia held his 80-year-old birthday banquet at Chengdu Hotel (now Meichen Hotel). Many students including ZHANG Qiangxin, CAI Tianxiong and others came to the banquet to express congratulations to their teacher. In the past ten years, the teacher was confined to the house, but that time he gave a painting to each of them as a gift. During the banquet, ZHANG Qiangxin stood in front of his teacher, held up the cup and drank three straight cups of alcohol as a toast to the teacher's birthday, saying with emotion, "The common saying goes as giving a plum in return for a peach. Teacher, I will always remember your earnest teachings." Seeing that the student was forthright and emotional, the teacher was so deeply touched that he produced a couplet which read, "Bravery for alcohol shocks these at the banquet; Brush with hardship moves those from all directions". Taking it a precious treasure, ZHANG put this couplet on the wall in his study until now as a motto and a life encouragement.

In 2000 when he was at the age of fifty-two, he served as executive president of Shanghai Painting and Calligraphy Academy. In the preface to the collection of his paintings *Thin Ink and Thick Smoke—Ink-wash Works by ZHANG Qiangxin*, he wrote, "In acquisition of knowledge, I've been working diligently to make progress bit by bit, not seeking to skip over the normal steps. Striving for recasting on the basis of numerous striking, I never devote my efforts to fanciness. I would rather clamber to another peak and travel a long distance with the help of horse and carriage."

The apartment of ZHANG Qiangxin is located at No. 14 in Alley 49 on Yongfu Road. The building is a multi-storey residential apartment with a structure of four-story masonry. Its architectural plane is rectangular. Light yellow paint decorates the outside wall surfaces. At the south façade there is a balcony with the structure of concrete cantilever and hollow cement fence. The entrance of the first floor is located at the north side of the building. The straight stairs with landing are of reinforced concrete and there are four houses on each storey. White paint is used for the inside walls. Stairs are seated in the middle and there are two households at both sides respectively. At the north side is the corridor. The layout of each floor is similar.

张强辛 （钱定华画） ZHANG Qiangxin （By QIAN Dinghua）

张瑞芳
（1918—2012）

祖籍北平，出生于河北保定，电影表演艺术家。1935 年考入北平国立艺术专科学校。1938 年至重庆，同年加入中国共产党。后入怒吼剧社、中华剧艺社等任演员。中华人民共和国成立后历任北京电影制片厂、中国青年艺术剧院、上海电影制片厂演员，上海电影演员剧团团长，上海电影家协会主席，上海市政协副主席。从艺 70 多年，先后参演了 40 余部话剧、近 20 部电影。其中话剧有《棠棣之花》《屈原》《家》等，电影有《南征北战》《母亲》《家》《李双双》《大河奔流》《泉水叮咚》等。1963 年获电影百花奖最佳女演员奖。1993 年获中国电影表演艺术学会特别荣誉奖。2005 年被授予“国家有突出贡献电影艺术家”称号。2007 年获上海国际电影节“华语电影终身成就奖”。

你是我们“农民的演员”

1961 年，张瑞芳接受在电影《李双双》中饰演女主角的任务。关于《李双双》，有人认为，作为喜剧似还不“喜”；也有人认为，剧本只是琐碎小事的组合，缺乏中心事件和冲突。但张瑞芳下乡听取农民意见后，却发现他们反应强烈，于是决心要演好这部戏。

电影在河南林县拍摄。张瑞芳和一位妇女队长刘凤仙交上了朋友。白天，张瑞芳跟着她去开会、组织生产劳动，还下田间学会了锄地、浇水、施肥、点种；晚上，她们促膝谈心，张瑞芳跟她学习纳鞋底儿、缝被子、擀面条……她们时常睡在一个帐子里，聊生活，谈看法。张瑞芳发现自己与妇女队长的距离在拉近，这使她对饰演李双双有了信心。当时导演十分大胆，就地取“才”，选用当地农民做群众演员，诸如评工计分、送公粮等戏都是采用实景拍摄。这一招果然增加了片子的真实性。

《李双双》上映后，全国轰动。1962 年，张瑞芳去日本后返回北京，受到周恩来总理的接见。总理握住她的手笑容满面地说：“我要请你吃螃蟹，你拍了部好片子啊！”张瑞芳的脸一下红了：“我……什么？”“《李双双》啊！有生活，艺术上也有新东西。”周总理如数家珍。张瑞芳激动万分，回招待所后，马上给编剧李准打电话。李准听到总理的评价高兴得差点跳起来。1963 年，第二届电影百花奖评选，《李双双》喜摘桂冠，张瑞芳获最佳女演员奖。在周总理参加的百花奖颁奖会上，陈毅高兴地说，我也投了《李双双》一票。

时隔 45 年后的 2006 年，当年的妇女队长刘凤仙来到上海。张瑞芳热情地邀请她到淮海中路的家中做客。姐妹俩分外亲热，两人有着说不完的话。刘凤仙说，《李双双》在我们那里几次重映，赞誉不绝。乡亲们都说，你演得太像了，是我们“农民的演员”。

张瑞芳听了欣喜地说：“这是我最爱听的！”原来周总理曾对她这样说过，不要以为历史剧难演，其实现代剧比它更难，因为现代人谁都可以评说你演得像与不像。多少年来，周总理的教诲一直在张瑞芳耳边回响。她演的角色被农民们承认了，这是对她最大的奖赏。

建筑简介：淮海中路1202号

张瑞芳旧居位于淮海中路1202号淮海公寓，原名盖司康公寓，又名万国储蓄会大楼，建于1935年，万国储蓄会出资建造，赉安公司设计，中法营造厂承建，以万国储蓄会大班盖司康名字命名。公寓分前后两排，主楼在后排，十三层钢筋混凝土结构。前排为二号楼，为五层公寓大楼。建筑占地面积4533平方米，主楼建筑面积9062平方米，辅楼建筑面积3318平方米，属现代派建筑风格的公寓住宅。主楼建筑立面为中轴对称，形体上由中部向两侧逐步跌落，中央有三条凸出的白色垂直带饰，入口挑出雨篷，卧入式阳台。一层青灰色大理石，以上外墙全部贴以米黄色面砖，仅各层阳台板为白色。二号楼底层为出租商号，二层以上为居住层，二间一套，每层六套，共二十四套。周谷城等著名人士曾经在此居住，瑞士、印度尼西亚驻沪领事馆也曾在此办公。1994年2月5日上海市人民政府公布主楼为市优秀历史建筑。1999年9月23日上海市人民政府公布二号楼为市优秀历史建筑。

ZHANG Ruifang

ZHANG Ruifang (1918–2012), a film artist with her ancestral family from Beijing, was born in Baoding in Hebei Province. She was admitted to Beijing National Art Academy in 1935. She went to Chongqing and joined the Communist Party of China in 1938. Then she became an actress in the Roar Drama Society as well as in the Chinese Drama Society. After the founding of the People's Republic of China, she served successively as actress in Beijing Film Studio, China Youth Art Troupe and Shanghai Film Studio, as well as head of Shanghai Film Artist Troupe, president of Shanghai Film Association and vice chairman of Shanghai Municipal People's Political Consultative Conference. She was engaged in the performing act for more than 70 years, during which she performed in over 40 dramas and nearly 20 films. Her dramas include *The Flower of Shadbush*, *QU Yuan*, *Family* and so on, and her films include *Fighting North and South*, *Mother*, *Family*, *LI Shuangshuang*, *The Great River Flows On*, *Bubbling Spring* and so on. In 1963, she won the Hundred Flowers Award for Best Actress. In 1993 she was awarded the Special Honorary Award by China Film Society of Performing Arts. In 2005 she was awarded the title of "National Film Artists with Outstanding Contributions". In 2007 she won the "Chinese Film Lifetime Achievement Award" at the Shanghai International Film Festival.

You are our "Farmers' Actress"

In 1961, she accepted the task of playing the heroine in the film *LI Shuangshuang*. About this film, some people thought that it was a comedy without enough "happiness"; some else considered the script as a combination of trivialities, which lacked central events and conflicts. However, she went to the countryside and listened to the views of farmers. She found that they responded strongly to this film, so she determined to try her best in the performance of the role.

The film was shot in Linxian County in Henan province. She made friends with a woman team leader LIU Fengxian. During the day, she followed her to have meetings and organize the labor of production and she also learned hoeing, watering, fertilizing and planting seeds. In the night, they often had a heart-to-heart talk. From her she also learned to stitch soles, sew the quilts, make noodles with a rolling pin ... They often slept in one tent and talked about their life and their ideas. Gradually, she found she became

张瑞芳出演电影《李双双》
ZHANG Ruifang acted in the film *LI Shuangshuang*.

more adapted to the life of the team leader, which made her confident in playing the role of LI Shuangshuang. At that time, the director was very bold, for he chose local farmers as the figurants. Scenes such as the evaluation of work points and the sending of public grain were all finished by live-action shootings, which intensified the authenticity of the film.

The release of *LI Shuangshuang* created a national sensation. In 1962, when ZHANG Ruifang returned to Beijing from Japan, she was received by Premier ZHOU Enlai, who held her hands with smiles on his face and said, "I want to invite you to eat crabs, because you have completed a good film!" She blushed, asking "I ... what?" "*LI Shuangshuang*! It's adapted from daily life and has created new things in art." Premier ZHOU was familiar with this film. She was extremely excited. She called the screen writer LI Zhun as soon as she went back to the hotel. When LI Zhun got to know the evaluation of the Premier, he was so happy that he nearly couldn't help jumping. In 1963, during the evaluation of the Second Hundred Flowers Award, *Li Shuangshuang* got the first place and she won the award for Best Actress. At the award granting ceremony of the Hundred Flowers Award which Premier ZHOU was present, CHEN Yi said happily that he voted for *LI Shuangshuang* as well.

After 45 years, LIU Fengxian, the then women's team leader, came to Shanghai in 2006. ZHANG warmly invited her to her house on Middle Huaihai Road. The two sisters were so intimate that they got endless words to talk with. The leader said that *LI Shuangshuang* had been replayed for several times in her hometown. Villagers spoke highly of this film and said that ZHANG performed vividly and she was a "farmers' actress".

"That is what I've expected to hear most!" ZHANG said with delight after hearing the evaluation. For Premier ZHOU had said to her that it was improper to think that historical dramas were hard to perform. Actually, modern dramas were more difficult because any modern person could make comments on whether you performed the role well or not. Many years have passed and the teachings of Premier ZHOU have been ringing in her ears. That her role was recognized by the farmers is the greatest reward for her.

The former residence of ZHANG Ruifang lies in Huaihai Apartment at No. 1202 on Middle Huaihai Road, which was formerly called Gascogne Apartments and also known as the International Savings Society Building. Built in 1935 by Sino-French Construction Company, it was invested by the International Savings Society and was designed by Leonard-Veysseyre-Kruze Architects. It was named after Gascogne, the manager of the International Savings Society. The apartments are divided into two rows—the front and back rows. The main building which has thirteen floors with a reinforced concrete structure is the back row. The front row is Building No.2, a five-story apartment. The building covers an area of 4,533 square meters, the main building has a construction area of 9,062 square meters and the auxiliary building has a construction area of 3,318 square meters. It is of modern architectural style. The facade of the main building is symmetrical, the two wings being one floor lower than the middle gradually, and the centre of the building has three white vertical belt decorations that are standing out. The entrance has projected canopy and balconies are receded. The first floor has cinereous marbles for walls while the exterior walls above the first floor are coated with beige tiles. Only the balcony plates at all floors are white. The ground floor of Building No. 2 has shops for lease and rooms above the first floor are for residence. There are two rooms in one suite and six suites on each floor and twenty-four suites in total. ZHOU Gucheng and other famous people once lived here. Consulates of Switzerland and the Republic of Indonesia in Shanghai once had their offices here as well. Both the main building and Building No. 2 became a Heritage Architecture, issued by the Shanghai Municipal People's Government on February 5, 1994 and September 23, 1999 respectively.

张瑞芳（戴晓明画）　ZHANG Ruifang (By DAI Xiaoming)

李白
（1910—1949）

湖南浏阳人。1925年参加农民运动。后加入中国共产党。1930年参加中国工农红军，到中央根据地举办的电讯训练班第二期学习。后在红一方面军从事电台通讯工作。1934年随中央红军参加长征。抗日战争期间，到上海设立秘密电台。曾被日军逮捕入狱。抗战胜利后继续从事秘密电台工作。1948年12月被捕后，在酷刑下仍严守党的机密。1949年5月7日在浦东被秘密杀害。

永不消逝的电波

1937年10月10日，李白受党中央委派，化名李霞从延安抵达上海，担任秘密电台报务员。为掩护地下电台，党组织安排23岁的绸厂女工、共产党员裘兰芬（改名裘慧英）与李白假扮夫妻，协助工作。

1938年4月，两人以“夫妻”名义住进法租界环境幽静的蒲石路蒲石村（今长乐路399弄）。白天李白外出打短工维持生活，晚上便去房后的小灶间工作。每天深夜十二时至凌晨四时，是李白与延安约定的通报时间。当人们酣睡时，李白挂上双层深色窗帘，将5瓦小支光灯泡蒙上黑布，戴上耳机，按动电键，通过用电波架起的空中桥梁，及时把延安党中央的指示传达给上海地下党，又把日伪的重要情报传递给中央。

盛夏酷暑，门窗紧闭，李白伏身在狭小的如同蒸笼般的灶间通宵达旦工作，衬衣湿透，便光着膀子，裘慧英边擦汗边替他打扇。寒冬腊月，不能生火取暖，就在收发报机旁放杯开水御寒，李白按电键的手指冻得僵硬肿大，每次发完报裘慧英都给他揉搓至发热。在为共同事业奋斗的岁月中，两人萌生了纯洁的爱情。1940年秋，经组织批准，两人结为正式伴侣。

太平洋战争爆发后，日寇占领租界，李白的电台曾数度转移。1942年9月、1945年3月，李白两次被捕，后经党组织营救保释出狱。

抗战胜利后，李白夫妇从浙江回到上海，继续从事党的秘密电台工作。1948年12月30日凌晨，国民党淞沪警备司令部稽查处侦察到秘密电台的方位，大批军警包围了他家所在的黄渡路107弄。正在15号三楼拍发一份标注“十万火急”情报的李白发现动静后，坚持发完报，最后发出一组电码“8873”（意即我已被敌发现），然后将电码稿撕毁吞下后被捕。

李白在狱中经受了严刑拷打、厚禄利诱等考验，始终坚贞不屈，保护了党的备用电台得以迅速启用。

1949年5月7日，裘慧英带着不满四岁的儿子在警局见了李白最后一面，当晚，淞沪警备司令部将李白等人秘密押至浦东杀害。这一天恰是李白39岁生日。1958年，以李白为原型的电影《永不消逝的电波》上映后，在全国观众中引起巨大反响。

建筑简介：长乐路339弄18号

李白旧居位于长乐路339弄18号底楼。339弄1至44号蒲石村，新式里弄，以蒲石路（今长乐路）命名，建于1934年，占地面积4080平方米，建筑面积7376平方米，共有砖木结构三层楼房42幢，二层楼房1幢，平房1间。入口上有轻薄雨篷，右侧开一小圆窗，二层局部有大转角窗，水泥拉毛外墙，坡顶，钢窗，硬木地板。李白烈士曾在此设立秘密电台，他的儿子李恒胜电话确认此事，他还回忆：曾带领中央电视台的记者来此地拍摄过。虹口区文史馆的同志介绍，此地址是烈士遗属裘慧英老人生前确认的。现列入上海市第三次全国文物普查不可移动文物名录。

LI Bai

LI Bai (1910–1949) has his ancestral family from Liuyang in Hunan province. In 1925, he participated in the Peasant Movement and then joined the Communist Party of China. In 1930 he joined the Red Army of the Chinese Workers and Farmers and attended the second phase of the telecommunications training courses organized by the Central Revolutionary Base. After that he was engaged in the radio communications work for the Red Army. In 1934, he took part in the Long March as a member of the Central Red Army. During the War against Japanese Invasion, he went to Shanghai and set up a secret radio station. He was once arrested and put to prison by the Japanese invaders. After the victory of the War, he continued to work for the secret radio. He kept secrets of the Party despite the torture after he was arrested in December, 1948. Unfortunately, he was secretly killed in Pudong in Shanghai on May 7, 1949.

The Radio Waves that Never Wear Away

On October 10, 1937, LI Bai, with the assumed name LI Xia, arrived in Shanghai from Yan'an to act as a secret radio operator under the appointment of the Central Committee of the CPC. To protect the underground radio station, the CPC arranged QIU Lanfen (renamed QIU Huiying), a 23-year-old silk factory worker and a communist, to disguise herself as LI Bai's wife in order to support his revolutionary work.

In April 1938, they settled in a quiet place on Pushi Road in Pushi Village in the French Concession (now named Alley 399 on Changle Road) as a "couple". During the daytime, LI Bai went out and did part-time job to earn a living. As night came, he would go to a tiny kitchen behind the cottage to work. Every day the period from midnight to four o'clock in the morning was the time for him to intercommunicate with Yan'an. When people were in deep sleep, he pulled down double-layer dark curtains and muffled the 5-watt small light bulb with black cloth. Then he put on headphones and pressed the button, transmitting the instructions from Yan'an Central Committee to the Shanghai underground party and passing the important information of Japanese invaders and the puppet government to the CPC through the air bridge set up by radio waves.

1946 年 1 月 19 日，李白全家合影于上海
Photo of LI Bai and his family, taken in Shanghai on January 19, 1946.

It was unbelievably torrid in summer. With doors and windows closed, he worked day and night in the narrow steamer-like kitchen. He would take off shirt since it was all wet and the wife would wipe off the sweat from his face and wave a fan by his side. Since they could not set fire to keep warm even in cold winter, they put a cup of hot water by the transmitter to keep warm. His fingers became frozen and swollen on account of pressing the key for a long term. Each time he finished reporting, she would rub his hands till they became warm. In the years of struggle for the common ideal, the two fell in love for each other. In the fall of 1940, they got married with the approval of the Party organization.

After the outbreak of the Pacific War, the Japanese occupied the Concessions. LI Bai moved several times with his radio station. He was arrested twice in September 1942 and March 1945 and later he was bailed out by the CPC.

After the victory of the War against Japanese Invasion, LI Bai and his wife came back to Shanghai from Zhejiang, continuously engaged in Party's secret radio work. On the early morning of December 30, 1948, the inspection office of the KMT Shanghai Garrison Headquarters detected the location of the secret radio and a large number of police quickly surrounded his home in Alley 107 on Huangdu Road. At that time, LI Bai was sending a message marked "urgent" on the 15th floor. After finding himself in an emergent condition, he persisted in finishing the telegram and finally issued a set of code "8873" (meaning I have been found by the enemy). Then he tore up the pieces of paper and swallowed them before he was arrested.

LI Bai endured great torture, temptation and other tests in prison but he never yielded, which ensured that the Party's standby radio could be quickly actuated.

On May 7, 1949, the husband and wife met in the police station for the last time with their nearly four years old son. During that night, the Shanghai Garrison Headquarters frog-marched LI Bai and others secretly to Pudong and slaughtered them cruelly. That day happened to be his birthday. In 1958, the film *The Eternal Radio Waves* based on the life story of LI Bai became a nationwide sensation after hitting the big screen.

The former residence of LI Bai is situated on the ground floor of Building 18 in Alley 339 on Changle Road. Buildings from No.1 to No. 44 in Pushi Village in Alley 339 are of a new alley style named after Pushi Road (now Changle Road). Built in 1934, it covers an area of 4,080 square meters with a construction area of 7,376 square meters. Totally there are 42 buildings of a three-story structure of brick and wood with one building of two stories and one bungalow. There's a light awning on the upper of the entrance and a small round window on the right. On the second floor, there are stuccoed exterior walls, pitched roofs, steel windows, hardwood floors and partly large corner windows. The Martyr LI Bai once set up a secret radio station here before, which his son LI Hengsheng confirmed on the phone. He also recalled that "I used to bring the reporters from CCTV here to shoot a documentary". According to a staff member in Hongkou District Research Institute of Culture and History, the martyr's wife QIU Huiying confirmed this place before her death. Now the residence has been included in the third census list of national cultural relics in Shanghai.

李白 （忻秉勇画）　　LI Bai （By XIN Bingyong）

李石曾
（1881—1973）

直隶高阳（今属河北）人，名煜瀛，字石曾，笔名真民、石僧，晚年自号扩武。1902 年赴法国就学，倾心于克鲁泡特金的互助论。1906 年与人发起组织世界社，出版《新世纪》周报。8 月加入同盟会。归国后，在天津出版《民意报》，参与成立进德会、社会改良会、留法俭学会。1915 年任华法教育会副会长。后任北京大学教授、中法大学董事长。1924 年国民党改组，任中央监察委员。后任北平大学校长、北平师范大学校长、北平研究院院长等职。抗日战争期间从事外交活动。1948 年被聘为总统府资政。1949 年去瑞士。1952 年当选为国民党中央评议委员。1956 年定居台北。1973 年 9 月在台北病逝。著有《石僧笔记》，另有遗稿《扩武自述》《石僧随笔》。

“世界社者世界之试验所”

作为中国留法第一人，李石曾认为开展世界文化运动方能实现其理想大同世界。1906 年，他与张静江、吴稚晖在巴黎发起创办“世界社”，以“传布正当之人道，介绍真理之科学”为宗旨，“欲从各方面为促进教育之准备”。主张撷取各国文化之精华，兼容并蓄，熔为一炉。1941 年，他在给杨家骆的信中说道：“我组织世界社，欲其成为立体与动作的百科全书，因而无事不举，由出版而至于学术教育；由理论而至于应用经济；由戏曲的舞台而至政治社会的舞台，无所不为。”“世界社者世界之试验所。”

1929 年，李石曾将世界社迁往福开森路（今武康路）393 号自己的寓所，和张静江及褚民谊负责主要事务。1932 年，李石曾发起创办中国国际图书馆，它是中国第一所国际专业图书馆，由坐落于福开森路 393 号的世界社图书馆改建而成，藏中外图书五万余册、中外杂志五百余种。1936 年，李石曾和张静江等知名学者在此兴办世界学校，作为培养留法学生的预备基地，其创办宗旨与世界社一脉相承，亦倡导青年走出国门、开阔眼界，学习欧美先进技术，科学救国、教育救国。

世界学校当时被誉为沪上最顶尖的“贵族学校”，对中国教育的现代化历程具有深刻而长远的影响。在校董李石曾的管理下，世界学校实行小学至初中毕业七年制，聘请著名学者授课，李石曾更亲力亲为，走上三尺讲台耐心地教授学生法语。抗战时期，世界学校坚持不使用汪伪课本，在国际图书馆设立救护站救助伤员及难民，组织学生慰问抗日官兵，接待流亡师生，学生们积极参与，以生命研修人道主义与反法西斯课程。

李石曾毕生为世界文化运动奋斗，设立了数十个隶属世界社的组织，致力于使“人人知世界、爱世界、行世界、成世界，亦可谓为人与世界成为一体”，推动世界文化的交流与发展。

建筑简介：武康路393号

李石曾曾居住于武康路393号，1929年，他创办的世界社迁至此处，1936年创办的世界学校亦设立于此。1950年初，世界学校中学部停办，校名改为私立世界小学。1956年，上海的私立学校全部改为公办，私立世界小学更名为淮海路第二小学，校址依旧。1965年，学校迁至不远处的武康路280弄2号。2008年，校名恢复为世界小学。武康路393号建筑由两部分组成：其一为矩形建筑，建于1912年，仿英式古典建筑风格；另一为三角形，具有典型装饰艺术风格，建于20世纪30年代。整幢建筑以花岗岩为墙角基础，底层筑有对称大理石露天台阶，立面以水泥仿石砌块衬托浅色横直线条，附以浮雕和装饰线角。南墙二、三层间镶有弓形花色水泥阳台，左右用厚实的"牛腿"加以支撑，兼具装饰效果。建筑南面是一座占地4亩的大花园。辛亥革命元勋黄兴曾于1916年在此居住。

LI Shizeng

LI Shizeng (1881–1973) has his ancestral family from Gaoyang in Zhili province (now Hebei) with a personal name of Yuying, a courtesy name of Shizeng and pen names of Zhenmin and Shiseng as well as a style name of Kuowu given by himself. In 1902, he went to France to study, losing his heart to the mutual aid theory of Pyotr Kropotkin. In 1906, he launched with others the organization of World Society, and published weekly *New Century*. In August he joined the United League of China. After returning home, he published *Public Opinion Newspaper* in Tianjin and participated in the founding of Progressive Virtue Society, Social Reform Society and France Work-Study Society. In 1915 he served as vice president of China Law Education Association and later as professor of Beijing University and chairman of the Sino-French University. In 1924, he served as member of the Central Supervision Committee when the KMT was reorganized. Later he served as president of Beiping University, Beiping Normal University and Beiping Research Institute. During the War of Resistance against Japanese Invasion, he was engaged in diplomatic activities. In 1948, he was appointed as advisor of the office of the president. In 1949, he paid a visit to Switzerland. In 1952, he was elected as member of the KMT Central Evaluation Committee. In 1956, he settled in Taipei, where he died in September 1973. In addition he was author of the book *Notes by Shiseng* and manuscripts *Self-Account of Kuowu* and *Essays by Shiseng*.

"World Society as Experiment of a World"

As the first Chinese to study in France, LI Shizeng thought that the world cultural movement could help to realize an ideal stateless world. In 1906, he together with ZHANG Jingjiang and WU Zhihui in Paris launched the founding of the "World Society", with a view of "spreading justified humanity and introducing the science of truth", "in order to promote the preparation of education in all aspects". He advocated the absorption of the essence of different cultures and the inclusion of everything from them. In 1941, he wrote a letter to YANG Jialuo, saying, "I organized the World Society in order to create a three-dimensional encyclopedia for action.

世界社的三位创办人（右一为李石曾）
The three founders of World Society (LI Shizeng at first from right).

Therefore nothing was not included, ranging from publication to academic education; from theory to applied economics; and from the stage of opera to the stage of the political and social society." "World Society was an experiment of a world."

In 1929, he moved the World Society to his apartment at No. 393 on Ferguson Road (now Wukang Road) and took charge of main affairs along with ZHANG Jingjiang and CHU Minyi. In 1932, he initiated the establishment of the China International Library, which was China's first international professional library and was reconstructed from World Society Library located at No. 393 on Ferguson Road. It had a collection of Chinese and foreign books of over 50,000 volumes in addition to Chinese and foreign journals and magazines of over 500 types. In 1936, he together with other famous scholars set up the World School here as a training base for students to go to study in France. The purpose of its founding came down in one continuous line with that of the World Society. It also advocated that the youth go out of the country to broaden their horizons and learn the advanced technologies from Europe and the United States for the purpose of saving the country by science and by education.

At that time, the World School was hailed as the top of the "exclusive schools", which exerted a profound and long-term impact on the modernization of China's education. Under the management of the chairperson LI Shizeng, the school implemented a seven-year system from primary school to junior high school, inviting well-known scholars to teach courses. The chairperson even went into classroom to patiently teach students French in person. During the War of Resistance against Japanese Invasion, the school insisted on doing many things such as avoiding the use of the textbooks by the puppet government of WANG Jingwei, setting up aid stations in the international library to rescue the wounded and refugees, organizing students to greet the officers and soldiers against Japanese Invasion, and receiving teachers and students in exile. Students actively participated in them to attend and research courses of humanitarian and anti-fascism.

He devoted his whole life to the world cultural movement and established dozens of organizations affiliated to the World Society, dedicating himself to enable "everyone to know the world, love the world, travel the world and create a world, i.e. the integration of people and the world", and promoting the exchange and development of world cultures.

LI Shizeng once lived at No. 393 on Wukang Road. In 1929, the World Society he founded was moved here. The World School he founded in 1936 was also established here. In the beginning of 1950, the high school in it was closed and its name was changed to the Private World Primary School. In 1956, all private schools in Shanghai were converted to public ones and it was renamed the Second Huaihai Road Primary School with the site remaining the same. In 1965, the school moved to No. 2 in Alley 280 on Wukang Road, not far away from its original site. In 2008, its name was renewed as the World Primary School. The buildings at No. 393 on Wukang Road consist of two parts. One is rectangular, built in 1912 with the British classical architectural style; the other is triangular with a typical style of art deco, built in the 1930s. The entire building is based on the granite as its corner foundation; its bottom has symmetrical marble open-air steps; and its facade uses cement imitation stone blocks to set off light-colored straight lines with reliefs and decorative lines. The south walls between the second and third floors are studded with bow-shaped concrete balconies, the left and right sides of which are solidly supported by corbel with decorative effect. In front of the building in the south there is a large garden with an area of four acres. HUANG Xing, one of the great heroes of the 1911 Revolution once lived here in 1916.

李石曾 （钱定华画） LI Shizeng （By QIAN Dinghua）

李国豪
（1913—2005）

广东梅州人，桥梁工程与力学专家、教育家、社会活动家。1936年毕业于同济大学。1938年至1945年在德国达姆斯塔特工业大学专攻桥梁工程和结构力学。1946年回国后，任上海市工务局工程师、同济大学教授。中华人民共和国成立后，历任同济大学副校长、校长，上海市第六届政协主席等。先后受聘为武汉长江大桥和南京长江大桥技术委员会委员、主任，宝山钢铁总厂工程技术委员会首席顾问，上海南浦大桥专家组组长，汕头海湾和虎门珠江顾问组组长等。1994年当选为中国工程院首批院士。其专攻的桥梁工程学科达到中国领先水平并在国际上具有显著影响，为世界十大著名结构工程专家之一。

解开“大桥晃动”之谜

1957年10月15日，中国万里长江第一桥——武汉长江大桥建成通车。浩浩荡荡的人群摩肩接踵，向大桥进发。突然大桥晃动了起来。是什么原因使大桥晃动？李国豪一直思考着这个问题。因那几年身负国防科研任务，实在没时间研究，就此搁下了。1968年，南京长江大桥通车的消息传来，他担心大桥会再次晃动。因为武汉长江大桥出现晃动后，为确保万无一失，修建南京长江大桥时，把钢桁梁加宽了4米，多用了4000吨钢。不过，大家心里还是没底，这能否起作用？

李国豪决定解开这个难题。他的脑中浮现出当年留学德国时运用的方法。他将一座复杂的多腹杆菱形桁架体系桥梁化成连续体系，用微分方程成功推导了刚度转换的等效关系，并用模型试验得到了验证。对，就用这个思路来研究大桥的稳定与振动问题。就这样，李国豪凭着极强的记忆力和扎实的基本功，根据两桥梁的基本数据，开始推算。

1971年4月，李国豪从理论上给出了大桥晃动的答案。但他知道，仅有理论计算不行，必须要由试验来验证。可当时没有制作钢桥模型的工具，他思来想去，决定用赛璐珞来替代。他女婿帮忙从中央商场买回了一大堆废赛璐珞计算尺。当晚李国豪急不可待地支上锅灶烧水，放入的赛璐珞变软了，他压、剪、拉，开始制作桥梁模型。一年后，李国豪的试验数据终于出来，和理论计算结果完全一致。1974年，在全国钢铁振动科研协作会议上，他报告了研究成果：武汉长江大桥通车时出现的晃动，是由于突然涌上大桥的人群荷载造成的桥梁弯曲、扭转共振，大桥自身结构没有问题。因此，南京长江大桥多用的4000吨钢没有必要。“困扰我们17年的谜解开了！”全场掌声雷动。

多年后，李国豪用通俗的语言解释大桥晃动的原因：“这就像坐小木船，当你一只脚迈上船时，船就会晃动；当你两只脚都上去后，船很快就不晃了。大桥的晃动，是很多人突然拥上出现的情况。而桥梁结构本身没有问题。”

1975年，11万字的《桁梁扭转理论——桁梁的扭转、稳定和振动》一书出版。1983年，这一成果获得国家自然科学三等奖。李国豪的这一理论为后人造桥大大节约了人力和物力。

建筑简介：复兴西路34号

李国豪旧居位于复兴西路34号卫乐公寓，原名卫乐精舍，建于1934年，赉安洋行设计，占地面积1720平方米，建筑面积3797平方米，汽车间附屋802平方米，属现代点式建筑风格的公寓住宅。建筑为十三层钢筋混凝土结构，两翼跌落一层，立面对称，竖三段布置，中间凸出，设一串挑出的半圆阳台为构图中心，两边为卧入式阳台形成竖向线条；水泥砂浆外墙，立面中部竖线条及突出的半圆阳台为暗红色粉刷，其余部分为浅黄色粉刷，山墙顶部及南侧有重复线条装饰。楼前有小花园。解放后，吕蒙与黄准夫妇、陈鲤庭、吴强、赖少其、峻青、王西彦等一批文化人在此居住。1994年2月15日上海市人民政府公布其为市优秀历史建筑。

LI Guohao

LI Guohao (1913–2005) has his ancestral family from Meizhou in Guangdong province. He was an expert in bridge engineering and mechanics, educator and social activist. In 1936, he graduated from Tongji University. From 1938 to 1945, he studied in Darmstadt University of Technology in Germany, specializing in bridge engineering and structural mechanics. After returning to China in 1946, he was appointed as engineer of Shanghai Municipal Bureau of Works and professor of Tongji University. After the founding of the New China, he served in succession as vice president and president of Tongji University and chairman of the sixth session of the Shanghai CPPCC. He was successively employed as member and director of the Technical Committee of Wuhan Yangtze River Bridge and Nanjing Yangtze River Bridge, chief adviser of the Engineering Technical Committee of Baoshan Iron and Steel Plant, expert group leader of Shanghai Nanpu Bridge, advisory group leader of Shantou Bay and Humen Pearl River. In 1994 he was elected as one of the first academician of Chinese Academy of Engineering. The discipline of bridge engineering he has been specializing in has reached the leading level in China and has a significant impact in the international arena. He is one of the world's top ten well-known structural engineering experts.

Unraveling the Mystery of "Bridge Vibration"

On October 15, 1957, Wuhan Yangtze River Bridge, China's first bridge across the Yangtze River, was completed and opened to traffic. Mighty crowds jostled each other and swarmed to the bridge. Suddenly the bridge vibrated. What caused the bridge to rock? He thought about this problem for a long time. Because of his national defense research missions in those years, he had no time to study it and put it aside. In 1968, the news that Nanjing Yangtze River Bridge was opened to traffic reached him. He worried that the bridge would vibrate once again. Years ago, Wuhan Yangtze River Bridge vibrated at its opening to traffic. This time, in order to be on the safe side, the construction of Nanjing Yangtze River Bridge widened the steel truss girders by 4 meters and used more steel

李国豪（左三）与朋友们
LI Guohao (third from left) and his friends.

by 4,000 tons. However, everybody was still unsure about the result. Would this work?

He decided to solve this problem. Methods he used when he studied in Germany crossed his mind. He converted a complex bridge of multi-column diamond truss system into a continuous one, successfully deduced the equivalence relation of stiffness conversion by using differential equation and verified it with model tests. Yes, he told himself to adopt this idea to study the stability and vibration of the bridge. In this way, he made use of the basic data of the two bridges to start calculation on the basis of a powerful memory and a solid foundation.

In April 1971, he theoretically gave the answer to bridge vibration. But he knew that theoretical calculations alone could not work and they must be verified by tests. At that time, however, there was no tool to make a steel bridge model. On a second thought, he decided to use celluloid instead. His son-in-law helped buy a lot of celluloid from the central mall. At that night, he could scarcely wait to prepare a stove to boil water. The celluloid he put into the stove softened. After pressing, cutting and pulling, he began to make bridge models. A year later, his test data finally came out, which was completely consistent with theoretical results. In 1974, he reported the results at the National Conference on Steel Vibration: the vibration when Wuhan Yangtze River Bridge was opened to traffic was due to the fact that the crowd of people suddenly gushed onto the bridge, resulting in a load which caused vibration and torsional resonance. But there was no problem with the structure of the bridge. Therefore, there was no necessity to use additional 4,000 tons of steel in the construction of Nanjing Yangtze River Bridge. "The mystery which troubled us for 17 years was solved!" The applause burst out at the conference.

Years later, he used plain language to explain the reasons for the bridge vibration: "This is like a small wooden boat. When you put one foot on it, it will shake; when you put both feet on it, it will not shake any more in a while. The bridge vibrated is due to the fact that a lot of people suddenly swarmed onto it, while there was no problem with the bridge structure itself."

In 1975, the book *A Theory of Truss Torsion: Its Torsion, Stability and Vibration* was published, which covered 110,000 words. In 1983, this achievement won the third prize of National Natural Science Award. His theory greatly saved manpower and material resources for later man-made bridge.

The former residence of LI Guohao is located in Willow Apartment at No. 34 on West Fuxing Road. Formerly known as Willow Court, it was designed by Leonard-Veysseyre-Kruze Architects and built in 1934, which covers an area of 1,720 square meters with a construction area of 3,797 square meters in addition to attached rooms of 802 square meters for garage. It is an apartment of point construction and modern architectural style. With thirteen layers of reinforced concrete structure, it has two sides lower by one floor. Its front is symmetrical with three vertical sections. The middle section protrudes with a series of semi-circular balconies for its center. On both sides are receded balconies to form vertical lines. Exterior walls have cement mortar. In the middle, the vertical lines and protruded semi-circular balconies are painted dark red and the rest is painted light yellow. Both the gable top and the south side have parallel lines for decoration. There is a small garden in front of the building. After the liberation, quite a number of intellectuals lived here. On February 15, 1994, it became a Heritage Architecture issued by the Shanghai Municipal People's Government.

李国豪 （邬海佳画）

LI Guohao （By WU Haijia）

李俍民
（1919—1991）

浙江宁波人，原名李恺，又名李星，翻译家。1937 年读中学时参加横河抗日救亡工作团。1942 年至淮北苏皖边区抗日根据地参加革命。1946 年入沪江大学外文系，两年后辍学，开始翻译苏联儿童文学作品。中华人民共和国成立后，专事文学翻译。历任少年儿童出版社、上海编译所、人民文学出版社上海分社编译所、上海译文出版社编译所等翻译。曾任上海市政府参事室参事、上海市政协委员。译著有长篇小说《牛虻》《斯巴达克思》《白奴》等，中短篇小说《游击队的儿子》《少女革命家——丹娘》《尼尔斯奇游记》《学校》《蓝杯》《铁木尔和他的队伍》等共数十部。

《牛虻》影响了几代人

李俍民的译著中最有影响的就是《牛虻》。

1897 年，英国女作家艾捷尔·丽莲·伏尼契受当时身边革命者的献身精神激励，写成了歌颂意大利革命党人牛虻参与反对奥地利统治者、争取国家独立统一的斗争，最后为之献出了生命的小说《牛虻》。

正在中学求学的李俍民读到了梅益翻译的《钢铁是怎样炼成的》，深受感动。作者奥斯特洛夫斯基在书中几次提到《牛虻》这本书，这使他对书中这位名叫牛虻的人物颇为好奇。此后，李俍民开始自学俄语，立志从事文学翻译工作，而最大的愿望就是要把《牛虻》译介到中国。20 世纪 50 年代初，李俍民读到了《牛虻》的俄译本和英文原版，于是他决定着手翻译。

书中，牛虻临刑前，在遗书中这样写道："我没想到他们这么快就重新动用审讯和处决的手段。我知道如果你们这些留下来的人团结起来，就会给他们猛烈的反击，你们将会实现为之奋斗的宏伟大业。至于我，对待死亡将会怀着轻松的心情，走进院子，就像是一个放假回家的孩童。我已经完成了我这一份工作，死刑就是我已经彻底完成了这份工作的证明。他们杀了我，因为他们害怕我，我心何求？"李俍民仿佛置身于狱中，边读边译，边译边读，无比激动。这段后来成为经典的"遗书"，他不知译了多少遍，改了多少遍，最后才定稿。

1953 年，《牛虻》中译本由中国青年出版社出版，很快风靡全国。这本书在全国人民尤其是青年中引起了轰动，影响了几代人。有人作过统计，从 1953 年到 1959 年，该书印行达 100 万册。从 1978 年 6 月《牛虻》重新出版至 1995 年 9 月，累计印刷 30 次，发行总量达 204 万册。李俍民翻译的《牛虻》成为我国几代读者喜爱和受益最多的译本。

"不管我活着，还是我死去，我都是一只牛虻，快乐地飞来飞去！"

牛虻在狱中给他终身挚爱的琼玛的那封信里，写的他们儿时熟稔的那首小诗，至今还有人在诵读。

李佷民旧居位于淮海中路1285弄上方花园，原名沙发花园，为英籍犹太人的私家花园。1933年浙江兴业银行购买后开发建造住宅，由马海洋行设计，至1941年共建成74幢三层砖木结构花园住宅。20世纪50年代沙发花园改名为上方花园，寓有幽静美好之意，由张元济题名。1992年6月1日上海市人民政府公布其为上海市文物保护单位。1994年2月15日上海市人民政府公布其为市优秀历史建筑。

LI Liangmin

LI Liangmin (1919–1991), native of Ningbo in Zhejiang province with a former name of LI Kai and another name of LI Xing, is known as translator. In 1937 when he was in high school, he participated in the Henghe Resisting-Japanese Salvation Work Group. In 1942 he went to participate in revolution in Jiangsu-Anhui Resisting-Japanese Border Base Area in north Anhui province. In 1946 he was registered in the Department of Foreign Languages of Shanghai University. Two years later he dropped out of school and began to translate children's literature of Soviet Union. After the founding of the People's Republic of China, he specialized in literary translation. Once he served in succession as translator of Children's Publishing House, Shanghai Compilation and Translation Institute, and translation office of the Shanghai Branch of People's Literature Publishing House and Shanghai Translation Publishing House. Also he once served as counselor of advisory office of Shanghai Municipal Government, and member of the CPPCC Shanghai Committee. His translations include novels like *The Gadfly*, *Spartacus* and *White Slave*, in addition to novelettes such as *Guerrilla's Son, Zoya: A Girl Revolutionist, Niels' Travel, School Blue Cup*, and *Timur and His Team*, which amount to dozens in total.

The Gadfly Which Influences Generations

The most influential among his translations is the Chinese translation of *The Gadfly*.

In 1897, the British female writer Ethel Lilian Voynich was inspired by the dedication of revolutionaries around her and finished

李俍民翻译的《牛虻》
The Gadfly translated by LI Liangmin.

writing the novel *The Gadfly*, eulogizing the Italian revolutionary Gadfly who participated in the struggle against Austrian rulers for national independence and reunification, and who finally sacrificed his life.

LI Liangmin, who was studying in high school, read the Chinese version of *How the Steel was Tempered* translated by MEI Yi and was deeply moved. The Russian writer Nikolai Ostrovsky made several references to *The Gadfly* in his novel, which left him quite curious about the character with the name of Gadfly. Since then, he began to learn Russian by himself with the determination to engage himself in literary translation and the greatest desire to introduce *The Gadfly* into China. In the early 1950s, he read the Russian translation of *The Gadfly* and its English original and decided to set about its translation.

In the novel, Gadfly wrote in a letter before his execution, "It didn't occur to me that they go back to secret trials and executions so soon. I know that if you who are left to stand together steadily and hit hard, you will see great things. As for me, I shall go out into the courtyard with as light a heart as any child starting home for the holidays. I have done my share of the work, and this death-sentence is the proof that I have done it thoroughly. They kill me because they are afraid of me; and what more can any man's heart desire?" As if in prison, he read it and translated it, very excited. This "letter before death" later became classic and he translated and revised and it for many times until the translation was finalized.

In 1953, the Chinese version of *The Gadfly* was published by China Youth Publishing House and soon swept the whole country. This book aroused a sensation among people in the New China, especially among the youth, and influenced generations. Statistics were made that, from 1953 to 1959, one million copies of the translation was printed. From June 1978 when it was re-published to September 1995, it was printed for 30 times and the total copies amounted to 2.04 million. The Chinese translation of *The Gadfly* produced by LI Liangmin had been a version most favored by and most beneficial to readers for generations in China.

"Then am I/ A happy fly, / If I live /Or if I die."

In his letter to Gemma, whom he loved in his lifetime, Gadfly in prison copied this little poem which they were familiar with in their childhood. It is now still read.

The former residence of LI Liangmin is at Shangfang Garden in Alley 1285 on Middle Huaihai Road. Formerly known as Sofa Garden, it was a private garden of a British Jew. In 1933, Zhejiang Industrial Bank purchased it for the development and construction of residential buildings. The design was made by Moorhead & Halse, a foreign company. Up to 1941, the garden house was constructed with a total of 74 three-storied buildings of wood and brick structure. In 1950s, the Sofa Garden was renamed as Shangfang Garden with the meaning of being quiet and beautiful. The title was written by ZHANG Yuanji. It became a Cultural Relics Protection Unit and a Heritage Architecture issued respectively on June 1, 1992 and on February 15, 1994 by Shanghai Municipal People's Government.

李俍民 （邬海佳画） LI Liangmin （By WU Haijia）

李家耀
（1935— ）

祖籍广东番禺，出生于上海，导演、国家一级演员。1959年毕业于上海戏剧学院表演系。曾主演话剧《吝啬鬼》《安东尼与克莉奥佩特拉》《生不带来死不带去》《无事生非》《渔人之家》等，在电影《模范丈夫》《多管闲事》和电视剧《孽债》《夺子战争》等多部作品中饰演角色。1976年开始，师从黄佐临转攻导演专业及戏剧研究。导演京、昆、沪、越、甬、滑稽戏等多部作品，并出任芭蕾舞剧、哑剧的艺术指导。著文有《喜剧表演浅说》《莫里哀笔下的滑稽人》《也谈莎剧戏曲化》《布莱希特与中国评弹》等。1996年获话剧研究会表演最高奖金狮奖。

中国评弹和布莱希特

中国戏剧大师黄佐临对李家耀的艺术才能十分欣赏，希望他转攻导演，并给以教诲："学导演'百听不如一看，百看不如一串'，实践为重，理论为辅。导演学最好的课堂在排演厅、演出场。戏剧艺术的学问，在于'为吃今天新鲜牛肉的观众演戏'（布莱希特语）。"

1978年，黄佐临接受中国青年艺术剧院的邀请，进京与导演陈颙联合执导布莱希特名作《伽利略传》。李家耀随师进京，不仅亲眼看到了大导演的执导风采，而且亲身体验了布莱希特表演体系在话剧实践中的运用。

毕业于上海戏剧学院的李家耀原本学的是斯坦尼的体验表演学。当他接受世界戏剧另一表演体系的布莱希特学说时，一时感到难以理解。这时，外国布氏学者来到中国参加学术研讨会，黄佐临让李家耀陪同这些学者去听评弹。被称作"说书先生"的评弹演员以说、噱、弹、唱、演见功。说书好评古论今，不时会和听众一起有感而发地来一番议论。评论完，"说书先生"马上回到剧中各个角色，继续说唱。没想到，这些布氏专家听后便说："这就是布莱希特！"这使坐在一边的李家耀豁然开朗。

1984年，上海举办布莱希特国际研讨会。李家耀为上海青年话剧团执导布氏剧作《潘弟拉老爷和他的男仆马狄》。他想到了"评弹"，便请来了评弹演员石文磊在半截子幕前担当评说者。幕布上写着布莱希特的名言："如果把什么都消化完了，给观众的只能是一堆大粪。"石文磊评说后拉开幕布马上投入剧情，扮演女仆。就这样，话剧和评弹合作的实验演出引起布氏学者的强烈兴趣。由此，国际布氏学会特别邀请李家耀参加在香港举行的国际研讨会。那天，李家耀作的学术报告就是《中国评弹和布莱希特》。他又请了评弹演员蒋云仙同行，他做报告，蒋云仙穿插评弹演唱，真是前所未有。沉闷的学术研讨被李家耀搞得活泼而生动，这是中国评弹首次在国际艺术论坛上亮相，而李家耀的学术报告将布莱希特学说诠释得有声有色。

建筑简介：淮海中路1390弄11号

李家耀寓所位于淮海中路1390弄11号。11号位于弄堂北端，为一幢独立的三层住宅楼。房屋为三层砖混结构，建筑平面呈矩形。外立面为涂料饰面，南立面设有悬挑阳台，部分外窗下方墙面贴有黄色面砖，平屋面。一层门厅位于房屋东南角，门口台阶为红缸砖饰面；楼梯间位于房屋东端，木楼梯，木扶手；一层东北侧为厨房间，楼梯间西侧区域为一户；二、三层楼梯间西侧均为两户。

LI Jiayao

LI Jiayao (1935–), native of Panyu in Guangdong province, was born in Shanghai and is known as director and national first-level actor. In 1959 he graduated from the Department of Acting of Shanghai Theater Academy. Once he played roles in dramas including *The Miser, Anthony and Cleopatra, Much Ado About Nothing, The Fisherman's House* and so on. Also he played various roles in films such as *The Model Husband* and *Mind the Business of Others* as well as TV series such as *The Debt* and *The War of Snatching Son*. Since 1976, he turned to study direction and drama under the guidance of HUANG Zuolin. Consequently he directed many works of Beijing Opera, Kun Opera, Shanghai Opera, Shaoxing Opera, Ningbo Opera and farces and served as art directors of ballets and mimes. In addition, he authors such books as *On Comedy Performance, Funny Characters under the Pen of Moliere, Also On the Dramatization of Shakespeare, Brecht and Pingtan in China* and so on. In 1996 he won the Golden Lion Award, the highest prize of performance issued by the Drama Research Society.

Chinese *Pingtan* and Brecht

HUANG Zuolin, master of Chinese drama, highly appreciated the artistic ability of LI Jiaoyao and hoped he turned to specialize in direction, offering him instructions, "'To watch is better than to listen' and 'to perform is better than to watch' in direction learning. Practice comes first and theoretical study comes second. The best classrooms for directors are rehearsal halls and theaters for performance. The knack of theatrical arts lies in the concept of 'performing for the audience who take today's fresh beef' (Brecht)".

In 1978, HUANG Zuolin accepted the invitation of China Youth Art Theater and went to Beijing to co-direct with CHEN Yong the famous masterpiece *Galileo's Biography* by Brecht. Going to Beijing together with his teacher, LI Jiayao not only witnessed the direction style of great directors, but also personally experienced the application of Brecht performance system in the practice of drama.

李家耀（左三）向戏剧大师黄佐临（左二）讨教
LI Jiayao (third from left) was consulting opera master HUANG Zuolin (second from left).

He graduated from the Department of Acting of Shanghai Theater Academy and originally studied Stanley's experiential performance. When he accepted Brecht's theory of another performance system in the world drama, he felt it difficult to understand for a moment. At this time, foreign scholars of this school came to China to participate in academic seminars. HUANG Zuolin asked him to accompany these scholars to listen to Pingtan. Known as "Mr. Storytellers", actors of Pingtan exhibited skillfulness in such aspects as speaking, loud laughter, flipping, singing and performance. After commentaries, they immediately returned to the roles in the play and continued to rap. Out of expectations, these experts of Brecht listened and said, "This is Brecht!" These remarks found LI Jiayao, who was sitting at the side, suddenly enlightened.

In 1984, Shanghai held a Brecht International Symposium. He directed *Mr Puntila and his Man Matti*, a play by Brecht, for Shanghai Youth Drama Troupe. He thought of the Pingtan, therefore he invited the Pingtan actor SHI Wenlei to be at the curtain to act as a commentator. On the curtain are written the famous words by Brecht, "If you have finished digesting everything, merely a pile of feces can be given to the audience." After commentary SHI Wenlei pulled apart the curtain to immediately get into the story and play the role of a maid. In this way, the experimental performances of combining drama and commentary aroused a strong interest among scholars of Brecht. As a result, the International Brecht Society specially invited LI Jiayao to attend an international seminar held in Hong Kong. That day, his academic report was "Chinese Pingtan and Brecht". He also invited the Pingtan actor JIANG Yunxian for company. As he delivered his report, the latter interspersed his report with Pingtan performance, which was really unprecedented. The dull academic research was made lively and vivid by LI Jiayao. That was the first time that Chinese Pingtan debuted at an international art forum, where his academic report made a vivacious and dramatic interpretation of the theory of Brecht.

The apartment of LI Jiayao is located at No. 11 in Alley 1390 on Middle Huaihai Road. No. 11 is situated at the north end of the alley and is an independent three-storey residential building. The building is of a three-storey mixed structure of brick and concrete and its plane is rectangular. Its facades are decorated with paints. The south facade has a cantilevered balcony. Part of the exterior surface under the window is decorated with yellow tiles. The roof is flat. The hall at the first floor lies at the southeast side of the house. Steps at the doorway are finished with red bricks. The staircase lies at the east side of the house with wooden steps and handrails. At the northeast side of the first floor is the kitchen. There is one household at the west side of the staircase and there are two at the west side of the staircase on the second and third floors.

李家耀 （邬海佳画） LI Jiayao （By WU Haijia）

李鸿章
（1823—1901）

安徽合肥人，字少荃，道光进士。1853 年在籍办团练抵抗太平军。1861 年奉曾国藩之命编练淮军。1862 年，带淮军至上海，升任江苏巡抚。1865 年署两江总督，次年任钦差大臣，先后镇压了东、西捻军。1867 年授湖广总督。1870 年继曾国藩任直隶总督兼北洋通商事务大臣，掌管清政府外交、军事、经济大权，成为洋务派首领。从 19 世纪 60 年代开始，先后创立江南制造局、金陵机器局、轮船招商局、开平煤矿、漠河金矿、天津电报局、津榆铁路、上海机器织布局等。又建立北洋海军，开办北洋水师学堂。谥文忠。有《李文忠公全集》。

微服私访　师夷长技

1862 年 4 月 8 日，李鸿章率领淮军乘船登陆上海。

4 月 29 日，李鸿章获悉有一支租界洋人聘用的西洋军将在南翔附近进行军事演习。对外国科技颇感兴趣的李鸿章想亲自见识洋枪洋炮的威力，便决定“微服私访”。他穿着便服，只带了三个随从，悄悄前往南翔实地考察。他发现在演习中浮桥、云梯、炮台等各项从未见过的军火都各具精工妙用，而两军对垒时，“洋兵数千枪炮并发，所向披靡，炮弹落地开花”，此等“神技”令李鸿章看得目不转睛、如痴如醉，不知不觉间越走越近，竟越过了军事演习的警戒线。洋人们不认识李鸿章，便悉数扣押此一行四人。

李鸿章的下属丁日昌闻讯后派遣翻译官前去交涉。年届不惑的李鸿章在当时可谓老人，翻译官便称这些人是喝完喜酒回南翔的，其中一位老先生身体欠佳，患有高血压、心脏病，恳请洋人们网开一面放了他。洋人们本欲让该翻译官顶替李鸿章赴国外受审，但后经观察认为他们不像间谍，也就不了了之，释放了李鸿章一行。

回到府邸后，心情久久难以平静的李鸿章致函恩师曾国藩，感慨西方军事兵强器利：“其大炮之精纯，子药之细巧，器械之鲜明，队伍之雄整，实非中国能及。”李鸿章立志将这些技术引进中国。曾国藩回信劝诫他不可迷信洋枪洋炮，更不能聘请洋教练。李鸿章生平首次“顶撞”恩师：“中国军器远不如洋人，鸿章深以为耻。若是长驻上海，反不能资取洋人长技，那才真叫悔之晚矣。”他向曾国藩保证自己将“用西人而决不被西人所用”。

李鸿章踏上了“师夷长技以制夷”“洋为中用”的征途，大力引进西式兵器及军事科技，使淮军迅速成长为清军中装备精良、英勇善战的地方武装，走在了中国近代军事现代化的最前列。

建筑简介：华山路849号丁香花园

丁香花园位于华山路849号，始建于1862年，由美国著名建筑师艾赛西·罗杰斯设计，占地面积2.04万平方米，总建筑面积2934平方米。有主楼和副楼两幢，假三层砖木结构。主楼为美式乡村式别墅，副楼为现代式花园洋房，属中西合璧式花园住宅。该园体现了19世纪后期美国式花园别墅的基调，又融进了我国南方园林建筑的特色。主楼正中凸出呈梯形，主楼南入口沿台阶而上为大平台，柱式门廊，A形地坪，三开间，底层前部三间为客厅、餐厅，后部为书房、扶梯间和浴厕间。二楼为起居室、卧室。上海解放初，丁香花园是中共华东局机关所在地，陈毅、潘汉年、陈赓等先后在此办公和居住。1952年，由政府投资兴建2层楼房1幢（现为二号楼）。后成为上海市老干部活动室。

LI Hongzhang

LI Hongzhang (1823–1901) has his ancestral family from Hefei in Anhui province. With a courtesy name of Shaoquan, he became a *jinshi* during the reign of the Emperor Daoguang of Qing Dynasty. In 1853, he set up and trained the Local Militia to fight against Taiping Army in Anhui province. In 1861, he formed an army called the Huai Army at the command of ZENG Guofan. In 1862, he brought his Huai Army to Shanghai and was promoted to the provincial Governor of Jiangsu. In 1865, he implemented the authority of the Governor-general of Jiangsu and Jiangxi provinces. He was appointed as the Imperial Commissioner in the following year, defeating the eastern and western Nian Rebellion Army. In 1867, he was appointed as the Governor-general of Hunan and Hubei provinces. Three years later, he took over the posts of Governor-general of Zhili Province and Beiyang Minister of Commerce after ZENG Guofan and acted as a leader of advocates of Westernization Movement, taking charge of foreign affairs as well as military and economic affairs of the Qing Government. Since the 1860s, he successively established the Jiangnan Manufacturing Bureau, Jinling Machinery Bureau, Ship Business Soliciting Bureau, Kaiping Coal Mine, Mohe Gold Mine, Tianjin Telegram Bureau, Tianjin-Shanhaiguan Railway, Shanghai Cotton Cloth Mill and so on. Later, he set up the Northern Navy and ran the Beiyang Naval Academy. His posthumous title is Wenzhong and his works was entitled *The Complete Works of LI Wenzhong*.

Pay Secret Visits and Learn from Foreigners

On April 8, 1862, armed with foreign guns, LI Hongzhang led the Huai Army, and landed in Shanghai by foreign troop ships.

On April 29, he learned that a western army recruited by foreigners in Shanghai Settlement would conduct military exercises near the town of Nanxiang. Interested in foreign science and technology, he would like to see the power of foreign guns and artillery in person. Dressed in plain clothes, he went there with three personal entourages to conduct an on-the-spot investigation. He found that these weapons used in maneuver, which he had never seen before, all had excellent workmanship and functions, such as the floating bridges, scaling ladders, emplacements and other munitions. When two armies were pitted against each other, foreign soldiers shot thousands of bullets concurrently and their artillery shells exploded upon falling onto the ground. Staring at these

淮军将领
Generals of the Huai Army.

entrancing miraculous weapons, he got closer and closer without his knowledge and even crossed the cordon of the military exercises. However, not knowing him at that time, foreign soldiers detained him and his three entourages.

After hearing the news, his subordinate DING Richang sent an interpreter to negotiate the issue. In his forties at that time, he could be regarded as an elderly. So the interpreter claimed that these people were on the way back to Nanxiang after attending a wedding feast and one elderly man of them was in poor health because of hypertension and heart disease. In view of this, the interpreter requested the foreign soldiers to release them. The soldiers intended to make the interpreter take LI's place to be sent abroad for a trial, but eventually decided to release all of them after careful observation to make sure that these people were not spies.

After getting back to his mansion, he was unable to calm down, so he sent a letter to his mentor ZENG Guofan, in which he praised the powerful armies and sophisticated weapons of Western countries, "The quality of their cannons, the fineness of their powder, the remarkableness of their weapons and the braveness and discipline of their troops are far beyond our reach." He was determined to introduce these technologies to China. However, ZENG Guofan exhorted him in his reply not to believe in foreign guns and cannons or to hire foreign coaches. He conflicted with his mentor for the first time in his life, saying, "I feel deeply ashamed that China's military power has been left far behind that of foreigners. If we cannot take advantage of the advanced technologies of foreign countries during our presence in Shanghai, we will regret sooner or later." He assured ZENG Guofan that he will learn from the Westerners rather than being manipulated by them.

Then he embarked on the projects of "learning from foreign countries for combating foreign invasion" and "adapting foreign things to serve China". He spared no effort to introduce foreign weapons and military science and technology to China, thus making his Huai Army grow up into a well-armed and brave local armed force and taking the lead in China's military modernization in modern China.

Lilac Garden is situated at No. 849 on Huashan Road. Built in 1862 and designed by the famous American architect Isaiah Rogers, it covers an area of 20,400 square meters with a total construction area of 2,934 square meters. There are main building and adjacent building, which are nominally three-storey structure of brick and wood. The main building is a villa of the American countryside style and the auxiliary building is a modern-style garden house, which integrates Chinese and Western elements. The garden not only reflects the fundamental key of garden villa of American-style in the late 19th century, but also blends with the architectural features of China's south garden landscape. The middle of the main building projects to form a trapezoidal shape, the south entrance of the main building leads along the steps directly to the big platform. It is characterized with column porches, A-shaped floor and a width of three rooms. The first three rooms in the front on the ground floor are the living rooms and dining room; in the rear there are a study, an escalator and a bathroom. The sitting rooms and bedrooms are on the second floor. In the initial period after the liberation of Shanghai, Lilac Garden was the location of East China Bureau of the Communist Party of China. CHEN Yi, PAN Hannian, CHEN Geng, etc, once lived and worked here. In 1952, a two-storied building (now Building No. 2) was built with investment from the government. Later it became the Activity Center for Retired Cadres in Shanghai.

李鸿章（桑麟康画）　LI Hongzhang （By SANG Linkang）

杨在葆
（1935— ）

安徽宿县人，电影表演艺术家。毕业于中央戏剧学院华东分院（现上海戏剧学院）。1959 年进入上海青年话剧团任演员。1965 年调入上海电影制片厂任演员。杨在葆富阳刚之气、阳刚之美，有"银幕硬汉"之称。自 20 世纪 60 年代在成名作《红日》中饰演连长石东根后，先后在《白求恩大夫》《年青的一代》《江水滔滔》《大刀记》《从奴隶到将军》《原野》《血，总是热的》《双雄会》《代理市长》《卧薪尝胆》等影视剧中饰演各类角色。1984 年，以饰演《血，总是热的》中罗心刚一角，获第四届金鸡奖最佳男主角奖、第七届百花奖最佳男演员奖。1986 年，以饰演《代理市长》中萧子云一角，获第九届百花奖最佳男演员奖。

血总是热的

1979 年，当话剧《于无声处》被拍成电影后，剧作家宗福先和贺国甫又推出了新话剧《血，总是热的》。1983 年，北京电影制片厂决定将它搬上银幕。在考虑了众多中国男演员后，导演文彦决定由杨在葆出演主角——厂长罗心刚。

可此刻，以打斗搞笑为主的香港影片已开始冲击内地的市场，而且颇有观众。所以，不少人劝杨在葆不要去演这个描写普通工厂生活的电影。那天晚上，刚拿到剧本的杨在葆打开剧本，朗读起来。当他读到剧中主人公罗心刚那段"没有退路"的精彩演讲时，他的热血好似也沸腾起来："……我们搞了 30 年不理想，万一再搞 20 年还不理想，中国怎么办，没有退路了。同志们，我们只有和党同心同德，拼出一个现代化的中国来。否则，我们这些人再被打倒了，就不会有人再为我们平反了。有人说，中国的经济体制像一架庞大的机器，有些齿轮已经锈住了，咬死了，可只要用我们的血做润滑剂，这话已经说烂了，不时髦了，没人要听了，可无论如何，我们的血总是热的。"

真是掷地有声！"这是人民的心声啊！作为一个演员，应该拍这样的影片。"于是，他毅然决定接下这部戏。这是部低成本电影，可杨在葆毫不懈怠，他与往常一样，用全部身心来演戏。功夫不负有心人，他成功地塑造了一个克服阻挠，带领大家力主改革的国有企业厂长形象。

"我不会为了挣钱而演戏！"这是杨在葆的艺术观。因此他宁可贫穷也不会迎合时俗去接他觉得不适合自己的角色。他穷得买不起烟，就自己卷烟吸。爱人和岳母病了，他因打不起车而背着她们上医院。1984 年，杨在葆获得金鸡奖最佳男主角奖和百花奖最佳男演员奖的桂冠。可当时他穷得连上台领奖的衣服也没有，临时在北影厂旁边的地摊上花 1 元零 5 分钱买了件黑色短袖 T 恤，就去济南领奖了。对此，他毫不介意，甚至引以为荣："没什么好丢人的，我是一个诚实的劳动者。我就是穿着龙袍，也当不成真的皇帝。我最看重我的事业，从不拿自己的事业开玩笑。"

当天晚上，从颁奖晚会回到宾馆，杨在葆写下了自己最真实的心声："我在银幕上塑造的人物形象，如果活在了观众心里，这是对我最大的奖赏，我才算是一个有了艺术生命的演员。"

建筑简介：五原路281弄15号

杨在葆寓所位于五原路281弄15号。五原路281弄为花园里弄，15号与16号是利用空地所建造的两幢新式里弄住宅。16号为电影艺术家、国家一级导演赵焕章寓所。

YANG Zaibao

YANG Zaibao (1935–) has his ancestral family from Suxian County in Anhui province and he is known as a film performance artist. He graduated from the East China Branch of the Central Academy of Drama (now Shanghai Theater Academy). In 1959 he entered the Shanghai Youth Drama Troupe to work as an actor. In 1965 he was transferred to Shanghai Film Studio to serve as an actor. In China's film industry, he was known with his masculine beauty and was entitled as "screen tough guy". Since the 1960s, he established his fame for his performance of the role of the company commander SHI Donggen in *The Red Sun*. After that he successively played various roles in films and television plays, including *Doctor Bethune, The Younger Generation, River's Water Surging, The Legendary Broadsword, From Slave To General, Fields, Blood Is Always Hot, Meeting of The Two Heroes, Acting Mayor,* and *Sleeping on Brushwood and Tasting Gall*. In 1984, he won Best Actor in a Leading Role of the Golden Rooster Award and Best Actor of the Seventh Hundred Flowers Award for his play of the role of LUO Xingang in *Blood Is Always Hot*. In 1986, he won Best Actor of the Ninth Hundred Flowers Award for his play of the role of XIAO Ziyun in *Acting Mayor*.

Blood is Always Hot

In 1979, when the drama *In the Silent Place* was made into a film, the playwrights ZONG Fuxian and HE Guofu launched a new drama *Blood is Always Hot*. In 1983, the Beijing Film Studio decided to put it on the screen. After considering a number of Chinese actors, the director WEN Yan decided to select YANG Zaibao to play the leading role LUO Xingang, the director of the factory.

But at the moment, Hong Kong films with the main characteristics of tussle and comedy began to impact the mainland market and were very popular among the audience. Therefore, many people persuaded him not to play any role in this film which described the life of ordinary factory. That night, he opened the script he got just now and read it aloud. When he read the part of the drama where the leading role LUO Xingang delivered a wonderful speech "no route for retreat", his blood seemed to be boiling up. "…

杨在葆
YANG Zaibao.

We've struggled for 30 years, but it has turned out be unsatisfactory. In case of another 20 years with still unsatisfactory result, what should China do? We have no way out. Comrades, we only have to be of one heart and one mind with the Party in order to fight for a modernized China. Otherwise, if all of us were defeated, there would be nobody who could redress our cases. Some say that China's economic system is like a huge machine and some of the gears have become too rusted to move. However, if only we would use our blood as lubricants. These words have been said for too many times to be fashionable and no one is willing to hear them any more, but in any case, our blood is always hot."

Really forceful and lofty! "This is the voice of the people! As an actor, I should participate in such a film." So he resolutely decided to take up the role in the play. The film was low-cost, but he could not be slack. As usual, he acted heart and soul. Where there's a will, there's a way. He successfully created an image of a director of a state-owned enterprise who overcame obstruction and led his people to brave the reform.

"I will not act for making money." This is his art outlook. So he would rather be poor than cater for the custom of the time to play a role which he thinks is not suitable for him. When he was too poor to afford cigarette, he would make some on his own. When his wife or mother-in-law was ill, he had to carry them to the hospital on his back since he could not afford to take a taxi. In 1984, he won best actor of both the Golden Rooster Award and the Hundred Flowers Award. But who would have expected that he was so poor at that time that he could not even afford a decent suit to accept the award on the stage. In that case he temporarily spent one yuan and five cents at a stall near the Beijing Film Studio buying a black short-sleeved T-shirt. Then he went to Jinan for the award. In this regard, he did not mind at all and even took pride in it, saying, "There is nothing to be ashamed of. I am an honest laborer. Even with an emperor's robe, I could never be a true emperor. I value my career most and never play a trick about it."

In the evening, he went from the award party back to the hotel, where he wrote down his most heartfelt aspiration, "I am on the screen to shape the image of characters. If they could live in the heart of the audience, this would be my greatest reward. Only in this case would I be considered an actor with artistic life."

The apartment of YANG Zaibao is located at No. 15 in Alley 281 on Wuyuan Road. The alley is one of a garden. No. 15 and No. 16 are two new residential buildings in an alley which were built by making use of open space. No. 16 is the residence of ZHAO Huanzhang, a film artist and national level director.

杨在葆 （汪观清画） YANG Zaibao （By WANG Guanqing）

汪观清
（1931— ）

安徽歙县人，连环画家、国画家。从事连环画创作30余年，并致力于国画的创作和探索。注重墨韵，笔下的山水、人物极富个性，尤以画牛著名。先后有十多幅作品被中国美术馆收藏。历任上海新美术出版社专业连环画创作员，上海人民美术出版社专职画家、副编审。现为中国美术家协会会员、上海文史馆馆员、上海文史馆书画研究社社长、安徽新安画派研究会顾问、黄山画院名誉院长、上海市民盟书画院院长等。代表作品有中国画《梦里徽州——新安江风情图》（60米长卷），《黄山天都云瀑歌》图卷，中国最大玉雕《万水千山》（重7.3吨，参与设计创作），连环画《红日》（获第二届全国连环画创作评奖绘画二等奖）等。著有《汪观清画百牛纪念封珍品集》《汪观清画集》等。

情系好八连五十载

在中国连环画的长廊中，《南京路上好八连》分外光彩夺目。这是50年前，汪观清联袂贺友直、郑家声、陶长华、端木勇、任伯宏、任伯言等一批上海画家亲临好八连创作，在当年就受热捧的连环画。

1949年上海解放后，中国人民解放军上海警备区某部八连进驻上海，身居闹市，一尘不染，助人为乐，全心全意为人民服务。1963年4月25日，中华人民共和国国防部授予该连“南京路上好八连”称号。毛泽东主席写下著名诗篇《八连颂》。汪观清大受鼓舞，在上海人民美术出版社组织下，与画家们一起下连队蹲点采风，为好八连画下了最精彩的故事。

50年过去了，还创作过《红日》《雷锋》《周恩来同志在长征路上》等军旅作品的汪观清，与好八连的情结再一次使他激动。他知道，今天的好八连虽已搬离了南京路，但他们的精神没变，好八连的战士依然谱写着令人感动的故事。他也知道，当年参与创作连环画《南京路上好八连》的7位画家尚有5位健在。于是，他提议，由当年老画家领衔，再创作一部反映新时期八连风貌的连环画，并将此作为献给“南京路上好八连”命名50周年的礼物。

汪观清的策划不仅得到老画家们的支持，而且受到上海文史馆书画研究社和上海民盟书画院画师们的响应。一个风和日丽的春日，汪观清等5位老画家携手100多位中青年画师来到位于宝山部队营区的八连驻地。官兵们以飒爽的军姿和精湛的武艺热情地接待画家。军事科目展示、参观连队设施、与战士们座谈，八连的先进事迹打动着画家们。当年5位连坛高手，如今都已届耄耋之年，可强烈的社会责任感和对八连的深厚感情，让他们顷刻化解了困难。老画家各自拿出了自己的作品。83岁的汪观清更是乘地铁、坐公交，深入到与八连长期结对的南京路云中居委会采访，回来后编写故事，构思画稿。中青年画家们为能够捕捉更真实生动的人物，前后三次下军营，真切地走近好八连，画出了现代科技无法捕捉的那份感动。

2013年春，在“南京路上好八连”命名50周年前夕，一部反映新时期八连风貌的连环画《南京路上好八连（二）》出版了，这是1963年版《南京路上好八连》的续篇。同时，由画家们创作的160幅画作在营部展览厅里展出。在“南京路上好八连”命名50周年之际，收到这两份大礼的战士们个个脸上绽放出笑容。

建筑简介：五原路212弄1号

汪观清寓所位于五原路212弄1号。五原路212弄为大华新村，新式里弄，1947年建造，共有17幢，占地面积5420平方米，总建筑面积7226平方米。建筑略具现代派风貌，三层砖混结构。平屋顶四周设置女儿墙，立面简洁，极少装饰。南部二层设有悬挑的阳台，下部为底层门廊。素色水泥砂浆外墙面均布钢窗，窗裙板仅以网格细槽略作装饰。楼内布局紧凑，功能齐备，原用锅炉水汀供暖。

WANG Guanqing

WANG Guanqing (1931–) has his ancestral family from Shexian County in Anhui province. Known as a comic artist and Chinese painter, he has been engaging himself in comic painting for over 30 years and has committed himself to the creation and exploration of Chinese painting. Focusing on ink flavor, he creates landscapes and characters with very strong personalities and he is especially well-known for painting cattle. Successively over ten of his works have become collections in the National Art Museum of China. He served in succession as professional comic painting creator for Shanghai New Art Publishing House and full-time painter and deputy editor for Shanghai People's Fine Arts Publishing House. He is currently member of the China Artists Association, assistant of the Shanghai Research Institute of Culture and History (SRICH), president of the SRICH Painting and Calligraphy Research Society, consultant of the Anhui Xin'an Painting School Research Institute, honorary president of the Huangshan Painting Academy and president of the Shanghai China Democratic League Painting and Calligraphy Academy. His representative works include Chinese paintings such as "Huizhou in a Dream—Landscape of Xin'an River" (a long scroll of 60 meters) and "Mount Huangshan Celestial Capital Peak Cloud Waterfall" (a scroll), as well as China's largest jade carving "A Myriad of Rivers and Thousands of Mountains" (7.3 tons in weight, participating in design and carving). He also published a comic book *The Red Sun* (which wins him the second prize for painting at the Second National Comic Painting Creation). Also he authors such books as *The Commemorative Treasure Collection of Cattle Paintings by WANG Guanqing* and *A Collection of Paintings by WANG Guanqing*.

Connection with the Good Eighth Company for Fifty Years

In the gallery of Chinese comic paintings, "Good Eighth Company on Nanjing Road" is exceptionally bright-coloured and dazzling. It was 50 years ago when he, together with some other painters from Shanghai including HE Youzhi, ZHENG Jiasheng, TAO Changhua, DUANMU Yong, REN Bohong and REN Boyan, went to visit the Good Eighth Company and created the comic book which was over-favoured in the same year.

After the liberation of Shanghai in 1949, a certain eighth company of the Shanghai Garrison of the Chinese PLA entered Shanghai and stationed itself there. Living in the downtown area, they maintained their original pure character, took delight in helping others and served the people wholeheartedly. On April 25, 1963, the Ministry of Defense awarded it the honorary title "Good Eighth Company on Nanjing Road". Chairman MAO Zedong wrote the famous poem "Ode to the Eighth Company". WANG Guanqing was greatly encouraged. With the organization of the Shanghai People's Fine Arts Publishing House, he and other painters went together

汪观清（左）在好八连采访
WANG Guanqing (left) had an interview in the Good Eighth Company.

to stay in the company for the collection of materials to write the most wonderful story of the Good Eighth Company.

Fifty years have passed. He has also created such works as "The Red Sun", "LEI Feng", "Comrade ZHOU Enlai on the Long March" and other military works. His connection with the Good Eighth Company once again excites him. He knows that the Good Eighth Company has moved out of Nanjing Road, but their spirit has remained unchanged and soldiers from the company are still writing touching stories. He also knows that five of the seven painters, who participated in the creation of the "Good Eighth Company on Nanjing Road" that year, are still in good health. So he made a proposal that, led by the elder painters, they create another comic book reflecting the features of the eighth company in the new era, which will be dedicated as a gift to the 50th anniversary of the naming of "The Good Eighth Company on Nanjing Road".

His planning not only gets the support of the elder painters, but also the response from the painters of the SRICH Painting and Calligraphy Research Society and the Shanghai China Democratic League Painting and Calligraphy Academy. On a sunny day in spring, he and other four elder painters together with more than 100 young artists came to the military camps at Baoshan where the Eighth Company is stationed. Officers and soldiers demonstrated their valiant military presentation and superb martial arts to express their enthusiastic welcome to painters. Such activities as military show, visiting facilities of the company and informal discussion with soldiers as well as the excellent achievements of the company touched the painters. The five master-hands of those years now have arrived at their eighties or nineties, but their strong sense of social responsibility and their deep feelings for the Eighth Company enabled them to instantly resolve the difficulties of age. Each of these elder painters produced works of their own. WANG Guanqing at the age of 83 even took subway or bus to get deep into Yunzhong Neighborhood Committee on Nanjing Road for interviews because of its long-term connection with the Eighth Company. As soon as they came back, they wrote stories and designed drafts of painting. Young and middle-aged painters went to the barracks for three times in order to be able to obtain more real and vivid images of character, really approaching the Good Eighth Company and reproducing the excitements beyond the capacity of modern technology.

In the spring of 2013 and on the eve of the 50th anniversary of the naming of "Good Eighth Company on Nanjing Road", a comic book "Good Eighth Company on Nanjing Road (II)" that reflects the features of the eighth company in the new era was published, which is a continuation of the 1963 edition. At the same time, 160 paintings by artists were exhibited in the exhibition hall in the barracks. On the anniversary, soldiers who received the two gifts had broad smiles like flowers on their faces.

The apartment of WANG Guanqing is located at No. 1 in Alley 212 on Wuyuan Road. Here is the New Dahua Village, which is featured with new style of alleys built in 1947 and embraces a total of 17 buildings, covering an area of 5,420 square meters with a total construction area of 7,226 square meters. With a bit of modern style, these buildings are of three stories with a mixed structure of brick and concrete. The flat roof is surrounded with parapets while the facade is simple with very little decoration. The southern part of the second floor has cantilevered balconies and the lower part has the bottom porch. The outside walls with plain cement mortar have steel windows and window skirt boards are only slightly decorated with fine mesh grids. The inside layout in the buildings is compact and full-featured, using the steam heat from the boiler for heating in old days.

汪观清 （钱定华画） WANG Guanqing （By QIAN Dinghua）

沈莱舟
（1894—1987）

江苏吴县人，字宏让，号弱余轩主。16岁时到上海久康洋杂货号当学徒、职员。1927年与人合伙开设恒源祥人造丝绒线号。1935年与同业合办裕民毛绒线厂，生产地球牌、双洋牌粗细绒线。次年被选为上海市毛绒商业同业公会主任委员，并被推为市商会委员。1937年被聘为亨达生洋行经理，后在沪西创办恒源祥公记染织厂。抗战胜利后开设原兴祥羊毛号，同时与人合办嘉旭钱庄和鼎新染织厂。1946年被推选为上海毛绒线商业同业公会理事长。1948年去香港筹集资金、订购机器原料，时上海解放在即，得悉中共经济政策后，毅然回沪筹办恒丰毛纺厂。中华人民共和国成立后，响应政府号召，热心参加各项社会活动，被选为上海市人民代表。暮年仍参加工商界爱国建设公司的集资活动，并教育后代为祖国建设尽力。

恒源祥的经营之道

20世纪30年代，沈莱舟历经坎坷终于将“恒源祥公记号绒线店”开在了绒线一条街兴圣街（今黄浦区永胜路）上。他敏锐地洞察到绒线编织技艺所蕴含的巨大商机，不惜以重金聘请著名绒线编织大师冯秋萍和黄培英来恒源祥坐堂，现场讲解绒线编织技巧，向顾客传授经验与诀窍。沈莱舟还斥资印刷《冯秋萍毛衣编织花样与技巧》小册子，免费赠予来店堂挑选绒线的顾客。为方便顾客编织，沈莱舟专门从日本进口了一批用于编织毛线的竹针，并以两根一副为单位重新进行包装，顾客只需在恒源祥买一磅绒线就奉送一副竹针。贴心周到的“买一送一”营销活动深受顾客青睐，使恒源祥在激烈的市场竞争中脱颖而出。

1945年8月抗日战争胜利后，上海妇女崇尚个性解放、追求自由民主的呼声日益高涨。沈莱舟审时度势，力邀因战乱沉寂多年的冯秋萍重出江湖，并大刀阔斧地买下知名电台的各档黄金时段，请冯秋萍将绒线编织技法娓娓道来。为扩大恒源祥的影响力，沈莱舟还高薪聘请上海小姐谢家骅、京剧明星李蔷华、电影明星张翠红等身着冯秋萍专门编织的新潮绒线时装担任模特儿，出版了配有明星穿恒源祥新款毛衣靓照的《秋萍毛线刺绣编结法》。这套共16册的图书由王晓籁、严独鹤等名家题签，恒源祥客户有机会在店堂免费获赠。

现代商业营销模式及明星效应被沈莱舟娴熟巧妙地应用于对恒源祥品牌的打造上。20世纪40年代，恒源祥店堂可谓星光熠熠。据沈莱舟的儿子沈光权回忆，沈莱舟先会在电台里做几天广告，向社会各界预告将有明星莅临恒源祥店堂试穿冯秋萍设计编织的毛衣。电台、报纸等媒介的强势传播，再加上一传十、十传百的口口相传，使得明星尚未抵达，恒源祥店堂里甚至店门外便已挤满了群众、各报记者甚至达官显贵，熙熙攘攘，热闹非凡。周璇、上官云珠、白杨、童芷苓、徐玉兰、尹桂芳等明星都曾被沈莱舟请到恒源祥店堂当模特造势。

沈莱舟说：所谓生意，就是你要生出新的（主）意来。他打破传统经营模式，勇于创新，在时代的风口浪尖弄潮，使恒源祥发展成社会大众喜闻乐见的绒线品牌。1948年，恒源祥总号日销售绒线高达一千磅，沈莱舟被誉为“绒线大王”。

建筑简介：东湖路56弄53号

沈莱舟旧居位于东湖路56弄53号，为近代花园住宅，约建于20世纪30年代中晚期。建筑为三层砖混结构，设计采用几何形块体组合，平面布局自由，立面多变化，略具现代风格。外墙水泥砂浆抹层饰横向线条，部分作水泥拉毛处理，入口处门楣别出心裁地作中式装饰。

SHEN Laizhou

SHEN Laizhou (1894–1987) has his ancestral family from Wuxian County in Jiangsu province with a courtesy name of Hongrang and a style name of Ruoyu Room Owner. At the age of 16, he went to Shanghai Jiukang Foreign Grocery Store and became an apprentice and clerk there. In 1927, he set up Hengyuanxiang Artificial Silk and Caddice Shop with partners. In 1935, he co-founded Yumin Plush Factory with others in 1935, manufacturing double knitting wool and fingering yarn with the brand names of Earth and Double Ocean. In the next year, he was elected as chairman of Shanghai Commercial Association of Plush and was recommended as committee member of Chamber of Commerce in Shanghai. In 1937, he was hired as manager of Henderson Foreign Firm and later started up Hengyuanxiang Dyeing and Weaving Factory in western Shanghai. After the victory of the War against Japanese Invasion, he set up Yuanxingxiang Wool Factory and co-founded Jiaxu Bank and Dingxin Dyeing and Weaving Factory with others. In 1946, he was elected as director-general of Shanghai Commercial Association of Plush. In 1948, he went to Hong Kong to raise funds and ordered raw materials for machines. At that time Shanghai was ready to be liberated. After learning the economic policies of the Communist Party of China, he resolutely decided to return to Shanghai to initiate Hengfeng Woolen Mill. After the founding of the People's Republic of China, he responded actively to the call of the government and was eager to participate in various social activities. He was also elected as representative of Shanghai Municipal People's Congress. Even in the twilight of his life, he still participated in fund-raising activities held by patriotic construction companies within industrial and commercial circles, and educated his descendants to contribute their efforts to building the motherland.

The Way of Running Hengyuanxiang

In the 1930s, he finally set up a shop named "Hengyuanxiang Caddice Shop" after ups and downs in the caddice street called Xingsheng Street (now Yongsheng Road in Huangpu District). He was insightful to find tremendous business opportunities in the technology of caddice knitting and hired the well-known caddice knitting masters FENG Qiuping and HUANG Peiying at great expenses for them to come to the shop to explain knitting skills on the spot and impart relevant experience and knacks to customers. He also spent large sums of money printing the brochure *FENG Qiuping's Patterns and Techniques of Sweater Knitting*. It was given as a gift to the customers who came to the shop to buy caddice. For the convenience of customers in knitting, he imported bamboo needles used for knitting from Japan and re-packaged them with two needles as a unit. Customers only needed to buy a pound of caddice and could get a pair of bamboo needles for free. The thoughtful marketing campaign of "buying one and getting one free" was favored by customers, so Hengyuanxiang stood out from the fierce market competition.

After the victory of the War against Japanese Invasion in August 1945, Shanghai witnessed an increasing demand for women

沈莱舟先生“海陆空”有奖销售（1947年9月25日与获奖者摄于上海龙华机场）
The “Sea, Land and Air” prize-giving sales by Mr. SHEN Laizhou (A photo with prize-winners at Longhua Airport in Shanghai on September 25, 1947.

to pursue the liberation of individuality, freedom and democracy. He seized up the situation and invited FENG Qiuping to resume her activity, who was not engaged in this business for many years because of the War. He also bought the prime-time of well-known radio stations for advertisement without hesitation and invited FENG Qiuping to share her experience about the skills of caddice knitting. In order to enhance the influence of Hengyuanxiang, he also hired several famous people with high pay as the models dressed in modern woolen fashions specially designed by FENG Qiuping, including XIE Jiahua, a Miss Shanghai, LI Qianghua, a Beijing Opera star and ZHANG Cuihong, a movie star. He published the book series entitled *The Knitting Methods of Wool and Embroidery designed by FENG Qiuping,* coupled with photos of celebrities dressed in new sweaters made by Hengyuanxiang. The 16-volume book series bore the inscription of WANG Xiaolai, YAN Duhe and other famous people. The customers of Hengyuanxiang had access to getting a book for free in the store.

Modern business marketing models and the celebrity effect were skillfully employed by him to shape the brand of Hengyuanxiang. In 1940s, Hengyuanxiang stores could be described as being star-shining. According to his son SHEN Guangquan, he first advertised in the radio station for a few days to foreshow all walks of life in advance that there would be stars coming to the Hengyuanxiang stores to try on the sweaters designed and knitted by FENG Qiuping. The news, forcefully spread by radio, newspapers and other media, together with words from mouth to mouth, transformed the Hengyuanxiang stores and even the places outside the store into hustling and bustling locations prior to the arrival of the stars, which were crowded with people, the reporters of newspaper and even dignitaries. Pop stars including ZHOU Xuan, SHANGGUAN Yunzhu, BAI Yang, TONG Zhiling, XU Yulan, YIN Guifang and others were all invited to serve as models for the store with the intention of strengthening its influence.

He once referred to the meaning of so-called business as coming up with new ideas. Through breaking the traditional business models and innovating, he stood in the forefront of the times and made Hengyuanxiang into a caddice brand loved by the public. In 1948, the daily turnover of the caddice sales of Hengyuanxiang headquarters was up to 1,000 pounds, so he was well-known as the “King of Caddice.”

The former residence of SHEN Laizhou lies at No. 53 in Alley 56 on Donghu Road. Built in the mid- and late 1930s, it is a modern garden-style house. The building itself has three stories of mixed structure of brick and concrete with a little bit of modern style. Geometric combination of blocks is applied in the design and the layout is well-organized. Exterior walls are coated with cement mortar and decorated with horizontal lines. Part of them is napped by cement. The lintel at the entrance is distinctive for its Chinese style.

沈莱舟 （刘为民画） SHEN Laizhou （By LIU Weimin）

言慧珠
（1919—1966）

北京人，原名芰莱。父言菊朋为著名京剧老生。12岁学戏，攻程派青衣兼学武旦。1935年首次登台。1939年在上海与父组织春元社（又称言家班）。1943年拜梅兰芳为师。1946年自组言慧珠剧团，任团长。中华人民共和国成立后参加上海京剧团。1957年调任上海市戏曲学校副校长。为中国剧协会员、中国农工民主党党员。擅演剧目有《玉堂春》《游园惊梦》《生死恨》等。

追求完美的佳人

1959年国庆十周年来临之际，言慧珠与俞振飞在周总理的提议下，合作排演了献礼剧目《墙头马上》，谱写了一曲歌颂婚姻自由的赞歌。为了成功塑造大胆追求爱情、敢于向封建家长挑战的“李倩君”这一艺术形象，言慧珠可谓煞费苦心。

言慧珠首先把李倩君和自己曾经饰演过的角色逐一比较、推敲，觉得李倩君开朗、豪放、活泼的性格与史湘云类似，而坚强、大胆、刚烈的一面折射出尤三姐的影子，当机立断、敢做敢当则颇具穆桂英之风。

言慧珠希望自己生平首次独立创造的艺术形象完美无瑕，她热忱地将众多小姐妹邀至家中，虚心听取她们的建议，群策群力甄选服饰及色彩搭配方案。戏装的料子是言慧珠在上海老介福精挑细选的。戏服的颜色与何种光片及花饰配套较为妥切合适，言慧珠反复思考斟酌。她还将自己珍藏的金条贡献出来，在翡翠头面和珠饰上镀真金，使之熠熠生辉，增强了舞台灯光下的演出效果。

为了传神展现李倩君的性格特征及《墙头马上》整出戏的意境，言慧珠与专家、学者反复研究苏轼《蝶恋花》首句“花褪残红青杏小”的含义。她潜心揣摩“墙里秋千墙外道。墙外行人，墙里佳人笑。笑渐不闻声渐悄。多情却被无情恼”所表达的心绪，设计了契合李倩君情感世界的身段、步法和唱念的语气、声调、节奏。

言慧珠将自身浪漫不羁的个性与传统昆剧艺术的张力有机结合，在宗法梅派的基础上巧妙创新，不拘泥于闺门旦的演法，而在出场时头梳歪髻、手执团扇，以近乎花旦的表演风格刻画李倩君天真活泼、无拘无束的神态，赋予李倩君鲜活的生命力，使《墙头马上》获得了巨大成功。《墙头马上》后被拍成电影戏曲艺术片在全国上映。言慧珠也因此登上了舞台表演艺术生涯中崭新的高峰。

建筑简介：五原路258号

言慧珠旧居位于五原路258号自由公寓，建于1933年，占地面积1200平方米，建筑面积1575平方米，附屋汽车间129平方米，属现代装饰艺术派建筑风格的公寓住宅。建筑为九层钢筋混凝土结构，立面中轴对称，饰简洁的竖向线条。水泥砂浆饰面的窗框、转角窗，与褐色面砖墙面形成虚实对比。建筑中间部分的窗套及两侧部分的窗下板为白色，立面中央有一白色垂直装饰带，成为构图中心，同时建筑顶部向后退、向中间收缩，形成台阶状。底层处理成粗石基座。楼前有小花园。1994年2月15日上海市人民政府公布其为市优秀历史建筑。

YAN Huizhu

YAN Huizhu (1919–1966) has her ancestral family from Beijing. She had a former name of Jilai. Her father was a famous actor playing the beared male role of Beijing opera. At the age of 12 she started to learn performance, specializing in black cloth character or martial female role in Chinese operas. In 1935, she had her debut performance. In 1939, she and her father organized the Spring Source Society in Shanghai (also called the YANs' Theatrical Troupe). In 1943 she started to learn from MEI Lanfang, an opera master. In 1946 she organized the YAN Huizhu Troupe headed by herself. After the founding of the New China, she joined the Shanghai Beijing Opera Troupe. In 1957 she was transferred to serve as vice president of Shanghai Drama School. She was member of China Theatre Association and member of Chinese Peasants' and Worker' Democratic Party. Her repertoire includes *The Story of Sue San, Peony Pavilion* and *Regrets of Life and Death*.

A Beauty in Pursuit of Perfection

When the 10th anniversary of the National Day in 1959 was approaching, with the proposal of Premier ZHOU, YAN and YU Zhenfei co-rehearsed a tribute repertoire of *On the Wall and Horseback* as a song of praise to eulogize the freedom of marriage. She could be said to have taken great pains in order to successfully create the artistic image, who boldly pursued love and challenged the feudal patriarchy in this opera.

In the first place YAN compared the heroine with those she had played and made a careful analysis. She thought that the heroine in this play was cheerful, forthright and lively, similar to SHI Xiangyun; she was strong-minded, bold and fiery which reflected the personality of YOU, the third sister; she also acted decisively and had the courage to bear responsibility, just like MU Guiying.

She hoped that the art image she independently played for the first time in her life would be perfect. Therefore she warmly invited many female friends to her home and listened to their advice with an open mind. They also pooled their wisdom and efforts to

言慧珠出演电影《墙头马上》
YAN Huizhu acted in the film *On the Wall and Horseback*.

decide on the selection of clothes and the color collocation. The cloth for stage costume was carefully selected by herself in Shanghai. She considered repeatedly the costume color and the matching of flower patterns. She also took out her collection of gold bars to decorate the jade head-ornaments and beadwork, which would shine brightly to enhance the effect of performance under the stage lighting.

To vividly demonstrate the personality of the heroine and the artistic conception of the whole play, she and other experts made repeated studies of the first poetic sentence quoted from SU Shi. She pored over the emotions to be expressed in the poetic lines in the original. On the basis of all this she designed the posture and gait in accordance with the emotional world of the character, and also designed the tone, intonation and rhythm of singing and speaking.

She also combined her own romantic and uninhibited personality with the tension in the traditional opera, making ingenious creativity on the basis of tradition. She did not get bogged down in the traditional acting of female roles, but took on a coiled bun and held a full-moon-shaped fan. She adopted a performing style similar to that of a young female opera character in depicting an innocent, lively and unrestrained manner, giving the character fresh vitality. The opera was a huge success. Later it was made into a movie and was released in the whole country. For that she also stepped onto a new peak in her stage performance career.

The former residence of YAN Huizhu is located in the Liberty Apartment at No. 258 on Wuyuan Road. It was built in 1933, covering an area of 1,200 square meters and a construction area of 1,575 square meters, with an attached automobile space of 129 square meters. It is a residential apartment with an architectural style of modern art deco. The building has nine stories of reinforced concrete structure and the front is symmetrical beside the central axis with the decoration of concise vertical lines. Window frames and corner windows with cement mortar veneer form a contrast with brown brick walls. The window casings in the middle and the lower window plates at both sides are white. The center of the front has a white vertical decorative band to form the center of the structure, while the top of the building recesses and contracts toward the middle to form a step. The bottom is treated as a field-stone foundation. In front of the building there is a small garden. On February 15, 1994, it became a Heritage Architecture issued by the Shanghai Municipal People's Government.

言慧珠 （钱定华画） YAN Huizhu （By QIAN Dinghua）

邵洵美
（1906—1968）

浙江余姚人，原名邵云龙，新月派诗人、散文家、出版家、翻译家，与徐志摩并称为“诗坛双璧”。1923 年初毕业于上海南洋路矿学校。1925 年入英国剑桥大学攻读英国文学。1926 年回国，开始写诗。1930 年投资上海新月书店，1931 年 4 月任新月书店经理。1932 年投资创办《大英夜报》，宣传抗日。1933 年编辑《十日谈》杂志，并发表第一篇小说《贵族区》。1934 年创办时代图书出版印刷公司。除出版张光宇主编的《时代画报》外，还创办《时代漫画》《时代电影》《人言》杂志，并任主编。1936 年至 1937 年 8 月主持《论语》半月刊编务。创办《自由谭》《直言评论》英文刊物，曾译载毛泽东的《论持久战》。中华人民共和国成立后，居家从事外国文学翻译工作。著有诗集《花一般的罪恶》，文论集《火与肉》。译作有雪莱的《解放了的普罗米修斯》《麦布女王》，泰戈尔的《家庭与世界》等。

《论持久战》从这里走向世界

邵洵美祖父为清末重臣上海道台邵友濂，祖母为李鸿章之女，母亲为盛宣怀之女。1926 年他从英国留学回来后，自己写诗、办杂志、开书店，还购置了当时德国最先进的印刷设备，成了一个慷慨助人的出版家，有“孟尝君”之美誉。1937 年“八一三”事变爆发，日军占领了上海。邵洵美举家避入法租界，几经周折，搬进霞飞路 1754 弄 17 号（今淮海中路 1768 弄 17 号）一栋西班牙风格的房子。

1938 年 5 月，毛泽东《论持久战》在延安发表，上海的地下党组织委托毕业于燕京大学的《大公报》驻外记者、中共党员杨刚翻译这部作品。当时邵洵美以美国《纽约客》杂志社驻中国记者项美丽的名义办抗日杂志《自由谭》，而项美丽与杨刚是好朋友。受领任务后的杨刚住进了霞飞路 1754 弄 9 号项美丽家中，一起翻译文章，遇到吃不准的问题，就找邵洵美帮忙。在邵洵美的帮助下，《论持久战》译稿从 1938 年 11 月 1 日第三期开始至 1939 年 2 月 9 日第六期，分 4 次在邵洵美与项美丽合编的《直言评论》上连载。此后邵洵美又策划了《论持久战》单行本的发行。毛泽东为单行本写了序言，题为《抗战与外援的关系》。邵洵美亲自为该序中译英，还负责译稿的秘密排印任务。单行本一共印了五百册。夜深人静之时，邵洵美和他的助手王永禄等人冒着生命危险，开车将这本小册子投递到霞飞路一带外国人寓所、别墅的信箱。《论持久战》英文本出版对当时在上海乃至国外的海外人士尽快了解中国抗战形势及中国共产党正确的抗战方针起到了关键的作用。据说，丘吉尔、罗斯福的案头上都放着《论持久战》英文本，斯大林的案头上则放着他专门请人翻译成俄文的《论持久战》文稿。邵洵美也因为此举，让日伪特务组织恼羞成怒，一度欲对其施以毒手。为安全起见，邵洵美随身带着一把小手枪，用以防身。

中华人民共和国成立后，邵洵美将他的全部德国进口印刷设备以低价转让给了国家。中华人民共和国成立后第一份画报《人民画报》即是由这台印刷机印出来的。

建筑简介：淮海中路1768弄17号

邵洵美旧居位于淮海中路1768弄（原霞飞路1754弄）17号，建于1930年，建筑面积6750平方米。建筑群为二至六单元联立式，假三层砖木结构，立面对称，中间凸出，底层并列弧拱门洞。建筑采用方形窗户，部分作弧拱券，红瓦四坡屋面，开弧顶老虎窗，檐下有叠涩线脚，浅黄色水泥拉毛墙面，有较大庭院。20世纪30年代，住户基本上是外籍人士，仅有两户中国人。一户住2号，是上海道台聂缉椝的后代，另一户是邵洵美全家。1994年2月15日上海市人民政府公布其为市优秀历史建筑。

SHAO Xunmei

SHAO Xunmei (1906–1968) has his ancestral family from Yuyao in Zhejiang province. He had former name of SHAO Yunlong and was known as poet of the Crescent School, essayist, publisher and translator. He was also known as the "two jades in poetry" together with XU Zhimo. In the early 1923 he graduated from Shanghai Nanyang Road and Mine School. In 1925 he was admitted into University of Cambridge in UK to study English literature. In 1926 he returned home and began to write poetry. In 1930 he made investment in the Crescent Bookstore in Shanghai and in April 1931 he served as its manager. In 1932 he invested to found the *British Night Newspaper* to publicizing the War against Japanese Invasion. In 1933 he edited the magazine Ten Days' Talk and published his first novel *Nobility Area*. In 1934 he founded the Times Book Publishing and Printing Company. In addition to publishing the *Illustrated Times* edited by ZHANG Guangyu, he also founded other magazines, including *Times Comic*, *Times Film* and *People's Words*, and served as their editor-in-chief. From 1936 to August 1937, he took the charge of the edition of the semimonthly *The Analects*. Also he founded English magazines such as *Free Views* and *Candid Comment*, which once published the English translation of *On the Protracted War* by MAO Zedong. After the founding of the PRC, he engaged himself in the translation of foreign literature at home. He authored the collection of poems *The Flowers of Evil*, literary essays *Fire and Flesh*, and translations such as *Prometheus Unbound* and *Queen Mab* by Shelley and *Family and the World* by Tagore.

On the Protracted War Making for the World from Here

The grandfather of SHAO Xunmei is SHAO Youlian, important official and municipal governor of Shanghai in the late Qing Dynasty; his grandmother is a daughter of LI Hongzhang; and his mother is a daughter of SHENG Xuanhuai. After he returned home from studying in the UK in 1926, he wrote poetry, founded magazines and ran bookstores. In addition, he also purchased the most advanced printing equipment from Germany and became a publisher generous to help others, reputed as "Gentleman Mengchang". When the "August 13" event broke out in 1937, the Japanese invaders occupied Shanghai. He along with his family took refuge in the French Settlement. After several twists and turns, he moved into a Spanish-style house at No. 17 in Alley 1754 on Xiafei Road (now No.17 in Alley 1768 on Middle Huaihai Road).

邵洵美全家合影
A family photo of SHAO Xunmei.

In May 1938, the works *On the Protracted War* by MAO Zedong was published in Yan'an. The underground party organization in Shanghai commissioned YANG Gang to translate it, who was a member of the CPC, the journalist of the *Ta-kung Daily* and graduated from Yenching University. At that time he founded the resisting-Japanese magazine *Free Views* in the name of XIANG Meili, journalist of American magazine The New Yorker stationed in China. The latter was one of the good friends of YANG Gang, who, after receiving the task of translation, went to live in one room of her apartment at No. 9 in Alley 1754 on Xiafei Road in order to translate the works together with her. When he encountered questions he was not sure of, he went to SHAO for help. With the help of SHAO, the translation of *On the Protracted War* was later published for four times in serial in *Candid Comment* co-edited by SHAO and XIANG from the third issue on November 1, 1938 to the sixth issue on February 9, 1939. After that SHAO made a plan to publish the works as a separate edition; Mao Zedong wrote a preface for the book, entitled "the relationship between war and foreign aids". SHAO not only personally translated the preface into English, but also was responsible for its secret composition and printing. A total of five hundred copies of the booklet were printed. When it was late at night, He along with his assistant WANG Yonglu and others risked their lives to drive a car to take the booklets and deliver them to the mailboxes of foreigners' apartment and villas along Xiafei Road. In this way, the publication of *On the Protracted War* in English played a key role for foreigners in Shanghai and even abroad to understand as soon as possible the situation of war in China and the correct war policy of the CPC against Japanese invaders. It was said that one copy of the booklet in English was placed on the desk of Churchill and Roosevelt. Moreover, on the desk of Stalin was placed a manuscript specially translated into Russian. Also because of this, SHAO aroused the anger of the spies of Japan and the organization of the puppet government, who once intended to apply murderous means to him. For the sake of safety, he carried a small pistol with him for self-defense.

After the founding of the PRC, he transferred all his printing equipment imported from Germany at a low price to the country. *People's Pictorial*, new China's first pictorial, was printed by the printing machine.

The former residence of SHAO Xunmei is located at No. 17 in Alley 1768 on Middle Huaihai Road (then Alley 1754 on Xiafei Road). Built in 1930, it has a construction area of 6,750 square meters. The building complex continues from unit two to unit six as connected ones with a nominally three-storied structure of brick and wood. Its front is symmetrical, the middle protrudes and the bottom has parallel arch doors. It adopts square windows with some being arched. The roof has four slopes coated with red tile and has tiger windows at the top of arches. Under the eaves there are overlapping corbels. Walls are napped with light yellow cement. There is a relative large garden. In the 1930s, households were basically foreigners with only two Chinese families. One family lived at No. 2, who was the offspring of NIE Jigui, the municipal governor in Shanghai; the other was for the family of SHAO Xunmei. On February 15, 1994, it became a Heritage Architecture issued by the Shanghai Municipal People's Government.

邵洵美 （钱定华画）　　SHAO Xunmei （By QIAN Dinghua）

邵滨孙
（1919—2007）

江苏太仓人，原名邵念慈，沪剧表演艺术家。1936年投师筱文滨学唱申曲，易名邵滨孙，后加入文滨剧团。1943年拜京剧大师周信芳为师，从京剧艺术中汲取营养，形成了邵派艺术唱做并重、声情并茂的表演风格。其邵派唱腔刚直高亢，铿锵有力，韵味浓郁，在沪剧男声唱腔中独树一帜。主演《杨乃武与小白菜》《白毛女》《母亲》《星星之火》等剧目，塑造了性格迥异的艺术形象。中华人民共和国成立后，先后担任上海沪剧院副院长、艺术顾问，上海市第五、六届政协委员等。曾荣获全国第一届戏曲观摩演出大会奖状、华东戏曲会演演员一等奖。

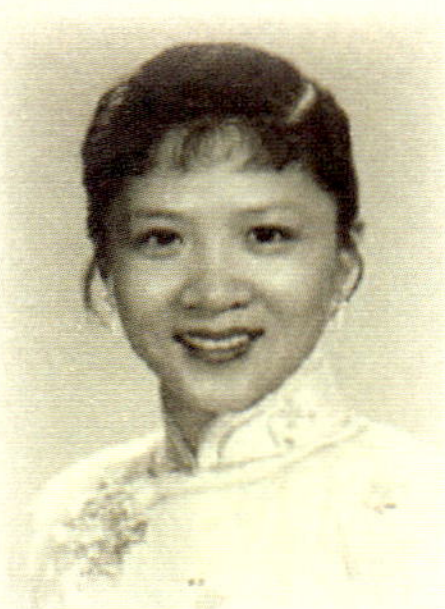

筱爱琴
（1928—1968）

江苏扬州人，原名吴彩珍，沪剧表演艺术家。幼年随母来沪谋生。10岁进婉社儿童申曲班学艺，与丁是娥、杨飞飞、汪秀英等同班。后在文滨、中艺等剧团担任演员。1946年与邵滨孙结婚。1952年参加上海沪剧团。曾先后在《白毛女》《罗汉钱》《雷雨》《杨乃武与小白菜》《母亲》《战士在故乡》《星星之火》等剧目中扮演主要或重要角色。曾任上海市政协委员、上海市妇联执行委员、上海市青联执行委员。1952年获第一届全国戏曲观摩演出大会演员二等奖。

夫妇同台　慷慨激昂

1959年，上海人民沪剧团（今上海沪剧院前身）创作演出沪剧《星星之火》，这是一部深受广大观众喜爱的优秀现代剧，同年被搬上了银幕。在这个戏里，筱爱琴和邵滨孙夫妇分别饰演日本纱厂女工杨桂英和地下党员刘英，两人出色的表演和精湛的唱腔，引来强烈的反响。

筱爱琴过去擅长扮演少女，从未演过中年妇女，但为了演好杨桂英，她背着铺盖，一头扑在排练场，与其他演员一起做小品、练唱、揣摩角色，连续奋战三十个日日夜夜。她每次排练，都当作正式演出一样对待，充满激情，排一场哭一场。该剧导演、上海戏剧学院著名教授朱端钧为此十分感动，上前与她握手，发觉她双手冰凉，连连说："像你这样的好演员实在难得！"戏中，筱爱琴和邵滨孙有一段"启发杨桂英"的对唱。唱段是精心设计的，为此，夫妻俩不断揣摩切磋。当时，在乌鲁木齐中路上，人们常常可看到两人一边散步一边比划哼唱。

邵滨孙是沪剧圈内唯一的麒门弟子。他在这个唱段中借鉴融合了京剧高拨子等一些音乐元素，糅合在"阳血"曲调里面，更为激扬，成功塑造了工人领袖刘大哥这一形象。筱爱琴演的杨桂英此时遭受失去女儿的磨难打击，心情沉痛，绝望悲凉。两人的唱腔一高一低，一刚一柔，一亮一暗，形成鲜明的对比。从"大嫂啊，你是否曾经想起过，你是苦海里长来苦海里生，为啥你在乡下越蹲越是苦，为啥你到上海未见好毫分？"开始，到"工人起来闹革命，为国为民为自身……"再到"仇恨岂止你一家人！"落腔，可谓慷慨激昂一气呵成。

建筑简介：乌鲁木齐中路179弄

邵滨孙、筱爱琴旧居位于乌鲁木齐中路179弄，建于1937年，初名麦琪里，以麦琪路得名。1943年麦琪路改名迪化路后，曾名迪化里。1954年迪化路改名乌鲁木齐路，改名乌鲁木齐里。弄内共有砖木结构2层楼房144幢，沿街3层店面房34幢，占地面积1.32万平方米，建筑面积1.57万平方米。麦琪里是上海市中心最经典的石库门小区，房屋结构统一，底楼称为“客堂间”，前后两间，前面连着“天井”（小院）。对应前客堂、后客堂楼上的二楼房间称为“前楼和后楼”，其中前楼朝南有四扇大窗，光线充足，冬暖夏凉，是石库门最好的房间；后楼则朝北。三层是人字型房顶的加层，俗称“三层角”，有老虎窗，也有前后两间。现已拆迁。

SHAO Binsun and XIAO Aiqin

SHAO Binsun (1919–2007) has his ancestral family from Taicang in Jiangsu province. With a former name of SHAO Nianci, he was known as a performing artist of Shanghai opera. In 1936, he studied Shanghai opera under the teaching of XIAO Wenbin and changed his name into SHAO Binsun. Later he joined Wenbin Troupe. In 1943 he formally acknowledged as teacher ZHOU Xinfang, master of Beijing opera, and drew on the opera art, forming a Shao art school whose performing style was characterized by a combination of singing and action as well as that of silver voice and deep feeling. His Shao-style singing was upright and high-pitched, sonorous and powerful, and rich with lasting appeal and flavor, being a unique male singer in Shanghai opera. He starred in such operas as *YANG Naiwu and Little Cabbage, White-Haired Girl, Mother, Sparks of Fire* and others, shaping the artistic images of quite different characters. After the founding of the PRC, he served in succession as vice president and art consultant of Shanghai Opera Theater, and member of the fifth and sixth sessions of Shanghai Municipal CPPCC. He once won the certificate of merit at the first conference of national opera performance for view and discussion, and the first prize for players of East China opera joint performance.

XIAO Aiqin (1928–1968) has her ancestral family from Yangzhou in Jiangsu province. With a former name of WU Caizhen, she was known as a performing artist of Shanghai opera. In her childhood, she came to Shanghai with her mother to make a living. At the age of ten, she attended Shanghai opera class for children of the Wan Society to learn opera art and was in the same class with such classmates as DING Shi'e, YANG Feifei and WANG Xiuying. Later she served as actress at theaters including Wenbin Troupe and Chinese Arts. In 1946 she got married with SHAO Binsun. In 1952 she participated in Shanghai Opera Troupe. Successively she played leading or important roles in such plays as *White-Haired Girl, Arhat Coin, Thunderstorm, YANG Naiwu and Little Cabbage, Mother, Soldiers in Hometown and Sparks of Fire*. She once served as member of Shanghai Municipal CPPCC, member of the executive committee of Shanghai Women's Federation and Shanghai Youth Federation. In 1952 she won the second prize at the first conference of national opera performance for view and discussion.

A Couple Singing with Passion on the Same Stage

In 1959, the Shanghai People's Opera (predecessor of Shanghai Opera Theater) created and performed the Shanghai opera *Sparks of Fire*, which was an excellent modern drama popular among the audience and was put onto the screen in the same year. In this play, the husband and wife respectively played the roles of a female worker YANG Guiying and LIU Ying, an underground

邵滨孙（左）、筱爱琴（右）演出沪剧《杨乃武与小白菜》
SHAO Binsun (left) and XIAO Aiqin (right) performed in the Shanghai opera *YANG Naiwu and Little Cabbage.*

member of the CPC in a Japanese cotton mill, whose excellent performance and exquisite singing attracted strong responses.

The wife was good at playing roles of girl in the past, but had never played a role of middle-aged woman. But she took her bedclothes and threw herself on the rehearsal in order to play the role well. She performed short acts, practiced singing and thought about the roles together with other actors and actresses, who worked continuously for thirty days. For each rehearsal she took it as a formal performance, full of passion and crying for each time. ZHU Duanjun, director of the opera and famous professor of Shanghai Theatre Academy, was moved very much and came up to shake hands with her only to find that her hands were cold. He commented that "you are a very good actress!" In the opera, there was a duet "Inspiring YANG Guiying" between the husband and wife. The aria was well-designed, for which the couple continued to consider and discuss. At that time, people often witnessed the couple taking a walk on the Middle Urumqi Road while making gestures and humming.

The husband was the only disciple of Qi School in the field of Shanghai Opera. In this aria, he borrowed and blended some music elements from Beijing Opera and mingled them in the tune of "Yangxue", which sounded more excited and high-spirited to successfully shape the image of a leader of workers Big Brother LIU. The female role YANG Guiying performed by the wife suffered the loss of her daughter at this time, depressed with deep feeling of grief and despair. The two styles of singing was in a striking contrast with one being high and one being low, one being strong and one being soft, one being bright and one being dark. The singing started from the "Dear sister, have you ever thought that you were born and brought up in a bitter background; why you lived an increasingly bitter life in the countryside; why you haven't got any better in Shanghai" to the point that "workers rise up in revolution for the country, for the people and for their own…" and then to the point "hatred is not only with your family!"—the whole process of singing was impassioning and exciting and was accomplished at one go.

The former residence of SHAO Binsun and XIAO Aiqin is located in Alley 179 on Middle Urumqi Road. Built in 1937, it had a first name of Maggie Alley named after Maggie Road. When Maggie Road was renamed as Dihua Road in 1943, the residence once had the name of Dihua Alley. In 1954 Dihua Road was renamed as Urumqi Road, so it was renamed as Urumqi Alley. In the alley there are totally 144 two-story buildings with a structure of brick and wood and along the street are 34 three-story buildings of store, covering an area of 13,200 square meters with a construction area of 15,700 square meters. Maggie Alley is the most classical neighborhood with stone gates in the downtown area in Shanghai. The structure of the building is unified. The first floor is called the "reception room", which has two rooms—the front room and the back room. The front one is connected with the "parvis" (a small courtyard). Rooms on the second floor corresponding to the two rooms are called "the front floor and back floor", among which the front floor has four large windows facing the south. Therefore there is sufficient sunlight and it is cool in winter and warm in summer. Also they are the best rooms in a stone gate building. The back floor faces the north. The third floor is an additional one under the herringbone-shaped roof, commonly known as the "third-floor corner" with a tiger window. There are two rooms including both the front one and the back one. Now it has been removed.

邵滨孙、筱爱琴 （钱定华画）

SHAO Binsun and XIAO Aiqin （By QIAN Dinghua）

陆久之
（1902—2008）

原籍湖南长沙。毕业于日本早稻田大学。青年时代受新文化运动和五四运动的影响，爱读《新青年》等进步书刊。1926 年，陆久之由中共党员徐梅坤介绍，进入由周恩来领导的上海地下总工会秘书处，担任联络员。曾任国民政府驻日大使馆专员、国民政府军事委员会专员、国民党第三方面军少将参议、《改造日报》社社长等职，长期搜集情报为中共地下组织工作。1946 年与蒋介石养女陈瑶光结婚，但他从不以“蒋家女婿”自居。1965 年被聘为上海文史馆馆员。1983 年任上海市第六届政协委员。晚年谢绝陈瑶光邀他前往香港定居之请。2008 年 2 月 12 日在上海逝世，被誉为“中共隐蔽战线的党外人士”。

汤宅策反

1927 年，陆久之申请加入共产党，但周恩来托人转告他说：“党欢迎你。但你留在党外，对革命贡献力量会更大。”1949 年 4 月，为了争取和平解放上海，中共中央决定策反汤恩伯，在福履理路（今建国西路）懿园，时任中共上海局宣传部长兼统战部长的沙文汉将此重任交付陆久之。虽然陆久之深感此行风险甚大，仍毅然决然地接受了这项艰巨的任务。

陆久之与汤恩伯青年时代便已相识，两人同在日本留学，陆久之还在汤恩伯考陆军士官学校寻举荐人时助其一臂之力，两人交情颇深。抗战胜利后，陆久之被时任第三方面军总司令的汤恩伯聘为少将参议，是蒲石路汤公馆（今长乐路 1221 号）的“座上宾”。为避开汤恩伯身边众多的耳目，陆久之决定直接到汤公馆找汤恩伯密谈，然而多次造访均不遇。重任在身的陆久之心急如焚，一天他与汤恩伯夫人王竞白商量后，索性住在汤公馆等候。第二天深夜，陆久之终于等到了从溪口匆匆返家的汤恩伯。

陆久之深知策反事关重大，容不得半点闪失。他先感慨对于时局的担心，试探汤恩伯一旦和谈破裂、共军渡江、南下淞沪该如何应对。汤恩伯以长江天险和上海防御工事“固若金汤”为由表示上海绝不会失守。陆久之指出目前人心厌战、军心涣散，劝汤恩伯效仿傅作义和平起义，顺应民心，弃暗投明。汤恩伯心头一惊，但并未训斥陆久之，在室内踱步半晌后向陆久之探询傅作义后来的境况。陆久之以傅将军受到共产党礼遇并深得民心的事实让汤恩伯放心。在如此长驱直入的“攻势”下，汤恩伯神色凝重，紧张地环顾四周，表示此事非同小可，须从长计议。翌日清晨，陆久之劝谏汤恩伯赶快拿定主意，不要置京沪杭人民的生命财产于不顾。汤恩伯不置可否，只是含糊其辞地表示万一淞沪告危，也将尽力确保上海免于战火。

陆久之及时将策反进展向党组织报告，并继续面见汤恩伯，恳切劝说。1949 年 4 月 23 日，南京解放，蒋介石父子三人抵达上海督战。蒋纬国的到来使陆久之只得先行辞别汤恩伯。随着蒋纬国入住汤公馆，再加上密布在汤公馆周围的中统和军统特工的监视，陆久之再也接近不了汤恩伯，策反功亏一篑。

没有完成党组织交付的重任，陆久之深感愧疚。沙文汉劝慰他说：“你敢于劝说汤恩伯做第二个傅作义，就可见你对党的忠诚了。尽管策反汤的工作没有完成，然而你对上海的解放是尽了全力、作出了贡献的。”

建筑简介：淮海中路1692号

陆久之旧居位于淮海中路1692号，为一幢双开间二层楼房。建筑整体风格朴素简约，大气沉稳，外观采用拉毛水泥饰面、红色砖饰，细部略具装饰艺术派特征。20世纪70年代，陆久之曾住在这幢楼房的二楼。

LU Jiuzhi

LU Jiuzhi (1902–2008) has his ancestral family from Changsha in Hunan province and graduated from Waseda University in Japan. In his youth he was influenced by the New Culture Movement and the May 4th Movement, fostering a liking for reading progressive books and periodicals like *New Youth*. In 1926, he was introduced by a member of the Communist Party into the secretariat of the Shanghai Underground General Union led by ZHOU Enlai and served there as a liaison person. He once served successively as embassy commissioner of the National Government stationed in Japan, commissioner of the Military Commission of the National Government, major general counselor of the KMT Third Army, and chief of the staff of *Reform Daily*. Over a long period of time he worked for the CPC underground organization to gather intelligence. In 1946 he married CHEN Yaoguang, adopted daughter of JIANG Jieshi, but he never considered himself as "son-in-law of the JIANG's family". In 1965 he was appointed as a librarian of Shanghai History Museum. In 1983 he served as member of the Sixth Committee of the CPPCC Shanghai Committee. In his later years, he declined the invitation from CHEN Yaoguang to settle in Hong Kong. He passed away in Shanghai on February 12, 2008, and has been known as "a non-Party personage in the hidden front".

Instigation of TANG into Rebellion

In 1927, LU Jiuzhi applied to join the CPC, but ZHOU Enlai sent word to him, saying that "you are welcome to the Party; but if you stay outside, you will do greater contribution to the revolution." In April 1949, the Central Committee of the Communist Party decided to instigate TANG Enbo into rebellion to strive for the peaceful liberation of Shanghai. In Yi Garden on Fulüli Road (now West Jianguo Road), SHA Wenhan, then minister of the Publicity Department and minister of the United Front Department of the CPC Shanghai Bureau, assigned this important task to him. Although he deeply felt the risk of the arduous task, he still resolutely accepted it.

Both LU and TANG were acquainted with each other in their youth, since both went to study abroad in Japan. The LU even gave TANG a helping hand when the latter was looking for recommenders to enter himself for an examination of an Army Academy,

陆久之在寓所
LU Jiuzhi in his apartment.

so a deep friendship was established between the two. After the victory of the War against Japanese Invasion, LU was hired as major general counselor by TANG who served as commander-in-chief of the Third Army. In this case he became "an honored guest" to TANG's mansion on Pushi Road (now No. 1221 on Changle Road). To keep away from the spies around TANG, LU decided to visit him in his residence to talk with him secretly. However, he paid severed visits, only to find TANG was not at home. Heavy task on shoulder, LU felt his heart torn with anxiety. One day after discussing with WANG Jingbai, wife of TANG, he simply stayed in the mansion to wait for him. Late at night the next day, he finally met TANG who hurried back home from Xikou, hometown of JIANG Jieshi in Zhejiang province.

LU was fully aware of the significance of instigation, which did not allow the slightest mishap. He first gave vent to his concern about the political situation, probing to know what TANG would do as an answer once the peace talk failed and the communist armed forces crossed the Yangtze River to advance south towards Shanghai. TANG believed that Shanghai would never fall with the natural barrier of the Yangtze River and the defenses in Shanghai "as strong as iron". LU pointed out that people were weary of war and the troops slacked in heart. He advised TANG to follow the lead of FU Zuoyi to start up a peaceful uprising, complying with the aspirations of the people and abandoning the shade for the sunlight. TANG was surprised at heart, but he did not reprimand LU. After walking back and forth for a long time, he asked about the recent circumstances of FU Zuoyi. With the courteous reception of General FU by the Communist Party and the fact that his uprising enjoyed the firm support of the people, LU asked TANG to set his heart at rest. After such a direct "offensive", TANG looked dignified, looking around nervously and saying that the matter was no trivial one which must be considered in a long-term view. The next morning, LU persuaded TANG to make a quick decision instead of leaving aside people's life and property. TANG did not express a clear opinion, but said ambiguously that, once Shanghai was in danger, he would try his best to ensure Shanghai would be free from war.

LU promptly reported the progress of instigation to the Party, and continued to meet TANG with earnest persuasion. On April 23, 1949, with the liberation of Nanjing, the father and sons of the JIANG arrived in Shanghai for personal supervision of war. The arrival of JIANG Weiguo forced LU to bid a farewell to TANG. His entering the mansion of TANG in addition to the surveillance of secret agents around made it impossible for LU to get close to TANG any more. Therefore the instigation was just one step short of success.

Not having completed the task of the Party, LU felt deeply uneasy. But SHA Wenhan soothed him, saying that "you've demonstrated your loyalty to the Party by bravely persuading TANG to give rise to a peaceful uprising. Though the instigation failed, you've done your utmost to the liberation of Shanghai."

The former residence of LU Jiuzhi is located at No. 1692 on Middle Huaihai Road. This two-storied building has a width of two rooms. Its overall simple and plain style features calmness and splendor. The exterior adopts napped stucco veneer and red brick decoration and the details mildly demonstrate features of decorative arts. In 1970s, LU once lived on the second floor of this building.

陆久之 （钱定华画）　　LU Jiuzhi （By QIAN Dinghua）

陈述
（1920—2006）

祖籍浙江上虞，出生于上海，原名陈致通，电影表演艺术家。1935年考入商务印书馆做练习生。1939年进入上海邮政管理局工作，业余参加上海基督教青年会少年剧团、中青剧团和邮务工会雁声剧团的演出。1948年任“文华”“大同”等影片公司特约演员，两年后辞去邮政局工作，正式开始其电影生涯。1952年进入上海电影制片厂。1954年在《渡江侦察记》中成功扮演了敌情报处长的角色，一举成名。从影以来，在近40部影片中饰演角色，先后参加了《斩断魔爪》《铁道游击队》《海魂》《黄浦江的故事》《聂耳》《难忘的战斗》《开枪，为他送行》《蓝盾保险箱》《摇啊摇，摇到外婆桥》等影片的拍摄，成为银幕上著名的反派演员。曾获1949—1955年文化部优秀影片奖个人一等奖，中国电影表演学会“特别荣誉奖”。著有传记画册《陈述的陈述》。

“情报处长”为秦怡画像

陈述以演技精湛、擅长扮演反面角色而享誉中国影坛。他扮演的第一位电影反派角色，是1954年拍摄的电影《斩断魔爪》中的外国神父。他多次去教堂，看神父做祈祷，观察其姿势、神态、表情，直到每一点细微之处都熟悉了，做到心里有底才表演，同年，《渡江侦察记》中敌情报处长一角选中了他。为演好这个人物，陈述从自己旧社会的经历中、从卷帙浩繁的资料中、从与一些当时在押的原国民党军官广泛接触甚至促膝谈心中取得了感受，然后他花工夫理清人物脉络，再设计人物动作。因此他的表演不仅生动地揭示了情报处长的阴险狡诈，而且演得真实可信。“情报处长”让他一举成名，后来竟成了他的代名词。

陈述的兴趣广泛、多才多艺在上影厂是出了名的，话剧、相声、小品、书法、摄影、配音和外语，样样在行。他酷爱体育，还是中国最早的体育运动解说员之一，曾担任过大型运动会电视实况转播的现场解说。年轻时，陈述还曾拜著名油画家、雕塑家张充仁为师，专门学习绘画。

陈述和秦怡是很要好的朋友，两人在影片《铁道游击队》里有过对手戏。陈述饰演凶残歹毒的日军队长岗村，秦怡饰演芳林嫂。据秦怡回忆，“那个时候整个剧组只有我一个女演员，大家特别照顾我。当时，拍戏任务很重，每天起早摸黑，很累。有天，趁着休息，陈述自告奋勇为我画像。”

秦怡开始有点不信，虽坐着，却不很听话，故意摇来晃去。当她用眼角的余光扫到画纸上，看到陈述画的自己还真有点像，便老老实实当起了模特。秦怡说：“他画得真不错，而且还是彩色的。”电影拍完，回到上海，陈述给画像配了相框，亲自送到秦怡家里。秦怡十分喜欢，当珍品挂在了客厅墙上。

没有想到，因一场意外，这幅画像被踩得粉碎。陈述得知后懊悔不已，直嘀咕：“早知道这样，当初就该留个底，我可以为你重画呀。”过了几天，秦怡突然接到陈述的电话：“嗨，那幅画，我留过照片（当时只有黑白照）。告诉你，找到了。”

陈述以此为秦怡重新画像。这幅画终于又回来了，不过是黑白的，它至今还保存在秦怡家里。

建筑简介：淮海中路1670弄

陈述旧居位于淮海中路1670弄中南新村。中南新村建于1941年，建筑面积8402.35平方米，属新式里弄住宅。建筑群为砖木结构，毗连式，前后错位，原有13栋，现存11栋。建筑入口架空为门廊，方形门窗，缓坡红瓦屋面，本色水泥外墙，横向窗间墙灰绿色面砖贴面，窗台上下有突出边框，强调水平线条，部分楼梯间外墙纵向窗间有几何图案装饰。每单元均有小庭院。当时多为商界人士及军政要员居住。1994年2月15日上海市人民政府公布其为市优秀历史建筑。

CHEN Shu

CHEN Shu (1920–2006) has his ancestral family from Shangyu in Zhejiang province. Born in Shanghai, he had a former name of CHEN Zhitong and was known as a film performance artist. In 1935, he was admitted to the Commercial Press as a trainee; in 1939, he worked for the Shanghai Postal Service and participated in the performances of Shanghai YMCA Youth Troupe, Middle-Aged and Youth Troupe, and Postal Union Goose Sound Troupe in his spare time. In 1948, he served as a contributing actor of such film companies as "Wenhua" and "Datong". Two years later he resigned from the post office and officially began his film career. In 1952, he entered the Shanghai Film Studio. In 1954, he successfully played the role of an enemy intelligence director in the film *Reconnaissance Across the Yangtze River*, and he made his fame at one stroke. Since his debut in the film circle, he played various roles in nearly 40 films, including *Cut the Evil's Claw, Railway Guerrilla, Sea Spirit, The Story of the Huangpu River, NIE Er, Unforgettable Battle, Shooting For His Farewell, The Blue-Shield Safe,* and *Beddy-Bye, Beddy Bye Over Grand-Ma's Bridge*. Consequently he became famous for roles of villains on the screen. Once he won the first individual prize for Best Films issued by Ministry of Culture from 1949 to 1955 and "special honor award" of China Film Society of Performing Arts. He got published one biographical pictorial album *The Account of CHEN Shu*.

"Intelligence Director" Painting a Portrait of QIN Yi

CHEN Shu enjoyed a fame of playing negative roles with his superb acting in the film circle in China. The first villainous role he played was a foreign priest in the film of *Cut the Evil's Claw* produced in 1954. He went to the church for several times to see the priest say prayers and observe his posture, demeanor and expression until he was familiar with the nuances of every point so that he was sure of the performance from the bottom of his heart. In the same year, the role of an enemy intelligence director in *Reconnaissance Across the Yangtze River* was assigned to him. To play the character well, he obtained understanding of the role from his social experience in the old times, from voluminous materials, and from broad contact and even face-to-face talks with some of the former KMT officers in custody at the time. After that, he spent time sorting out the context of his character and then designed the actions of the character. In the event his performance not only vividly revealed the insidious cunning intelligence of the director, but

陈述在《渡江侦察记》中扮演国民党军情报处长
CHEN Shu acting as the KMT intelligence director in the film *Reconnaissance Across the Yangtze River.*

his acting was trustworthy and credible as well. The role of "Intelligence Director" won him fame overnight and later became his code name.

His wide range of interests and versatility were widely-known in Shanghai Film Studio. He was not only expert at drama, comic crosstalk, sketch comedy, calligraphy, photography, voiceover and foreign languages, but also had a great liking for sports. He was one of the first sports commentators in China, once serving as commentator of live television broadcasting of large-scale games. In his youth, he took ZHANG Chongren as his teacher, a well-known oil painter and sculptor, in order to specialize in painting.

CHEN Shu and QIN Yi were very good friends and both played roles in the film *Railway Guerrilla*. The former played the role of Okamura, a cruel and vicious Japanese captain, while the latter played the role of Fanglinsao. According to the recall of QIN Yi, "At that time the whole film crew only has one actress, i.e. me and others took special care of me. But the task of shooting was very heavy and everyone was tired out every day for working long hours. During the break one day, he volunteered to paint a portrait for me."

In the beginning she didn't believe to some extent that he could paint. Though being seated, she did not cooperate so much, deliberately shaking from side to side. When the corner of her eye swept over the paper and saw that the portrait he made was really like her, she then conscientiously served as the model. She said, "His painting was really good and moreover the painting was in colors." The film was finished and she returned to Shanghai. He prepared a frame for the portrait and personally took it to her home. She appreciated it very much and took it as a treasure to put it on the wall in the living room.

Out of expectation, an accident happened that the portrait was crushed to pieces. After he learned of the accident, he regretted a lot, whispering, "If I could have known it earlier, a copy would have been kept. However, I can paint another portrait for you." After a few days, she received an unexpected call from him, "Hey, for that portrait, I've kept a photo (only black-and-white photo at that time). I've found it actually."

Based on this photo, he painted another portrait for her—the painting finally came back, but it was black-and-white, which is still preserved in her home.

The former residence of CHEN Shu is located in Central South New Village in Alley 1670 on Middle Huaihai Road. Built in 1941, the Central South New Village is a new-style alley residence with a construction area of 8,402.35 square meters. The building complex is of the structure of brick and wood with buildings adjacent to each other in horizontal rows and mutually dislocated in longitudinal rows. There were originally thirteen buildings and only eleven of them are still extant. The building has an entrance with a porch built on stilts and has square doors and windows, a roof of gentle slope with red tile, and exterior walls coated with natural cement. The horizontal spaces between windows are coated with a veneer of gray green face bricks, above and under windowsills are installed with projected frames, laying emphasis on horizontal lines. Between the longitudinal windows on exterior walls of some staircases, there are decorations of geometric patterns. Each unit has a small courtyard. Formerly these buildings were mostly occupied by business people and military and political officials. On February 15, 1994, it became a Heritage Architecture issued by the Shanghai Municipal People's Government.

陈述 （钱定华画）　　CHEN Shu （By QIAN Dinghua）

后记

湖南路街道因缘际会存留了厚实的历史底蕴和丰富的文化资源。这几年街道党工委和办事处为了进一步挖掘历史资源、传承历史文化，专门成立了编委会并组织人员收集整理历史资料，为众多曾经生活在这一地区的政治、经济、文化界等人物，以“人物简介、人物故事、人物旧居、人物画像”，勾勒一幅幅人物剪影。经过漫长艰苦的努力，克服了人物住址难找、旧居资料难查、故事情节难写的重重困难，最终编撰成这套《200031——一个历史街区的文化记忆》。

在资料收集过程中，目前已发现曾经居住于湖南路街道的各界人物 300 余位。由于资料翔实程度不同，现整理出 111 位人物及其旧居的资料，按照人物姓氏笔画排序，先行出版两册，其余的我们将继续充实资料，抓紧编撰，分批出版。

这套书的出版，首先要感谢上海文史馆馆员、上海民盟书画院院长、上海梧桐画社名誉社长汪观清先生及其他参与的画家。汪老是居住在这个区域，对湖南路街道有着深厚感情的一位德高望重的艺术家。他非常关心支持社区公共文化事业，不顾八十七岁高龄，不仅组织上海梧桐画社众多画家为本书配画，还亲自为巴金一篇创作题为《真爱》的画像，并对所有绘画作品把关。这些佳作为本书内容增光添彩。

对建筑作介绍是一项专业性要求极高的工作。我们参考书籍、调阅档案，并邀请上海市房地产科学研究院李占鸿、周云、代红超、李承根，以及上海石库门文化研究中心娄承浩等专家现场勘查，撰写部分建筑介绍，并请同济大学钱宗灏教授审阅部分内容。感谢他们从专业的角度，为本书出版付出的辛勤劳动。

还要感谢上海教育出版社原社长包南麟、中国中福会出版社副总编辑陈苏，他们不仅在体例规划、内容编写、稿件统筹上给予指导，还以湖南路街道老居民的真实情怀提供了很多有益的帮助。感谢上海大学上海美术学院汪大伟院长、上海市档案馆冯绍霆老师、上海市档案局郭红解老师、上海书店出版社完颜绍元老师的热心指教。感谢参与此书资料收集、资料整理、照片拍摄、文章撰写、稿件翻译等工作的所有人员，感谢上海图书馆、上海教育出版社、上海市徐汇区档案馆、众多人物的家属以及社会热心人士，不仅为我们提供了许多宝贵的线索和建议，还帮助我们查找资料和图片。书中引用的许多资料、图片，出自众多作者之手，难以一一详述，只能在此一并致谢。

本书编写历经数年，其间我们对资料反复调查、核实、修改、筛选，数易其稿，力求事实可靠、内容可读，具有艺术欣赏价值。然而，毕竟许多人和事年代久远，当事人大多已不在人世，虽经努力，难免挂一漏万。加之编者水平有限，书中错误和疏漏之处在所难免，敬请广大读者指正。也希望曾生活在这个区域的各界人士给我们提供有益的线索，以便再版时修正及使后续编撰工作进一步完善。

Postscript

Thanks to chances and opportunities, the Hunan Road Residential Subdistrict has accumulated handsome historical information and rich cultural resources. In order to further dig up historical resources and inherit the history and culture, the Party working committee and the subdistrict office specially set up an editorial board and organized personnel to collect and sort out historical documents and sketch the silhouettes for many people in the fields of politics, economy and culture who have lived in this area. The silhouettes have been materialized in the forms of "profile, story, former residence and portrait". After long and arduous efforts we have overcome various difficulties in looking for the addresses of people, searching for information about their former residences and writing the plots of their stories. Finally we have finished the compilation of this series with the title *200031—Cultural Memories of A Historical District*.

In the process of material collection, we have found at present over 300 celebrities from all walks of life who once lived in Hunan Road Residential Subdistrict. Due to the different degrees of fullness of information, we have now sorted out materials of 111 people and their former residences and put them in the order of stroke numbers of their surname. Two volumes are to be published first. We will continue to enrich the information of other people and lose no time in the compilation and writing. In the future more volumes will come out.

For the publication of these books, we are first of all indebted to Mr. WANG Guanqing, librarian of the Shanghai Research Institute of Culture and History, president of the Painting and Calligraphy Academy affiliated to Shanghai Committee of the China Democratic League and honorary president of Shanghai Wutong Painting Society, and our thanks also go to other artists involved. Mr. WANG is a highly respected artist who lives in this area and has a deep feeling for the Hunan Road Residential Subdistrict. He has much concern about and support for the public cultural undertakings of the community area. Regardless of his age of eighty-seven, he has not only organized many artists from the Shanghai Wutong Painting Society to prepare paintings for the books, but also personally created a portrait with the title of "True Love" for the passage BA Jin. In addition he has also made the final examination of all the paintings, which are the highlights of the books.

Writing introductions of architectures is a highly demanding job as far as professional knowledge is concerned. We have referred to books and read archives. Also we have invited such experts as LI Zhanhong, ZHOU Yun, DAI Hongchao and LI Chenggen from the Shanghai Real Estate Science Research Institute, and LOU Chenghao from Shanghai Stone-frame Gate Culture Research Center to make on-site investigations and write part of introductions of the architectures. In the meanwhile we have asked Professor QIAN Zonghao from Tongji University to read and approve part of the content. Therefore thanks go to all of them for their hard work for the publication of the books from a professional point of view.

We would also express our thanks to BAO Nanlin, former president of the Shanghai Educational Publishing House and CHEN Su, deputy editor-in-chief of China Welfare Institute Publishing House. They have not only given us guidance in the style and planning, content preparation and overall planning of manuscripts, but also provided a lot of useful help with the authentic feelings of the old residents of Hunan Road Residential Subdistrict. Our thanks still go to WANG Dawei, dean of Shanghai Academy of Fine Arts of Shanghai University, FENG Shaoting from Shanghai Archives, GUO Hongjie from Shanghai Archives Administration and WANYAN Shaoyuan from Shanghai Bookstore Publishing House for their warmhearted advice and instructions. We would also like to express our thanks to all people who have participated in the information collection, sorting out of documents, photo shooting, article writing, manuscript translation and so on. We would further like to extend our thanks to Shanghai Library, Shanghai

Educational Publishing House and Shanghai Xuhui District Archives, as well as family members of many public figures and warm-hearted people, who have not merely provided a lot of valuable clues and suggestions for us, but also helped us find information and pictures. A lot of the information and pictures cited in the books come from the hands of many writers, while it is difficult to elaborate one by one. We cannot help but express our thanks once for all.

The compilation of the books has lasted for several years, during which we have repeatedly investigated, verified, modified and sifted and the manuscripts have been revised for several times in order that the contents are reliable and readable along with values for artistic appreciation. However, many people and things are of the remote past and most people concerned are no longer alive. With all of our efforts, it is inevitable that the information is far from being complete. In addition editors are limited in one aspect or another. Therefore errors and omissions in the book are unavoidable. We sincerely invite all readers to point out mistakes so that they can be corrected in the future. Also we hope that people who have lived in this area provide us with useful clues so that revisions are to be made at the time of reprinting and that the subsequent compilation can be further improved.

图书在版编目（CIP）数据

200031：一个历史街区的文化记忆. 1 / 中共上海市徐汇区湖南街道工作委员会，上海市徐汇区人民政府湖南路街道办事处组织编写. — 上海：上海教育出版社, 2017.12
ISBN 978-7-5444-7858-8

Ⅰ.①2… Ⅱ.①中… ②上… Ⅲ.①城市道路—介绍—徐汇区 Ⅳ.①K925.13

中国版本图书馆CIP数据核字（2017）第285563号

责任编辑 严 岷 隋淑光 林 翘
装帧设计 王 捷 金一哲
封面设计 陈世东
封面绘画 钱定华
插页设计 邬海佳

200031：一个历史街区的文化记忆（1）

中共上海市徐汇区湖南街道工作委员会
上海市徐汇区人民政府湖南路街道办事处 **编**
陈世东 主编

出版发行 上海教育出版社有限公司
官 网 www.seph.com.cn
地 址 上海市永福路123号
邮 编 200031
印 刷 上海盛通时代印刷有限公司印刷
开 本 890×1240 1/16 印张 15 插页2
版 次 2017年12月第1版
印 次 2017年12月第1次印刷
书 号 ISBN 978-7-5444-7858-8/G·6472
定 价 （精装）148.00 元

如发现质量问题，读者可向本社调换 电话：021-64377165